D0006867

M-Business

The Race to Mobility

Ravi Kalakota

Marcia Robinson

McGraw-Hill

New York Chicago San Francisco
Lisbon London Madrid Mexico City Milan New Delhi
San Juan Seoul Singapore Sydney Toronto

McGraw-Hill

A Division of The McGraw·Hill Companies

Library of Congress Cataloging-in-Publication Data

Kalakota, Ravi.
  M-business : the race to mobility / Ravi Kalakota & Marcia Robinson.
    p. cm.
  ISBN 0-07-138078-7
  1. Electronic commerce. 2. Internet. 3. Mobile communication systems.
  I. Robinson, Marcia. II. Title.

HF5548.32 .K354 2001
658.8'4—dc21   2001044340

Copyright © 2002 by Ravi Kalakota and Marcia Robinson. All rights reserved.
Printed in the United States of America. Except as permitted under the United
States Copyright Act of 1976, no part of this publication may be reproduced or
distributed in any form or by any means, or stored in a data base or retrieval
system, without the prior written permission of the publisher.

1 2 3 4 5 6 7 8 9 0 DOC/DOC 0 7 6 5 4 3 2 1

0-07-138078-7

Printed and bound by R. R. Donnelley & Sons Company.

McGraw-Hill books are available at special quantity discounts to use as
premiums and sales promotions, or for use in corporate training programs.
For more information, please write to the Director of Special Sales,
Professional Publishing, McGraw-Hill, Two Penn Plaza, New York, NY
10121-2298. Or contact your local bookstore.

 This book is printed on recycled, acid-free paper containing a
minimum of 50% recycled, de-inked fiber.

To my mother, Anasuya, and sister, Sharada, for teaching me a lot about life. To my nephews, Vijay and Vinod, for making me constantly think about the future.

—Ravi

To my parents, Bill and Judy, for teaching me the value of hard work. To my sister and brother, Shelley and Roby, for their love and support.

—Marcia

Contents

Preface

Fortune is like the market, where many times, if you can stay a little, the price will fall.

—Francis Bacon

The twentieth century is a distant memory. The e-commerce hype has barely subsided, and the media, venture capitalists, and stock markets have already moved on to the mobile Internet. Everywhere you turn—newspapers, magazines, television, even the sides of city buses—you encounter debate about mobile business (or m-business). With the countless mobile scenarios being envisioned, managers have to correctly evaluate trends, avoid faddish solutions, and sort through the many options available to them. Indeed, accurate judgment of the short- and long-term value of the multitude of offerings requires careful consideration, a keen eye, and informed skepticism.

The most challenging question confronting business executives tasked with keeping their companies competitive is not "Is mobile business going to happen?"; it's "What form is it going to take and how do we use the technology to continuously innovate and improve?" At first glance, m-business can seem like yet another buzz-word. But if you look closer, you'll find there is a significant difference: M-business is not a business fad tied to a single method or strategy, but rather the next step in the technology curve. It is simply a way for improved customer interaction and new operational efficiencies. It builds on all the investments in e-business.

M-business, like many so-called revolutions, offers the spectacle of a succession of companies, products, and even industries getting their few minutes of fame and then fading away. It's like riding a roller-coaster as technologies, consumer tastes, financial conditions, and competition change ever more quickly. It seems that the mobile environment is changing faster and becoming more uncertain with each turbulent day, and questions are emerging from everywhere. In this high-risk environment, the need for a cogent roadmap that can help navigate through the chaos and anticipate the next change is very obvious.

What This Book Is About

Why this book? Why now? Most of the discussion about the mobile Internet is about consumer applications—portals, instant messaging, or streaming media. The implications of mobility on enterprise solutions—customer-facing, employee-facing and supplier-facing—have not been explored in detail. This is a significant gap as the mobile Internet moves from a "toy" to a "tool" in its evolution.

M-business, not m-commerce, is the focus of this book. Most C-level executives are grappling with the following questions as they think about the future: Is m-business for real? What application scenarios are most promising? How can existing multi-million dollar investments in ERP and CRM solutions be leveraged? What new solutions can be built on the emerging mobile platforms that will have a positive return on investment (ROI)?

Also, a core strategic question facing many companies: What comes after e-business? If "m" comes after "e," how do they relate? It seems intuitively obvious that e-business is evolving from a PC-centric model to a multi-device, multi-channel, and mobile model (m-business). But what is not so obvious is how the current landscape of enterprise applications will evolve and where the opportunities are in the near and long term. What new value propositions will companies look to create in their never-ending quest to become more competitive and customer-focused? How can companies further improve internal operations and employee processes? These questions form the basis for this book.

The goal of *M-Business: The Race to Mobility* is to provide a business perspective of the m-business landscape that is insightful and useful for managers. Our goal in this book is to dispel mobile myths that are causing companies to waste billions of dollars creating poorly conceived solutions. This is not a technical manual; plenty of other books cover the nuances of 3G broadband, mobile protocols, and new programming languages. This book will, however, help anyone understand the basics of m-business and how it should be applied.

The focus of this book is practical: helping senior management plan for and manage m-business investments. In our mission to demystify m-business, we hope to provide a complete picture of what's behind the m-business innovation cycle; discussion of how different companies are developing go-to-market strategies; and insights and examples from real companies. At the same time, our goal is to provide a flexible framework for thinking about m-business that you can apply to your business context.

Who Should Read This Book

This book's timeliness and insights into the structural changes in enterprise solutions make it useful to a broad audience:

- Senior management and strategic planners charged with developing business strategies
- Consultants helping corporate executives shape their companies' competitive future
- Information technology managers leading their teams with strategic decisions

This book is a must-read for all managers, consultants, entrepreneurs, and business school students who have been discussing and reading about the mobile revolution and who are interested in knowing how they can capitalize on the next wave of business innovation.

How This Book Is Organized

Chapter 1 describes the emergence of mobile as a new variable affecting business. We discuss the lessons learned from e-commerce and also lay out the structure of the mobile marketplace. Chapter 2 describes the broad trends that are driving the mobile economy. A framework for thinking about the mobile landscape is presented in Chapter 3.

Chapters 4 through 9 explore the various elements in the mobile framework. The goal is to identify clear, rational, strategic design choices that are responsive to evolving customer and employee needs. Each chapter describes the various business scenarios in which mobile applications are useful.

The last chapter is prescriptive, focusing on the challenges of becoming mobile by describing the design process and explaining how to undertake it. In today's business environment, the stakes are high and failure is swift. How an organization mobilizes itself into constructive action will determine its ultimate success.

Finally, if there is one thing that should become clear beyond a shadow of a doubt as you read through this book, it is that fundamental structural changes in technology, business applications, and competition are taking place. Mobile business is moving from the fringe to the mainstream. Although many of us are not quite prepared mentally to deal with yet another technology wave, we must. Our customers and companies will demand it, and we will need to respond. So buckle up and get ready for another roller-coaster ride!

Acknowledgments

We have learned much through our research, speaking, consulting, and executive education engagements and extend thanks to the many people to whom we have talked—in particular, Peter Zencke, Peter Wesche, Howard Beader, Dave Robbins, Dan Pantaleo, Keith Wright, Alan Tripp, Shirish Netke, Philip Bernosky, Macy Andrews, Hemant Taneja, Gary Rohr, Vipanj Patel, Larry Roshfeld, Nagesh Vempaty, Fred Tanzella, Richard Welke, Diyakar Pushkoor, and Ananth Rao.

Thanks to the many people at McGraw-Hill who made this book possible—in particular, our editor, Michelle Williams, whose enthusiasm for this book was contagious. To Keith Gribble, thank you for your patience and expertise in editing our book. At e-Business Strategies, we thank Pavan Gundepudi for his help. And finally, thanks to all our family and friends, in particular Lynn Lorenc for her friendship and advice.

Ravi Kalakota
ravi@ebstrategy.com

Marcia M. Robinson
marcia@ebstrategy.com

M-Business

Structural Migration:
From E-Business to M-Business

- Why is Microsoft so focused on transforming itself from a PC firm into a multi-platform infrastructure services company? Does the company perceive a migration away from a PC-centric to a multi-device model?
- Why is Intel so intent on transforming itself from a leading microprocessor producer into a manufacturer of mobile networking and communications products? Are they anticipating the impact of emerging mobile innovations on the hardware ecosystem?
- Why is Nokia reinventing itself to become a major player in the mobile economy instead of a narrowly focused cell-phone manufacturer? Are they positioning themselves to become the Cisco of the mobile economy?
- Why is NTT DoCoMo—the leading wireless operator in Japan with over 25 million subscribers—exporting its i-mode mobile Internet service to the U.S. and Europe? Do they expect to leverage their first-mover advantage and dominate these emerging markets?
- Why is Sony attempting to make on-the-go, in-hand entertainment the next gaming frontier? Is Sony quietly becoming a dominant handset and content player in the mobile space?

- Why is AOL Time Warner investing billions of dollars to ensure that their information services are accessible on any device, anywhere? Do they perceive increasing demand for easy ways to stay connected to friends and family while on the go?

Why are these leading firms and others like IBM, SAP, and Bertelsmann repositioning themselves? What is behind this corporate migration toward mobility? Are these firms expecting the mobile Internet to be the main catalyst toward a new kind of computing and a new kind of Internet? Are they anticipating that a new technology infrastructure is emerging to supersede the Web and form the bedrock of the next economy?

The changes the companies discussed above are making illustrate a pattern of structural migration from tethered PC-centric models toward mobile person-centric models. What does this mean for business? Within the next decade, mobile computing devices will become commonplace as broadband access and new wireless networks become increasingly available. As the lethal combination of computing and wireless gets embedded into everything from cars to toys, current business models have to morph to derive competitive advantage.

Mobility will change customer interaction in unforeseen ways and place traditional profit and revenue models on uncertain ground and at potential risk. Why? Today, customer relationships are characterized by a tethered, desktop-confined way of thinking. As new technologies and trends slowly shift the center of gravity from tethered to untethered models, a change-wave is unfolding. The companies anticipating this change-wave are moving quickly to reinvent themselves.

Historically, the emergence of new customer priorities and expectations resulted in new business opportunities and market structures. Astute entrepreneurs are aware that customer priorities have a tendency to shift in response to new technologies. As a result, entrepreneurs and venture capital firms are racing to create new companies to fill the perceived gaps. *In your industry, do you see any gaps due to the shift in technology or customer priorities?*

Changing customer priorities weaken existing industry structures, often forcing change. The history of technology is rich with examples of market leaders who were unable to make the necessary adjustments to ride the new wave. The railroad, steel, automotive, mainframe, minicomputer, and the Internet infrastructure industries each have experienced volatile changes in what customers want and expect. As a result, entrenched players are rendered vulnerable to attack from new entrants better positioned to address customer needs.

Structural Migration: Are You Ready?

A silent revolution is affecting dozens of industry sectors in the world economy. The emergence of the mobile Internet capable of interconnecting numerous devices and multiple information webs represents a global megatrend. It represents a new phase in enabling the knowledge worker. As a result, a substantial new creative cycle predicated on the marriage of the Internet, wireless technology, and e-commerce is upon us.

Sure, you're thinking, I've heard that before. Well, think again. It's true that in the 1990s wireless networks burst onto the scene with promises of big payoffs that rarely materialized. But today, the industry is broader and healthier, thanks to five key developments: huge advances in the infrastructure, advances in software, abundant capital, a more interested consumer, and the burgeoning demands of real-time business. The players are no longer just the geeks and early-adopters; they include mainstream users, and these users are demanding mobility. Mobility means fully portable, real-time access to the same information resources and tools that, until recently, were accessible only from your desktop.

Figure 1.1 illustrates the five cascading structural changes that have taken place over the last two decades. These decades are pretty unique in terms of the scope and pace of change. The first two structural shifts—system integration and business reengineering—required a major internal retooling of the corporation. For instance, in the steel industry, foreign competition and the demand for more efficiency forced a dramatic restructuring in the United States through competitive pressure. The automotive industry had to go through a similar structural migration by engaging in cost-cutting, restructuring, and reengineering.

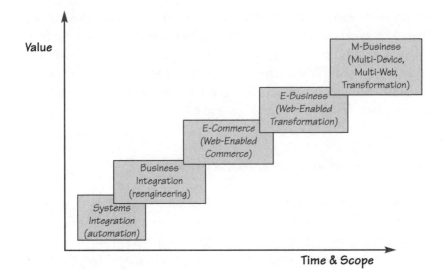

Figure 1.1: Market Evolution

Since 1995, we have seen literally three major structural shifts in rapid succession: e-commerce, e-business, and m-business. Interestingly, the structural changes caused by these shifts are not restricted to the four walls of the enterprise but have impacted the boundaries of the enterprise. E-commerce has had tremendous impact on how companies interact with their customers. E-business has had similar impact on the supplier and employee side. Since it is too early to definitely say, one can only speculate that m-business will have even more impact since its tentacles spread everywhere. M-business is unique since its effects are going to be evident at three levels: infrastructure and devices, applications and experiences, and relationships and supply chains.

M-Business: Vision Becomes Reality

To put it bluntly: Mobile applications will change the way we all live, play, and do business. No hyperbole. Let's look again at the evolution taking place:

- Phase 1—the user going to the computer's location (PC-centric)
- Phase 2—the computer is wherever the user is (person-centric)

The most significant economic consequence of this evolution will be the increased real-time interaction between companies and their customers, employees, and suppliers. Management everywhere must assess how the person-centric megatrend will alter their existing business models and develop proactive scenarios for deriving the greatest benefit from the technological changes taking place.

The leadership at many major firms is aware of the gravity of this technological shift and is making significant efforts to transform their business designs and competencies in order to successfully adapt to this new environment. Take, for instance, Microsoft, which has embraced mobility with a vengeance. From chief architect Bill Gates on down, the company is championing the extension of its desktop and server operating systems into the new generation of mobile devices and services. In addition, its .NET strategy is intended specifically to address the needs of multi-device and multi-network computing. In mid-1999, the company updated its product strategy to read "empowering people through great software anytime, anywhere, any device." The product that once defined Microsoft—the personal computer—is an aging starlet. Mobility is a young ingenue whose future promise is so enticing that Microsoft is racing with many initiatives to take a prominent position.

Companies like Microsoft anticipate that mobile computing will continue to enjoy strong growth for two primary reasons: First, it allows people to control the way they communicate by offering multiple devices, applications, and tools from which to select. Second, it permits people to control the time and frequency with which they obtain information. In Great Britain almost half of children age seven to sixteen now have a mobile phone. Text messaging is rapidly becoming the favorite method of communication, with an average of 2.5 messages per phone sent every day.[1] Mobile-phone users are increasingly accessing the Internet during downtime—short periods of free time such as sitting on the bus or during a coffee break. In other words, the Internet is ubiquitous.

Mobile computing represents the first wave of applications to take advantage of the ubiquitous computing trend. Vincent Cerf, one of the inventors of the Internet's technological underpinnings, once said that the Internet (and the Web) would become so ubiquitous it would disappear. Late-night talk-show jokes about ubiquitous computing—like your refrigerator sending you an e-mail when your kids drink your beer—are becoming today's reality. Computing is so pervasive that the computer is receding into the background. This ubiquity represents the gradual maturity of a technological innovation. For instance, we don't think about the electrical infrastructure when we turn on a lamp. Just like electrical power, the Internet will soon be accessible from anywhere. That is the central theme of the mobile economy.

The Rise of the Mobile Economy

Gradually but relentlessly, the structure of computing is changing. Although the dominance of tethered business will remain in the short term, a shift of seismic proportions is under way. The multi-channel customer revolution coupled with the development of mobile technology in its many manifestations is going to have a profound effect. No one is in any doubt about that. Where the uncertainty lies is in precisely when and how a new order will be imposed and which companies will emerge as the winners and losers. Consider the following:[2]

> Over 1 million vehicles in the United States are equipped with satellite tracking and communication devices, mostly new OnStar-equipped GM vehicles. Among other things, OnStar offers automatic notification of air bag deployment, tracking of stolen vehicles, emergency services, roadside assistance, remote door unlock and diagnostics. OnStar has about 800,000 subscribers in the United States and Canada, and expects more than 4 million vehicles to be equipped with the service by 2003.
>
> Subscribers to OnStar service will be able to track, manage and trade stocks while behind the wheel, under GM's alliance with Fidelity Investments. Fidelity Investments will offer in-vehicle access to quotes and market information to all subscribers of OnStar's Virtual Advisor. The service will allow customers to retrieve their account balances and do wireless trading. The OnStar service uses voice-activated, hands-free software, allowing drivers to keep their eyes on the road as the information is read to

them. Virtual Advisor also offers Web-based information such as e-mail, news, sports reports and weather. While the investment services will be offered for free to Virtual Advisor users, OnStar subscribers still will have to pay for bundled cell phone minutes.

The mobile economy (m-economy) is both inevitable and imminent. Businesses are at the threshold of an innovation tidal wave offering unforeseen technical and process capabilities. This m-economy is facilitated by the convergence of the Internet, e-business, and the wireless world where customers can go online anytime, anywhere, and using any device. This vision is often referred to by a variety of labels—Evernet, Supranet, X Internet, and Hypernet[3]—the next-generation multi-network, multi-content Internet will be accessed by millions of people using mobile devices.

As a result, the nature of customer interaction and speed of business is bound to change in the next decade. Businesses in the m-economy will have to deliver existing and next-generation services and applications with greater speed, intelligence, interactivity, and personalization than ever before. To support this vision, a new value chain is emerging that focuses on the blending of mobile device types, wireless access, and content.

The early phases of the m-economy will likely be chaotic. The adoption of technological innovation by the business world is seldom a neat, linear process. When a company first adopts an innovation, it can come as an abrupt shock. The period immediately following the adoption is often tumultuous and disruptive to the existing social and business processes. However, this period is typically short-lived and the technological and process changes soon diffuse throughout the organization in a steady and gradual manner. This is particularly true for larger firms. How technological and process diffusion occurs within companies will be a major issue as the rapid proliferation of mobile devices and new Internet appliances sets the stage for the mobile business boom.

Certain media spin-doctors portray the transition to the m-economy as nothing less than a total and complete upheaval in the way that every company and every industry currently conducts business. Other observers—those who lived through the roller-coaster years of the new economy or were burnt by the "E revolution"—view the transition as a gradual evolution of existing business landscapes wherein corporate cultures steadily absorb the new innovations over time. The truth about the m-economy combines aspects of both perspectives—it is a mix of revolution and evolution.

Internet + Wireless + E-Business = M-Business

It is useful to define the commonly used concepts associated with the rise of the Internet over the past decade in order to clarify key distinctions in the business realities they represent. These concepts are e-commerce, e-business, m-business, and m-commerce.

E-commerce is simply the buying and selling of products and services over the Web. The larger concept—e-business—represents all the technological applications and business processes enabling a company to service an e-commerce transaction. In addition to encompassing e-commerce, e-business includes both the front- and back-office applications that form the core engine driving contemporary business transactions. In the broadest sense, e-business is the overall strategy of redefining old business models, with the aid of technology, to maximize customer value and profits.

However, nearly all e-commerce and e-business applications envisioned and developed so far assume fixed or stationary users with wired infrastructure. This paradigm of fixed e-commerce is evolving with the emergence and widespread adoption of wireless data networks into m-commerce. Mobile commerce refers to business transactions conducted while on the move. M-commerce's growth is due to users seeking to conduct business, communicate and share information while away from their desktop computers.

M-business, on the other hand, is the application infrastructure required to maintain business relationships and sell information, services, and commodities by means of the mobile devices. Think of m-commerce as the facade and m-business as everything that is happening behind the scenes. M-business is also the logical extension of e-business to address new customer channels and integration challenges.

Note that mobile business can take place even if devices are not connected to the Internet. It would be disingenuous to assume that all mobile devices are going to be online all the time.

The Meaning of Mobile

Mobile implies portability; a device such as PalmPilot travels with you. Mobile is also commonly used to imply that the device has an "always on" connection to the Internet. So, the term "mobile" is being used to denote two different scenarios: offline and online.

- **Mobile but offline** means that you can use the device to run self-contained programs while not connected to the Internet. You can "sync" with a PC to download software, e-mail messages, and other content onto your personal digital assistant (PDA) for portable reading or offline reference. Data collected on the road can be synchronized with a PC once you get back to the office or uploaded when a live Internet connection is established.
- **Mobile but online** is commonly called wireless. This implies that the experience is based on a real-time live Internet connection via satellite, cellular, or radio transmitters. An online device will be "always on" in the presence of any wireless data network—seamlessly connecting to the Internet so it can exchange e-mail and instant messages and retrieve Web content.

The distinction between offline and online affects how m-business applications are designed and used. For instance, if real-time data is involved, such as a salesperson checking inventory availability, it is important to design an application to work with a direct connection to the back-office server. On the other hand, if you download an e-book and read it in an airport, then there is no need to dial up your server. The user is able to work offline without the need for a live connection. M-business covers both online and offline scenarios.

Mobile Business: The Quest for New Value

Applying mobile access to computing creates both tremendous commercial opportunity and complexity simultaneously. As the mobile Internet raises customer expectations and drives competition, companies are bound to discover that pretty fast is not fast enough. It will not be enough to move quickly: Successful businesses must operate in real time. In the face of such a large-scale structural change, entrepreneurs, corporate managers, and investors alike must act quickly and proactively to design their strategies for addressing the complexities of real-time business.

In defining their m-business strategy, the key first step for each of these players is to assess where the most value is created and captured. For the entrepreneur, the greatest value is created during the innovation phase by being first to market with new value propositions. For managers, the most value is created in the technology-infusion phase by being first to market with value-adding applications—using mobile technology to better deliver services and manufacture products. For savvy investors, value is created in both phases—investing in new market leaders (the next Cisco) and investing in new value leaders (the next Schwab). Clearly, we will see a period of rapid growth in the number of new entrants into the mobile space, followed by a period of shakeout and consolidation. *Are you reengineering your investment portfolio?*

The next generation of successful business leaders will be those who embrace the entire mobile concept, rather than a specific product or a service, as the starting point of mobile innovation. The history of business has shown repeatedly how, in times of technological creation and change, market leadership accrues to those who understand and implement strategies for creating new value. Market leaders compete not on the basis of products or services but on the basis of value creation. Market leaders don't tinker with cost cutting; they create new opportunities that can lead to exponential growth.

The emergence of the mobile economy will once again confirm this historic pattern. Fundamental business models and maxims that have been in place for decades will be under siege. As the global economy transitions to the mobile economy, existing business processes will be further streamlined, disintermediated, and reintermediated anew. In order to make sense of the coming changes, managers everywhere will need a fresh perspective on the technology, customer behavior, business models, and applications enabling the mobile economy.

Learning from the Fruit Flies

In following new things, we sometimes show a surprising tendency to delude ourselves into believing that history doesn't apply. This time it's different! So, as the economy stands at the threshold of another change, it is important to pause and reflect on how such changes have been handled in the past in order to avoid the same pitfalls. We believe there are important lessons to be learned from rapid-growth industries such as the personal computer and e-commerce. We also believe the pattern of this growth can be used to understand how the m-economy will evolve.

The implications of mobility on business are notoriously difficult to evaluate, because of the mass of material and the problem of distinguishing the significant event from the insignificant. So how do we go about making sense of it all? From the fruit flies. Biologists study the fruit fly because of their fast rate of development. They grow rapidly from one stage of life to the next, and this permits scientists to gain insight more quickly into comparable stages in slow-paced human morphology. In 1906, Thomas Morgan, a Columbia University zoologist, conceived the idea of using fruit flies for genetic research. In addition to their rapid breeding, the flies require little food and have many easily observed characteristics. Morgan is quoted as saying: "The fly could be bred by the thousands in milk bottles. It costs nothing but a few bananas to feed all the experimental animals; their entire life cycle lasts 10 days and they have only four chromosomes."[4] Later, fruit flies were used in mutational research, which settled the question as to whether evolution could successfully result from genetic mutation.[5]

The researchers sped up the mutational process in the flies by introducing genetic changes into the species. However, even with this speed-up of the mutational process, the experiment has not produced a new species—only more fruit flies. After decades of study, the researchers have identified 400 different variants in their subjects. None of these resulted in changing the fruit fly into a different species. The most important result of these experiments is the demonstration of the upper and lower limits within which fruit flies have their unique identity but beyond which they'll never go. So just like the fruit flies, business principles, no matter how many technology variants, will remain the same.

These same morphological limits exist when we examine the evolution of a business. A company's interactions with its business environment shape its distinctive nature as it shifts its business models and responds to the environment over time. On the surface, the adoption of a new business model can make it seem as though a firm has undergone mutation. In reality, the underlying features that define a successful business never change. Effective, customer-focused value creation and profitable customer satisfaction are the core principles all successful firms share.

Comparing fast-reproducing biological species and rapidly transforming industries is compelling. Let's analyze the life cycle of e-commerce for the same reasons a geneticist would study the life cycle of the fruit fly. Because these flies reproduce so quickly, their entire life span is over within a period of a few weeks. Similarly, e-commerce business models seemed to be ephemeral. In fact, during the period 1994–2000, hundreds of e-commerce mutations appeared in the form of new business models. However, these mutations in many cases were simply extending or enhancing certain core business models. Like fruit flies, these e-commerce start-ups went through a rapid cycle: birth, venture funding, breakneck growth, reality, and bankruptcy.

Studying e-commerce mutations may provide insight into understanding how m-business may evolve and the pitfalls to avoid.

Past as Prologue: Learning from the E-Commerce Fruit Flies

The excitement of m-business feels like déjà vu. If e-commerce is entering its adolescence, then m-commerce is in its infancy. This baby has a great deal to learn from the personal computer and e-commerce generations. The general development of the mobile economy will follow a pattern similar to the beginning of the computing, PC, and e-commerce industries.

Let's look at the computing industry and see what evolutionary lessons can be learned. In four decades we have seen four major shifts in the computing industry. From the mainframe to the minicomputer, to the PC, and now to the handheld, we have experienced the change from centralized to decentralized to networked computing. With each shift, cheaper computing systems appeared and people gained greater control of their computing capabilities. Interestingly, no one firm dominated from one generation of computing technology to the next. Each became wedded to its legacy systems, customer base, and cash flow and was reluctant to pursue a course of radical, constant technological innovation.

In contrast to the computing evolution, the PC industry's evolution involved three distinct phases. In the industry's early years, value was primarily placed on hardware/infrastructure products and services. But over time, the value shifted—first to enabling technologies such as operating systems, and software and services for managing the interactive environment—and ultimately to programming, content, and aggregation. Although the PC was *Time* magazine's Man of the Year in 1982, its actual e-business impact took more than two decades to unfold. The PC industry transformation can be measured by three factors: the rate of change in product development, process creation, and organization renewal. With increasing speed of evolution, competitive advantage became more temporary and tentative.

If the PC industry evolution was fast, it was nothing compared to the breakneck pace set by the e-commerce industry. E-commerce evolution involved four distinct phases. In the early years, value was placed on network infrastructure and dial-up access products and services. Companies such as Cisco, Ascend (bought by Lucent), and U.S. Robotics (bought by 3COM) represented this sector. Building on the network developments of the early years, the industry's access providers experienced significant growth. Companies such as UUNET, Netcom, and America Online represented the industry's value focus during the second phase of the Internet's evolution.

During the third phase the value focus shifted to the software enablers such as browser providers Spyglass and Netscape and to server companies such as OpenMarket. In the fourth phase, the value shifted from the software enablers to the e-commerce enablers search engine and security offerings, such as Yahoo and Verisign, respectively. The e-commerce enablers prepared the foundation for the Internet applications, content, and programming.

On the applications side, e-commerce has evolved into three major mutations: business to consumer (B_2C), business to business (B_2B), and business to employee (B_2E). The evolution of these three mutations offers valuable insight into how m-commerce applications will likely evolve in the coming decade. Charles Schwab, the do-it-yourself investment firm, is an example of a B_2C e-commerce mutation.

In the mid-1990s, Schwab's management realized that American consumers were now purchasing more PCs than television sets. This fact, together with the growth of the Internet, made it clear to

Schwab how basic retail communication was changing. As a result, they undertook an e-commerce initiative and in 1996 added Internet trading to the company's offerings. The firm also consolidated its online business into one package, offering all customers full-service Internet trading for one standard per-trade fee. There were significant risks associated with this decision because of its potentially serious impact on revenues. However, in spite of the risks, Schwab proceeded. It maintained a long-term focus because it believed the only way to build a successful business over time was to attract and retain satisfied loyal customers. As a result of this decision, Schwab saw a dramatic increase in customers, significantly increased trading, and realized tremendous, bottom-line growth.

The mobile economy is evolving in a very similar way to the e-commerce wave. Hardware and infrastructure lead software and applications. As in real-world commerce, the basic infrastructure—transportation, gas and electric networks—is critical before actual commerce can happen. Likewise, a solid infrastructure is critical for supporting the complex array of mobile devices and applications. However, as in the development of the PC market where the focus shifted away from hardware to software, m-business will be less hardware dependent and more software and application dependent as the industry matures.

While the mobile economy is exciting, not all promises will come to pass. Many of the analysts projections are simply too optimistic. In recent years, the mobile Internet has lifted expectations way too high, while reality has lagged considerably. The myths have hurt the industry and dampened some of the near-term opportunities. It's going to take a little time to recover. The long-term prospects of the mobile economy are extremely exciting. But it would be irresponsible to ignore the historical precedents with which we're all familiar. The rise and fall of the e-commerce revolution is a caution against too quickly denouncing the old and thoughtlessly embracing the new.

Rapidly changing industries such as computers, application software, semiconductors, and even consulting usually pass through predictable stages: an inflection point or a trigger, an era of widespread experimentation and turbulence, and convergence to a new, stable structure. We expect m-business to follow a similar pattern. However, there are three major pitfalls that m-business companies should avoid:

- **Speed kills.** A fast-growth mania seized the e-commerce companies, creating a voracious appetite for capital. As a result, companies were always planning for the next round of financing. This type of operation is a recipe for disaster.
- **Fashion and glamour don't make a business.** The glamour of a booming e-commerce marketplace and rosy outlooks helped start-up companies raise obscene amounts of money from venture capitalists and other sources. Creating a sustainable business takes a lot more than funding.
- **Diffusion of innovation takes time.** It almost always involves some degree of social, economic, company, and individual dislocation. Change takes time and patience.

Unfortunately, these same patterns appear to be repeating with the early mobile companies.

Unfolding the Mobile Ecosystem

The adage "Nature abhors a vacuum" holds true when an untapped opportunity for new profits exists. The mobile marketplace is giving rise to an array of new businesses at an extremely fast pace. Consider the following:

> Texas Instruments (TI) is investing $100 million in software developers writing wireless Internet software for its Open Multimedia Applications Platform (OMAP) over the next 12 to 18 months. Several potential areas of focus for developers include mobile commerce, multimedia, messaging, encryption and interactive gaming. OMAP is essentially a blueprint—based on TI's digital signal processors (DSPs)—for building next-generation cell phones and other wireless devices that will access the Internet. TI wants to ensure it enjoys a prominent place in the wireless ecosystem as it is created over the next few years. By seeding the market for OMAP-friendly applications, TI will, the theory goes, have an easier time persuading cell phone manufacturers, among others, to adopt its chips.[6]

What TI is doing is not unique. They are attempting to nurture and create a TI-centric mobile ecosystem composed of hardware, software, and original equipment manufacturers (OEM). Other manufacturers like Intel are creating their own parallel ecosystems. Microsoft is attempting to create its own ecosystem. Instead of focusing on each one of these ecosystem variants, it is important to understand what the overall mobile ecosystem looks like from a broad perspective and which areas—infrastructure, software, hardware, or services—deserve attention.

To help entrepreneurs, managers, and investors make sense out of this chaos, we have classified these emerging companies into seven main business areas. One interesting and unusual aspect is that the mobile industry has a number of the leading companies (Nokia, for example) that participate in more than one of the business areas. The areas are:

- **Network Infrastructure.** Companies providing the hardware, fiber networks, wireless communications towers, and satellite networks to enable the convergence of telecommunications and IP networks. This is about replacing hardware-based switching and proprietary service platforms with open network protocols, next-generation mobile switching centers, and high-capacity base stations. The typical business model is based on hardware sales or leasing to telecom companies. Examples include American Tower, Ericsson, Motorola, and Alcatel.
- **Access.** Companies selling dial-up and/or dedicated network connections to provide mobile access to Web services. The typical business model is based on monthly fees, which are determined by the speed of the connection and/or the volume of data flowing through it. Examples include Palm.Net, GoAmerica, OmniSky, AT&T Wireless, and Cingular.
- **Content.** Companies providing everything you see when you go online. These firms include both "portals and syndicators," which organize, aggregate, and provide access to content created by other companies, and "destinations," which create specialized content—for example, news and sports. The typical content business model is based on advertising and subscription fees. Examples include Yahoo!, Infospace, and I3 Mobile.

- **Commerce**. Companies selling merchandise or information, or facilitating the matching of buyers and sellers. The typical business model resembles that of a retailer or auctioneer, although as the industry develops it will likely begin to encompass advertising as well. Commerce companies operate in three arenas: consumer to consumer (C2C), business to consumer (B2C), and business to business (B2B). Examples include Amazon.com, Grainger, and eBay.

- **Software**. Companies selling software to facilitate inter- or intra-enterprise communication and commerce. The software area includes operating systems, security, and applications software customized for the wireless world. The typical business model is composed of software license fees, software maintenance fees, consulting services, and, increasingly, software hosting and operation services. Examples include Qualcomm, Microsoft, and Tibco.

- **Hardware**. Companies selling hardware like handheld PCs or networking equipment to facilitate mobile applications. This also includes some complementary markets, namely PCs, servers, semiconductors, and telecommunications service and equipment, which will benefit indirectly a hardware company's success. This business model is based on selling hardware directly to users or network operators. Examples include Handspring, Compaq, HP, and Sun Microsystems.

- **Applications**. Companies providing a wide variety of services necessary in the online ecosystem, including hosting, application rental, transaction processing, information databases, consulting, design, and implementation. It is to be noted that mobile commerce may require significantly different approaches in design, development, and implementation of applications due to the inherent characteristics of wireless networks and mobile devices. The typical business model is based on software license, "per-click" transactions, time and materials, or subscription fees. Examples include Aether, Air2Web, and Mobilicity.

Each of these segments interrelates and contains numerous subsections. For example, software for the mobile Internet can be further broken down into operating system software, security, compression, application software, and network management. Combining elements from each of the seven areas gives rise to solutions. The potential market for mobility solutions is enormous, and it's growing. While a number of the businesses operating in these areas will be new, others will have their origins in more than a decade of enterprise-level IT expenditures and more recent Internet technology investments.

How Will the Mobile Solutions Evolve?

These seven areas—network infrastructure, access, content, commerce, software, hardware, and applications—will have to come together to create value for customers. Customer value creation will most likely occur in five solution phases based on continuous improvements in mobile technology. These phases are:

- **Phase 1—Messaging**. The ability to interact with others. Short messaging services (SMS) have proven to be extremely popular on two-way pagers and mobile phones. Sources estimate that more than 80 percent of worldwide wireless data subscribers subscribe to SMS. The next stage in the development of messaging technology is direct access to corporate e-mail accounts. However, significant improvements in the data rate, memory, and storage capacity of wireless devices need to occur before corporate e-mail access displaces SMS as the messaging tool of preference.
- **Phase 2—Info-connectivity**. The ability to access and retrieve information from the Web. Unlike messaging, this requires a mobile device to maintain a real-time connection to the Internet. While such a capability already exists, the quality of information currently available is poor. Much of the information is free and often trivial. At a minimum, wireless browsers should become commonplace before this phase takes off.
- **Phase 3—Transactions**. Business transactions begin to take place via the mobile channel. Rather than applying a quick-fix approach to achieve a wireless Web presence, corporations need to develop an m-commerce strategy for extending and growing revenue-generating wireless transactions. The customer is a different entity in the mobile business model. They are identifiable,

locatable, and immediately in "buying mode" once they turn on their wireless device. Growth in the third phase will occur in unpredictable ways. It is very much dependent on a few killer applications. It is a common occurrence in Phase 3 for strategies to evolve, morph, and mutate.

- **Phase 4—Transformation.** The interconnection of business processes—inside the company and between organizations—takes place. For the notion of "business without boundaries" to prevail, back-end applications and data must be reengineered to take complete advantage of the features mobility offers. Implementing mobility-enhanced internal and external business processes will be the most difficult and challenging aspect of the m-business revolution. It is also where the largest gains in true economic and business value will be found.

- **Phase 5—Infusion.** The company absorbs mobility into its way of doing business. Mobility is no longer separated from the normal course of doing business. Infusion requires a shift from a culture in which technology is merely occasionally present, to one in which technology is an accepted part of business. Infusion requires a company, its employees, its suppliers, and even its customers to once again reengineer their business processes and relationships in order to acclimate the company's culture to the technology's presence. During this phase there will most likely be tremendous industry consolidation. Weak players either die or get bought out, as with the business-to-consumer e-commerce consolidations that occurred in 2000 and business-to-business e-commerce consolidations that occurred in 2001.

Mobile companies today are in Phase 1. However, the period when messaging and e-mail applications will dominate wireless communications will be short-lived. As noted earlier, how quickly and completely the mobile Internet is adopted and used will be determined by how well the software applications it provides meet real customer needs.

Shifts from one phase to another are rather difficult to predict. In 1985, had you asked people if they were ready for fax machines, cell phones, or personal computers when they first came out, they probably would have said they weren't going to fall over themselves to buy the technology. Most customers don't buy technology. They buy applications to solve a need. The mobile industry has responsibility for demonstrating its products and services usefulness to the consumer. If this demonstration provides compelling business and personal reasons for adopting a mobile business lifestyle, sales will take care of themselves. Let's look at some business applications that appear to be taking root in the mobile space.

Business Applications, Not Technology

What do customers really buy? Not operating systems, processors, or architectures. They buy applications, performance, and useful solutions. It is widely acknowledged that the usefulness of the mobile channel will largely be driven by new applications that enhance the overall customer value. Consider the following "applications" of technology to solve a business problem:

- While traveling, a sales representative for a pharmaceutical manufacturer receives a customer request for a larger-than-anticipated order. She uses a pocket PC to immediately confirm the availability of additional inventory and the timing for delivery in order to capture a larger sale.
- After notifying its customers of an investment opportunity in a software company's initial public offering, an online brokerage service receives and executes a buy order sent from a customer's Web-enabled phone while she commutes from work.
- At the customer's location, a field service technician for a semiconductor company is repairing a flat-panel display and uses a personal digital assistant to identify the appropriate replacement part, confirm availability at the nearest warehouse, and place the order.
- An on-the-go executive monitors e-mail via her cell phone. Basically, the cell phone is set up to poll her e-mail accounts. Once the email has been received, she can access it via a toll-free number. E-mail is read to her by a text-to-speech utility.

Clearly, the framework of applications is morphing from "nice-to-have" personal information management applications to "need-to-have," mission critical, or strategic to the corporation applications.

The convergence of the Internet and wireless connectivity offers companies the opportunity to leverage their existing Web infrastructure investments and extend the reach of their Web-based applications and content to their mobile customers, employees, suppliers, and business affiliates. The applications that once resided exclusively on the desktop—everything from word processing to industrial-strength enterprise software packages—are being modified to be delivered across wireless networks to a variety of devices, including laptops, palmtops, and tablets.

The major challenge facing all mobile applications will be the ability to deliver as holistic a user experience as is currently attainable online through the limits of a handheld device.

Mobile Infrastructure: The Access Race Is On

We've discussed several potential uses of the wireless Web, and there are obviously many more. But it is equally important to consider how we attain this mobile world. To that end, there are a number of infrastructure issues that must be considered when seeking to enable the next generation of m-business solutions.

Today, the development of the mobile Internet infrastructure is in its infancy. It is at the same level of development as was the railroad system in America in the 1860s. Imagine it's 1865 and railroad tracks are just beginning to be deployed. You've been offered the option of investing in (a) a group of five companies that have a near monopoly on railroad ties, or (b) one of ten capital-intensive start-ups that want to control railroad traffic in different regions. Which one would you choose? Similarly, if you were given the option of investing in mobile infrastructure enablers—Nokia, Cisco, Ericsson—or infrastructure builders—AT&T Wireless, Sprint PCS—where would you put your dollars?

The mobile infrastructure is at a similar level of development as the "wired" Internet's infrastructure was in the early 1990s. During those early years, visionaries expected more than a decade of infrastructure build-out and technology challenges to surmount in order to deliver the Internet access to a mass audience. Think about it. In 1992, Internet communication was via a primitive e-mail service using the SLIP protocol with a 386 computer and 9.6-Kbps modems. The major innovation and catalyst for the Internet revolution, however, came when engineering students at the University of Illinois unleashed their "Mosaic" browser, which was later commercialized as the killer application Netscape.

Internet content vendors from weather stations to bookstore operations established an online presence as more and more users accessed the Web. Internet "browser" technology improved significantly to include rudimentary formatting conventions such as tables, and enhanced technological capabilities such as Java scripts. At the time, many companies could almost taste the ensuing build-out aimed at stepping up the data bandwidth while cutting out online latency or delays. The phone companies, with their primitive "circuit-switched" networks that had not changed significantly from the days of the early switchboard operators, found themselves well behind the demand curve. They witnessed their networks crash when users around the world would stay connected for days at a time. As ISP's such as America Online built out higher-speed modems or "fatter pipes" (9.6 Kbps, 14.4 Kbps, 28.8 Kbps, 56 Kbps), the data "bottleneck" migrated from the network's edge to its core—the fiber transmission backbone—which had to be upgraded again and again to meet bandwidth demand. As a new generation of entrepreneurs stepped forward to fill customers' data requirements, a new cycle of infrastructure innovation was initiated.

Just like the Internet infrastructure build-out, the mobile infrastructure build-out will be gradual. The market will be composed of companies that are addressing different problems:

- **Mobile Data Networks**—How to increase coverage? How to increase wireless data bandwidth? How to increase capacity of existing networks?
- **Mobile Internet Infrastructure**—How to create new technology that enables the convergence of telecommunications and IP networks? What transmission protocols and content languages are required to make this happen?
- **Mobile Internet Service Providers**—How to provide mobile Internet connectivity to the masses?

As communications technology changes its focus from the old mode of "connecting to a fixed place" to the new model of "connecting to a person on the move," billions of dollars in spending will be required to obtain last-mile access for both fixed and mobile applications. However, the infrastructure investments have to be closely aligned with the mobile devices.

Mobile Devices: The Race for Radical New Products Is On

The traditional PC industry is at a crossroads, if not heading into a decline. Few, if any, significant changes in PC design have occurred in recent years. More important, no new, truly useful mainstream applications have been introduced since the advent of Microsoft Office Suite. The absence of change within the PC industry during the past five years reflects a mature market. The sudden availability of tens of thousands of mobile computing appliances would further threaten the industry's standing and render the desktop PC even less relevant for conducting business today. The days of assembling commodity PCs with fat profit margins and eager buyers are long past. One certainty about the PC's future: It will become increasingly portable.

Figure 1.2 depicts the Internet's evolution from time-share to the embedded model. This also represents moving away from a PC-centric dependence and toward a next-generation multi-device accessibility. Tomorrow's Internet will be accessed from a legion of new digital devices, including personal digital assistants (PDAs), handheld PCs, digital cameras, MP3 players, handheld gaming devices, and many more. Simply put, we are witnessing an evolution where Internet access will be embedded in an endless variety of appliances. An Internet appliance, or information appliance, as the future will show, is any non-PC device that leverages the capabilities of the Internet to extend content, services, and applications to the users.

There have been previous attempts to create new mobile devices. Early endeavors, such as Apple's Newton, failed because they were too heavy and cumbersome, and had poor screen resolution, a short battery life, and poor handwriting recognition capability. Many of these early design issues have been resolved through recent improvements in technology. Today, the PDA is essentially a pocket PC on steroids used to store, access, and organize whatever information you choose. Most PDAs work on either a Windows-CE or Palm operating system. Basic PDAs allow you to store and retrieve

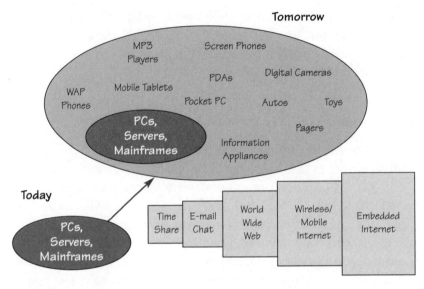

Figure 1.2: Evolution of Internet Access

addresses and phone numbers, maintain a calendar, create to-do lists and notes, play music, and record voice memos. More sophisticated PDAs can run word processing, spreadsheet, and electronic book reading programs, and also provide e-mail and Internet access. *What is the PDA going to evolve into next?*

Embedded Internet appliances will appear in the familiar form of the washing machine, television, and remote control. Others will resemble gadgets seen only in science-fiction films. Whatever their form, these devices will extend the Internet further into the interactions of daily life. Internet appliances, in theory, appear ready to revolutionize the way that information is currently used and accessed. However, it is not clear what form of appliance will be widely adopted.

The most successful appliances will be easy-to-use, task-oriented devices that leverage the benefits of Internet access to enhance their core functionality. Most likely, these appliances will not be loaded with every conceivable application and function, since this would defeat the design goals of ease of use and simplicity. If consumers want a PC, they will buy a PC. There is no reason to believe that televisions, gaming consoles, and telephones will stop being used for entertainment, gaming, and communication, respectively. Appliance-relevant content and services such as programming guides for Web TVs, online gaming services for gaming consoles, and directory services for telephones are examples of potential enhancements. Access providers will need to bundle and update relevant content or service with their appliance in an effort to attract and retain subscribers. Clearly, new business models are needed.

M-Business: What Stage Are We In?

Business models for competing in the m-economy are in the early stages of development. This is evident in scathing media reports highlighting the limitations of what is understandably an immature industry. These reports criticized the mobile industry for not having resolved issues of low bandwidth, differing communications and equipment standards, the presence of multiple carriers, and a myriad of devices, all of which decrease the ability of service companies to present users with a satisfying experience. This criticism is unwarranted and reflects a historical ignorance of how new technology is developed and adopted by society. There are no shortcuts. Building infrastructure takes time. The wired Internet industry had to address similar issues, including busy signals, the World Wide Wait, and insecure browser technology. The issues the mobile industry faces are significant, but they are also normal growing pains for every technology.

Technological visions often suffer from an enthusiasm that conveniently overlooks the practical reasons why they won't actually happen as quickly as the promoters would like them to. To overcome this vision-to-reality mismatch, it is important to understand where the technology is in the diffusion curve—a kind of social change, defined as the process by which an innovation is adopted through certain channels over time.[7] The technology diffusion curve has several key phases: visionary, missionary, ordinary, commodity, and maturity. We anticipate that mobile technology will follow a similar pattern.

In the visionary phase, technology is a novelty—sounds great, but don't know what to do with it. Entrepreneurs normally bloom when a technology is in the visionary phase. They anticipate new opportunities and create value propositions to address perceived gaps in the marketplace. During the visionary phase, few companies make money from technology, at least not initially. During the California gold rush, the story goes, the only people who made money were the ones selling shovels. M-commerce during the innovator phase will mirror the times of the California gold rush. A good example of this is the third-generation (3G) infrastructure build-out. Few telecom companies truly understand how to make money from their investments. On the other hand, systems integrators and software vendors will make money constructing the foundation and infrastructure.

During the missionary phase, executives—IT managers, R&D geeks, and "radical" employees—are the typical buyers of the new technology. They see business value that others cannot. As a result, they become increasingly vocal proponents of mobile solutions. They preach the vision to others in their company—many new types of devices and their connecting technologies will soon enable consumers to have ubiquitous access to whatever content and applications they want, where and when they want them. Other missionary adopters include innovative end-users who either build their own solution or customize a prebuilt solution to meet their standards. Innovative users embrace innovation for innovation's sake. They are motivated to sample new technology just to see if it works.

During the ordinary phase, the mainstream users begin to see value in the technology. For instance, ordinary users are beginning to adopt mobile products, such as PalmPilots. The increasing use of these devices by consumers and corporate officers illustrates how these specific mobile devices are no longer novelties or innovations but are becoming increasingly mainstream tools for conducting m-business transactions. Also, during the ordinary phase, previously isolated "islands of technology" will be connected, providing users with an expanding stream of rich digital content. In this phase, m-business increases its market penetration because it improves productivity while building on prior e-commerce investments. Its roots are in more than a decade of enterprise-level IT expenditures. These previous implementations automated and integrated the once separate internal departments within an enterprise with powerful comprehensive applications and Intranet solutions. The m-commerce infrastructure is the logical extension of these previously installed technologies into new areas.

Commodity markets are represented by technology such as personal computers. Cell phones are currently in the mass market or commodity phase of the cycle. As recently as 1990 there were only 5 million wireless subscribers in the United States. By 2000, this number had increased to 90 million, and by 2005 the number is likely to approach 140 million. Increasingly, cell phones are categorized as a commodity technology. However, that is true on the voice side. On the mobile data side, many mobility applications are still in the visionary phase.

Maturity is represented by technology such as printers and fax machines. Maturity represents a market where little or no innovation is taking place. Mature markets, such as long-distance telephone carriers, are usually characterized by consolidation with a few players jockeying for market share.

In each phase, technology adoption is not smooth. Each stage in the adoption life cycle is separated from each other stage by gaps in the process. The most significant gap in adoption is the one that separates the missionary of a technology from the ordinary users of the same technology. Geoff Moore calls this "crossing the chasm" in his best-selling book. Making sure a technology's user base progresses beyond the missionary stage is the key to achieving sustainable growth and long-term shareholder value.

Crossing the missionary to ordinary phases takes courage and persistence. Given the history of other types of so-called revolutions, we are likely to see a "boom-bust-boom" cycle for mobile companies, where rapid growth is followed by a slowdown, skepticism, lack of momentum, and investor fears about competition. Successful companies will ride these out until they catch the next wave of positive investor sentiment, consolidation, increasing share, and real profit generation. Thus, after an initial burst of energy followed by some fits and starts along the way, a handful of leading mobile brands will likely emerge as great companies.

A Final Thought

Yesterday is not ours to recover, but tomorrow is ours to win or lose.
—Lyndon B. Johnson

Like it or not, the ecosystem for the mobile Internet will be created during the next few years. Every CEO wants to ensure his or her company a prominent place in it. Within two years, the mobile economic landscape will be much clearer. The pure-play first-movers, such as Palm, and the traditional companies who have gone mobile, such as Microsoft, will offer one another strong competition in the months ahead. In the interim, corporate leadership should be selective when investing in this emerging sector, choosing a mixed portfolio of enhancing existing strategies and experimenting with new ones to ensure their companies are well positioned to capitalize on both stable and riskier opportunities.

With technology-enabled business models, strategic opportunities can shift like the wind, making timing crucial. Leadership is about inspiring your organization to take bold steps and push the limits to go where no one has gone before. As we mentioned at the beginning of the chapter, leading organizations like Microsoft, Intel, and Sony are transforming themselves while simultaneously creating a shared picture of the mobile future. Creation of this shared vision is critical to any business venture's success, but particularly so during times of rapid socioeconomic and technological change.

As Peter Senge writes in *The Fifth Discipline*, "One is hard pressed to think of any organization that has sustained some measure of greatness in the absence of goals, values and missions that become deeply shared throughout the organization. IBM had service, Polaroid had instant photography; Ford had public transportation for the masses and Apple had computing power for the masses. Though radically different in content and kind, all these organization managed to bind people together around a common identity and sense of destiny."

When there is genuine vision, people excel, not because the vision statement tells them to, but because they believe in the cause. *Does your company have a vision of what it will be like to do business in a mobile economy?*

Trends Shaping
the Mobile Economy

In January 1975, *Popular Electronics* published a cover story on a computer kit called Altair 8800 that sold for less than $400. Microinstrumentation & Telemetry Systems (MITS) of Albuquerque, New Mexico, designed the Altair. It didn't look anything like the sleek machines of today. There was no monitor, no keyboard, and no mouse. The MITS Altair 8800 was a simple box with switches and small lights, designed for scientific calculations. It appealed mainly to hobbyists.[1]

The MITS was typical of first-generation technology. Many industry executives did not see a need for it. In 1977, Ken Olson, founder, president, and chairman of Digital Equipment, was quoted as saying, "There is no reason anyone would want a computer in their home." Even consumers did not see any need for it. If someone said, this would be great for calculations and accounting, people would laugh and say, "This would never replace the HP-35 four-function calculator." Or if someone said, this would be great for word processing, people would say, "This will never replace a typewriter." Clearly, the most troublesome aspect was not the technology per se but gauging the scale and speed of user acceptance.

Few could have foreseen what was to come. From that ordinary start in 1975, the PC industry has exploded into a $500-billion-a-year business. In a twenty-five-year period, the PC became an integral part of life—a word processing tool, accounting tool, messaging device, and entertainment center. The PC industry's fortunes increasingly sway the direction of the global economy. How did this industry become so influential so fast? There are four reasons: Customers found creative uses for the PC. PC software steadily improved in its price/performance ratio. The processor speed followed Moore's Law, doubling roughly every eighteen months or so. Lastly, the Internet greatly increased PC use.

There is reason to believe the evolution and adoption of mobile technology will follow a similar path. There will be intense skepticism followed by grudging adoption. As the prices of mobile devices and services drop, reliability improves, applications that they support get better, and demand will explode. Consider this: Today, more than 100 million households worldwide have access to the Web. There are already well over 1 billion cell phone users. Handheld sales are beginning to eclipse PC sales. It's only a matter of time before mobile becomes mainstream.

One thing is clear: The mobile economy is inevitable. However, few business gurus, visionaries, and prognosticators can predict the shape and form of mobile innovation. Though the future cannot be foreseen, it is possible to generate insight about the mobile economy by developing plausible scenarios, based on recognizable patterns. Scenarios are relevant to the problem of creating sustainable business models constructed from various elements—an understanding of current conditions, an identification of driving forces for change, and a vision of the future.

Mobile Trends: What's Around the Corner?

"Prediction is very difficult," wrote Nobel laureate Niels Bohr. "Especially about the future." Take the classic case of cell phones. AT&T hired McKinsey and Co. in the early 1980s to assess the market for cellular phones. The study opposed entry into the market because "the total market for mobile cellular phones will be 900,000 subscribers by the year 2000." By 1996, there were more than 90 million such devices and AT&T had to enter the market via an expensive acquisition of McCaw Cellular.[2]

Predicting what customers will buy, and how they will think and spend their time, is hardly an exact science. Still, it's difficult to develop effective business strategies without looking ahead. For instance, Motorola in the late 1970s foresaw the wireless world and this drove its strategy for its cellular, satellite, and pager businesses. Strategic thinking is always future-oriented; it is concerned with reaching goals and objectives that have not been attained. By analyzing emerging trends—processes, technology, latent customer needs, or new markets—executives can prepare business strategies to shape their plans for growth. Companies can no longer afford to believe that today looks like yesterday and tomorrow will be more of the same.

Yet, one of the hardest things for busy managers to do is stop and think about disruptive trends. Also, it is hard to distinguish between significant trends and flavor-of-the-month business "fads." Such analysis is critical when investing in technology. For example, Hewlett-Packard foresaw the need for high-resolution printing much better than Xerox did. Trend analysis allows a company to discern which emerging customer needs their technological solutions must address. This requires foresight in anticipating the future before it arrives.

The social, technological, and economic forces shaping the business landscape are quite varied. Some characteristics of this new business world include extreme connectedness, ultra-quick supply chains, unpredictable swings in customer taste, users who believe "free" is normal, chaotic venture and capital markets, and a lack of loyalty among customers and employees. Analysis of these forces and the trends as they relate in particular to mobile business models has been minimal. This chapter attempts to fill this void by identifying a set of trends and directions emerging in the mobile Internet landscape. For clarity, Figure 2.1 groups these trends under broader themes: changing customer priorities, new hardware/device innovation, and new infrastructure innovation.

However, the synthesis of these broad themes into sustainable mobile business models is truly a complex phenomenon that is bound by invisible fabrics of interrelated trends, which often take years to fully play out their effects on each other. Often, when we are in the middle of it all, it's hard to see the whole pattern of change. Instead, we tend to focus on snapshots of isolated problems and wonder why we were unable to see the whole picture. Innovation in the mobile economy will be no different.

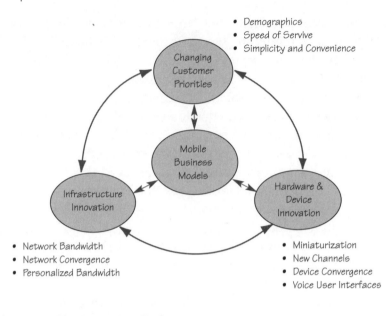

- Demographics
- Speed of Servive
- Simplicity and Convenience

- Network Bandwidth
- Network Convergence
- Personalized Bandwidth

- Miniaturization
- New Channels
- Device Convergence
- Voice User Interfaces

Figure 2.1: The Innovation Circle

Changing Customer Priorities

To paraphrase an old proverb: "Customer necessity is the mother of invention." Customers make choices based on their priorities. These choices have tremendous influence on what products get created. As technological innovations present customers with new options, customer priorities evolve. As a result, customers make new choices and reallocate their loyalty. Their changing priorities, and the way they interact with new technology and business capabilities, are what trigger, enable, and facilitate new innovation. Take, for instance, Nokia, which saw the emergence of digital mobile phones in the early 1990s before its competitors. Or the case of Dell Computer, which foresaw the need for the direct-to-customer business model. Dell leveraged the reach of the Internet to create a powerful new channel and a zero-inventory supply chain that enabled them to dominate the low-margin PC business.

Customer priorities are changing. For instance, customers are looking for solutions that help them manage stress—the always-rushed-and-never-enough-time syndrome. And while there's no simple way to deal with stress, the consequence of pretending customers are not looking for new experiences to relieve stress means that companies are not listening to their customers. *In your industry, what is the changing pattern of what customers need? What is their pain?* Many firms often overlook the "pain of the customer," leaving great opportunities languishing on the sidelines and presenting significant openings for new entrants.

However, the companies that anticipate and lay the groundwork for gradual change in customer priorities do very well in the long-term. Take, for instance, retailing. In the past four decades, retail has been about lifestyle simplification and efficiency for consumers. For example, Sam Walton, the founder of Wal-Mart, saw the rise of self-service and capitalized on it before anyone else. Consumers were willing to accept self-help in return for lower prices. As a result, forward-looking Wal-Mart and Kmart seized the trend long before department stores and were rewarded with significant market share. Clearly, the successful retailers understood the value proposition from the customer's perspective. Performing a thorough analysis of customer trends does help companies eliminate the business fad *du jour* mentality and identify new opportunities.

So, what are the developments that may alter the way mobile solutions get built? The three customer trends that we believe will be influential in shaping the mobile economy are:

- **The Connected Society.** Customers want continuous communication and information access regardless of locale. It was said that the airplane brought the people of the world closer together. Similarly, wireless is making the 24/7 world commonplace for the next generation.
- **Increasing the Speed of Service.** Customers are tired of waiting for service. Customers want technology to eliminate queues and shorten the length of time they must wait. Queue buster (Q-busters) applications permit customers of service-providing firms such as airlines, car rental companies, and hotels to avoid waiting in line.
- **More Simplicity and Convenience.** Consumers have always placed high value on products and services that are easy and

convenient to use. In the mobile environment, they expect significant improvements in self-service. Companies must determine for themselves if mobile technology can aid in this quest for simplicity and convenience.

Demographics and the Connected Society

There was a time, not so long ago, when mobile phones were regarded as executive toys. But now mobile communications are within the reach of most of the world's population. As society becomes more mobile, consumers and professionals are demanding the same capabilities on the go that they are used to having in their homes and offices. But instead of creating one-size-fits-all solutions, companies must acknowledge and address systematically the on-the-go needs of different customer segments.

The demographic trends of the modern era are pretty well documented—aging population, working women, changing household makeup, single parents, declining real income, teens with spending power, and an exploding ethnic population. These customer segments have needs that current solutions are not addressing. Customers want the Internet to follow them into their cars, in the airport, on vacation, while shopping—whatever they're doing, wherever they happen to be. Large numbers of people now take it for granted that they can access whatever and whomever they want—whenever they want, wherever they are. There are no information blackout zones. As a result, companies need to customize solutions by delivering devices with new applications to meet the needs of customers, enabling them to work and function on the go.

A good example of this is the teen market. Teenagers around the world are using mobile devices to socialize, chat, or arrange meetings with friends. Instant messaging could well be the dial tone of this generation. Instant messaging allows "synchronous," or real-time, conversation between online parties. Users tap out messages to each other on their keypads. The messages then appear instantaneously on the screens of the intended recipients. The pace of live interaction between parties is limited by the agility of the typists on either end of the conversation. All told, more than 100 million people use instant-messaging to zap short missives back and forth.

With the addition of voice and video capabilities, as well as the broader footprint of high-speed wireless connections, instant messaging usage will become even more widespread than it already is.

Increasing teen usage is also leading to a ramp-up of entertainment content for wireless Internet services. Games target the younger generation, who are more impressionable and more open to seeking new experiences. Games have proven to be a popular mobile altractor in Scandinavian countries as well as in Japan. Games also represent new revenue streams for carriers, such as those from flat-rate pricing, ad-based games, pay-per-session games, and tie-in merchandising. The more sophisticated the game, the more likely these new layers of revenue become. Interactive games and music on wireless phones are growing in popularity, with the likes of Bertelsmann, Vivendi, Sprint PCS, Sony, and Sega rolling out new strategies. But the jury is still out on what applications are going to succeed, who wants them, and what customers will pay for.

In addition to the teen market, another fast growing segment is the mobile workforce. With the speed of business being what it is, there is a need for being connected to work, the need to have communication and Internet access at all times. This scenario of a 24/7 work environment is not just restricted to workaholics anymore, it is pretty much every worker. This creates a strong demand for e-mail, news, and other types of corporate information on the go. This corporate transition requires a shift from a PC-centric workforce to one that has the efficiencies and benefits of the PC anywhere, anytime. This customer segment wants information, education, communication, and entertainment on the fly.

Mobile applications such as short message services (SMS) are leading to interesting social issues. It is well known that mobile phone users are making and breaking dates by typing SMS message into their handsets. But, in certain countries they are getting divorces. In Malaysia, an Islamic cleric triggered a national debate by saying that a SMS phone message sent from a husband to his wife to declare their divorce is a valid first step to legal recognition of the split. In the United Arab Emirates, a Dubai court accepted an SMS message as a form of written divorce. Under Islamic law, husbands were obliged to tell their wives to their faces that they wanted a divorce before it gained any religious recognition. It appears the mobile phone text messages may soon take the place of face-to-face encounters.[3]

Over time the declining costs of service results in mass market adoption across all customer segments. As the cost of service declines, it will become a mass-market product rather than a luxury good. Also, Economics 101 makes it clear that the increase in the number of competitors in each market will lead to price declines, which should draw in more users. *From your experience, what are three demographic trends that will accelerate mobile innovation?*

Increase Speed of Service: For the Customer, Time Is Money

Attention-deficit customers. Multi-tasking customers. For customers, time is of the essence. We live in a time of extraordinary stress, and no matter how hard we try to keep up, the to-do list always seems to grow faster than our ability to whittle it down. The situation reminds us of a scene in Charlie Chaplin's 1936 movie *Modern Times* where an assembly-line worker who is tightening bolts every few seconds all day long, desperately struggles to keep up as the production line goes haywire.

In today's "modern times," people respond to mounting stress by relying more and more on faster service. Just look at the success of drive-through oil changes, drive-through fast food, overnight delivery of packages, and other quick-turnaround businesses. Thomas Middelhoff, chairman and CEO of Bertelsmann, was quoted in their annual 1998 report as saying that "We're all competing for the most precious and least replaceable asset the consumer has—time."

As discretionary time quotas shrink, customers count speed of service as a key reason why they do business with certain companies. People today are increasingly frustrated with delays of any sort and become particularly upset at delays in service. A simple example is the wait at the supermarket checkout. Studies have shown how checking out is the least pleasant experience involved with store shopping. Customers dislike every aspect of checking out—from standing in line to having to watch the checker's actions. The process is even more intolerable during peak hours and holidays.

As customers expect increasingly faster service, they are less willing to accept delays. The message to the marketplace is clear: In order for companies to ensure success, they must streamline their purchase and fulfillment processes by compressing the number of steps required to properly serve their customers. By reducing the processing time associated with product search, selection, order placement, and fulfillment, a company can demonstrate its respect for the limited time available to customers.

The business community is beginning to listen to customer expectations, as new trends in the online banking, retailing, travel, and entertainment industries confirm. For example, the airline industry is undertaking significant change. To many, the frequent business traveler represents the epitome of a consumer frustrated by service delays. There is also no more mobile a customer base in the world. The airline industry is racing to implement wireless technology to provide improved, faster service. Some airlines are offering basic wireless capabilities such as access to flight schedules and customer frequent-flier mile records. More advanced capabilities include the following: Travelers can change their seat assignments or reservations while on the go, or buy tickets and check in via cell phone or hand-held PC. But the ultimate experience will be when you arrive at the airport and your PDA receives a message: "Flight 10 to Tokyo is on-time. Upgrade to business class available. Confirmed seat 2D." We are all anxiously waiting for this development to arrive!

So what does this trend mean for mobile solutions? Mobility can offer the opportunity for businesses to radically cut the time required to service their customers. It can help them differentiate in a business environment characterized by the demands of busy, time-starved consumers; the threat of hostile competition; low margins; and countless sales outlets selling similar products. For instance, Frito-Lay, a pioneer in mobile applications, anticipated these trends in the early 1980s. They developed a system of handheld computing devices for field sales reps to manage the inventory on the shelves in the grocery stores. This process innovation—vendor-managed inventory—helps their busy customers optimize assortment per store, allowing just-in-time merchandising. This helped Frito-Lay dominate the snack food market.

Faster service, however, needs to be balanced with service quality. One of the ironies in the last few decades is that average product quality has improved with TQM (total quality management) and ISO 9000 practices. But service quality has actually decreased in many cases as consumers have been presented with more choices. Increasingly, business processes, regardless of the applications supporting them, must also be retooled to expedite customer service. Customers now penalize companies that infringe on their time through delays, mistakes, or inconveniences. If companies don't expedite processes, customers will go to someone who does it faster. If a company doesn't make it easy for the customer to do business, another one will.

New Experiences: Simplicity and Convenience

Customers are increasingly seeking new experiences. To deliver these new experiences, it is important to view the world through a different lens. This is what MTV did by asking what teens wanted as music entertainment. In-N-Out Burger developed a cult following by sticking to a basic menu—burgers, fries, shakes—and doing it well. Virgin Atlantic, started by Richard Branson in 1984, became a roaring success because Branson saw flying as an experience, not a monotonous mode of transportation. His airline was the first to offer free wine to all passengers, nonstop video and audio, Nintendo games, and goodie bags for children.

Great service has two components: new experiences and consistent processes. Mobility holds great promise in providing customers and employees with real-time experiences that create new possibilities. For example, location-based service is unique to the mobile world. At present, the wireless network infrastructure can locate individuals within certain geographic cells. However, current technology can determine a person's location only within several hundred meters, the typical radius of small cells. The next-generation wireless network infrastructure will locate individuals within 50 to 100 meters. Future enhancements will include GPS (Global Positioning System) enabled handsets to track users with even greater precision.

GPS-enabled handsets and cars are paving the way for new location-based m-commerce services. With a GPS receiver in your phone, a location-based service can send you advertising, coupons, and specials based not on where you live but on where you are at the moment. For example, you are driving past the mall when your cell phone alerts you to a special sale at Macy's. Or consider the example of Vindigo, a location-based m-commerce service. Vindigo is a free directory service for the Palm PDA used to find restaurants, retailers, and movies in specific cities. Once you tell the service where you are, it displays suggestions, with relevant content such as the Zagat's Guide, directions, phone numbers, and ads for stores along the route. You can also search for a specific business type, like a flower shop, by entering the street, intersection, or neighborhood, and then Vindigo will return a list of flower shops with details such as products, prices, reviews, and directions. The road to more useful features lies ahead.

Mobile services need to be backed by new processes that can deliver a consistent experience. Consider QVC, which turned home shopping into a multibillion-dollar business. QVC founder Joe Segel focused on what the public wanted. He recognized that TV shopping had to be simple. Just turn on a TV set and dial a telephone. No complicated keypads, no special buttons to push, no computer or modem to install. QVC also invested carefully in the back-end of direct marketing—order processing, fulfillment, customer service, warehousing, and inventory control. By combining direct marketing basics with new technology, QVC succeeded whereas other highly interactive, technical experiments conducted by companies such as Time Warner failed.[4]

What does this trend mean for companies? Newly designed customer processes must make the experience of real-time service exciting and consistent before mobile solutions will be widely adopted. Take, for instance, bill-payment on-the-go. Mobile bill-payment will require large-scale changes in a company's back-office functions. Companies may have to move away from their ERP-based batch-model architecture toward a real-time computing model driven by a need to be in constant communication with its customers. Each company must define what real-time service means for its business processes. Then it must look at mobilizing these processes.

Hardware and Device Application Innovation

New and more powerful technologies are arriving at a dizzying pace: Yesterday's innovation becomes today's standard, then tomorrow's outdated concept. Steadily declining component costs and increases in mass production economics are driving down the average price of new technology. These price declines make mobile devices affordable to a broader set of consumers, greatly increasing the market penetration rate and creating user profiles more reflective of society at large.

In the face of this relentless change, the first task of top management is to understand the direction and velocity of technological innovation in its industry. Without such an understanding, diligent effort by thousands of employees is misdirected. Even worse, thousands of jobs and billions of dollars of market value are placed at unnecessary risk. Also, scarce resources will be invested without producing any returns and opportunities for more profitable growth are lost.

So a fundamental line of inquiry is: *What is the changing pattern in technology that is disruptive?* Disruptive technology is emerging in the following areas:

- **Miniaturization**. Handheld computing demands continuously increasing functionality in compact, power-efficient packages. The trend toward miniaturization in microelectronics is occurring simultaneously in handset, screen display, data storage, and power supply technologies.
- **New Channels**. New customer interaction channels are emerging in the form of smart things—cars, appliances, or toys. For instance, telematics brings the Web into the car. The automobile, the largest mobile device, is increasingly becoming viable as a distribution channel for information, transaction, and entertainment services.
- **Device Convergence**. Device convergence is occurring at breathtaking speeds. Examples include the smart phone platform, the convergence of the phone and computer, the convergence of the PC and the pager, and Handspring's successful combination of the PDA with the phone.
- **Voice User Interfaces**. Device interaction patterns are changing as new "easy-to-use" capabilities such as speech recognition and synthesis become available. Emerging technologies enable businesses to integrate voice access into enterprise applications using a broad selection of speech recognition technologies and telephony interfaces.

Miniaturization Trends

In the world of wireless, smaller is better in four areas: handsets, screen displays, data storage, and power supply technologies. The key to this miniaturization has been the development of extremely compact, power-efficient electronic devices and components—the building blocks of mobile hardware of all kinds.

Handset Miniaturization. Mobile phones have dramatically reduced in size since the mid-1980s. In 1986, a cell phone weighed about 800 grams. By 1997, the weight was down to 50 grams. The handset is currently constrained by several factors, including processing capability, input methodology, and screen form-factor. Next-generation phones will have fatter clients, such as Java Virtual Machine (JVM), which enables these devices to do limited "processing." In essence, such devices could lessen data traffic over a network, since basic formatting and logic can be done on the device itself. In order for Palm's PDA devices to succeed in the application market, they must decrease in size and increase their computational ability.

System-on-a-Chip. Three long-running miniaturization trends typify the microchip industry. The first trend is feature size. This is the width of the wires that provide connections inside the microchip. It continues to shrink. Depending on the type of chip, the features in the newest generation will be 0.13 microns—a micron is ten-one-millionths of a meter—down from 0.25 microns. The second trend is the shift to 300-millimeter wafers. Traditionally, chips are cut from 200-millimeter platters of pure silicon, each yielding 100 chips. The shift to the larger size—moving from salad-plate to dinner-plate dimensions—will enable 225 chips to be cut from each wafer. The third trend is the shift from aluminum to copper as the principal metal for the wires inside the chips.[5]

One interesting example of miniaturization is the Seiko-Epson's wearable personal computer called "Ruputer." It is a wrist watch-sized PC-compatible computer weighing 67 grams with a 16-bit processor, 128 Kb RAM, 512 Kb ROM, and 2 MB flash memory. The 102 x 64 pixel liquid-crystal display can show five rows of 16 ASCII characters with two input/output (I/O) ports for exchanging data with a PC. An infrared link can also be used to transfer data between two Ruputers. Powered by two coin-sized batteries, the operating time is 300 hours for continuous use or four months when using the display for one hour per day. The user interacts with the device using a joystick and four buttons, which work well with menu-based applications. However, entering data is cumbersome, limiting the usefulness of the Ruputer to information browsing.

Flat-Panel Displays. The trend toward ultra-compact size is illustrated in flat-panel-display technology. Today's displays—cathode-ray tubes or the advanced flat panels found in laptop computers—are invariably rigid, glass-encased devices. There is tremendous demand for very small, high-resolution displays for use in head-mounted gear and other mobile applications. For example, the U.S. firm Kopin manufactures a 320 × 240–pixel liquid crystal display (one-fourth the pixel count of a desktop VGA resolution monitor), which measures only 0.24 inches diagonally. Colorado MicroDisplay has developed a liquid-crystal-on-silicon (LCOS) display, which supports a full 800 x 600 pixels in a unit measuring 0.47 inches diagonally.

Scientists are working on new approaches to displaying information that use, for example, chemical polymers rather than electronic transistors. This means that screens could be printed on flexible pieces of plastic that could be rolled up and stuck in a back pocket. It might also be possible to mount a computer display on a curved surface, or even on existing objects like walls or cars. While they are still in the laboratory stages, these new display technologies might one day allow for astonishing portability.

Data Storage. Disk drives have gone from the large "disk packs" used with mainframe computers in the 1960s and 1970s to the 8-inch- and 5.25-inch-diameter drives in early PCs, to the 3.5-inch or smaller drives used in laptop computers. At each stage, the size of the drive itself has not only shrunk, but the densities at which data can be stored have increased dramatically. The smaller drives actually store more information than their larger predecessors. Take for instance, IBM's Microdisk, the world's smallest and lightest hard drive, can store up to 1 gigabyte of data on a disk the size of a matchbox. Weighing only 20 grams—less than a standard AA battery—the Microdisk can hold more than 200 times the data or images held by a standard floppy disk. The Microdisk can be used in most digital cameras, PDAs, laptops, or PC systems with PCMCIA card slots.

In a continuation of this trend, DataPlay offers miniaturized optical storage—about the size of a quarter with 250 MB to 500 MB capacities. This digital media is designed to record and permanently store up to five hours of CD-quality music or up to eleven hours of MP3 files. DataPlay has also designed a high-capacity micro-optical engine that integrates with next-generation mobile devices such as digital cameras and PDAs. A single DataPlay digital media will play and record multiple types of data—everything from music to digital images to electronic books and beyond. It is designed for use in digital music players, electronic book readers, PDAs, digital cameras, portable games, personal computers, wireless devices, and more. The micro-storage industry bears watching.

Next-generation technological devices should include three core design features: compact form, high performance, and low power consumption. The power supply is the heart of any electronic system. In space-constrained devices, the size of the power supply and power consumption becomes a crucial issue. Users expect electronic devices to work for long periods without recharging. A number of firms are working to develop ultra-low-power devices that could run for months on the tiniest of batteries.

Telematics: Cars as Mobile Channels

Automobile manufacturers are beginning to offer wireless services to drivers. Most in-car-communications capabilities are still pretty basic: Usually it's a built-in phone linking the driver to a service center operator, who provides the driver with emergency assistance, directions, or other basic travel information. Car makers will increasingly bring wireless capabilities—downloading music, returning e-mail, and on-the-road shopping—to their vehicles. Why? The million hours a week drivers spend in their cars makes them a large—and captive—audience.

Telematics is the basic technology behind products such as GM Onstar, Ford RESCU, and Mercedes-Benz TeleAid. The term originated in the European automotive industry to describe automotive communications technologies. Mercedes-Benz was one of the first companies to use the term, and others quickly responded. Telematics refers to a complete solution—from the hardware and software to the service center's support.[6]

How does a Telematics system work? The heart of the system is the Telematics Communications Unit (TCU), located in the car and connected (wirelessly) to a central service center. The TCU serves as the central command center. It communicates location-specific information to a central service center, and in turn the center helps deliver support services to a driver via the cell phone. The TCU is also connected to the engine control unit—the car's onboard computer—which enables enhanced services such as remote engine diagnostics and automatic airbag notification.[7]

Analysts predict Telematics will become a multi-billion dollar industry in a few years. The growth in the global in-vehicle information system (IVIS) market can be attributed to several factors. First, a large number of new entrants from the automotive and wireless industries are positioning themselves in the market. In addition, IVIS development has benefited significantly from recent advances in intelligent transportation system (ITS) applications such as fleet management systems, in-vehicle navigation systems, collision avoidance systems, and adaptive cruise control.

Telematics represents the first major revolution since the radio for content delivered to the automobile. Combining personalization and Telematics will allow companies to deliver real-time traffic alerts, specialized news programs, and targeted ads based on an individual's location and profile.

The future of Telematics shows promise. As market penetration increases and the demand for enriched content grows, Telematics becomes viable as a channel of information and entertainment. Eventually, Telematics channels will permit us to communicate with the office and home, in ways well beyond simple voice conversations. Drivers will be able to turn on home lights, start and stop the sprinkler system, and set their office and home security systems—all via their Telematics systems. With a platform so flexible, the potential scenarios are endless.

Device Convergence: Mobile Devices Get Web-ified

Until recently, PDAs weren't much more than electronic calendars and address books with tiny keyboards and murky displays. But they are rapidly changing into multi-purpose devices. For example, the

Hewlett-Packard Jornada PDA doubles as a mobile phone. Once considered separate and distinct, the wireless, Internet, and computer industries are rapidly converging. However, convergence is truly a complex phenomenon that is bound by interrelated innovations, which often take years to fully develop. Companies like Microsoft are accelerating convergence by setting *de facto* standards.

The dynamics of convergence are both complex and challenging. For instance, manufacturers have to compromise to get enhanced functionality plus acceptable form factors, e.g., the size and weight of their products. However, end users are less eager to purchase a device with enhanced functionality if it is accompanied by increased size and weight. At the same time, the relentless pace of technical and stylistic evolution generally keeps a device's life cycle short. Therefore, producing pricey, multi-functional devices with too many bells and whistles may not make financial sense. The typical response to such concerns is that the main market for these devices is the business executive who is looking for integrated functionality. Perhaps, but there is a wider problem that may be more difficult to ignore.

Creating convergent devices requires a deep understanding of mobile users' needs and behavior. For instance, cell phones and PDAs involve very different usage patterns. When accessing one service, it is virtually impossible to use the other service simultaneously. Headphones address this problem, but it is questionable whether people are willing to change their behavior anytime soon. In other words, it may be relatively simple for manufacturers to merge device functionality, but it may be difficult for users to merge a device's multiple uses.

This dilemma can be resolved by articulating a clearer, more focused vision of the device's purpose. For example, PDA-like features such as personal information management (PIM) should be included in mobile phones. However, the phone shouldn't attempt to totally replicate a PDA's more robust functionality, better data-entry mechanisms, and larger screen. Instead, the design focus is on improving and integrating communication between the two devices to permit users to perform integrated functions seamlessly.

The BlackBerry pager, developed by Research in Motion (RIM), illustrates how useful a convergent device can be. RIM provides wireless solutions for the corporate e-mail market. The popular Black-

Berry pager has a thirty-five-key QWERTY keyboard, roller-wheel scroll button, and instant messaging capability. The device provides real-time e-mail by integrating its devices with corporate e-mail systems and provides PIM tools, such as calendaring, contacts and to-do lists. Many corporate users have grown attached to their Black-Berry pagers, which allow them to always be connected with information in their corporate networks.

The success of the mobile Internet market will be determined by the ability of mobile devices to integrate with the Web. Mobile devices have already begun to evolve from single-function to multi-function devices. Many today are capable of voice, data, PIM, and basic computing. Once stand-alone tools, mobile devices are now being connected or synchronized to PCs. As a result, security is also becoming an increasingly important issue. In addition, the ability to download software onto mobile devices is important for enabling m-commerce. *What is your ideal mobile device?*

Voice User Interfaces

If mobile devices are to succeed, usability will be a major factor. Consumers want devices with which they can interact in as natural a way as possible. These devices should be equipped with intuitive interfaces, making technology transparent to users. Take, for instance, the Nokia cell phone, the most widely used mobile product. This product was successful because of its elegant but simple interface.

Mobile devices are struggling to get away from the tyranny of the desktop user interface. Until recently, the needs of most desktop computer users were satisfied by what is referred to as the WIMP model— a graphical user interface (GUI) based on *W*indows, *i*cons, *m*enus, and a *p*ointer. While the GUI is an improvement on the text user interfaces, it is cumbersome to use on a small mobile device. Over time, we anticipate that the WIMP model will probably be displaced as more natural, intuitive interfaces become technically feasible.

One trend that is taking hold is the speech-driven user interface. Speech frees users from the mouse and the keyboard. Speech recognition is likely to be the major enabling technology for the so-called "post-PC era."[8] Voice-enabled car phones and navigation systems are already available. Toys, games, and both industrial and house-hold voice-commanded automation are in the works.

Development of new speech recognition technologies, along with breakthroughs in PC speed and performance, have made voice user interfaces a reality. Speech is better for applications that use a constrained set of key words. It's good at collapsing menus, but it's not good for pointing. For many applications, it's easier to have information on a screen. But the biggest issue with speech applications is scalability. What if a million people call at the same time? Can the system handle the processing? Speech portals are excellent for enterprise applications. For example, companies such as Fidelity Investments and American Airlines currently use speech recognition technology to reduce the costs associated with using live operators to answer customer questions and provide information. Furthermore, these companies report high levels of user satisfaction with their systems.

Speech recognition technology is just now reaching the market. In the next few years, it will become a major presence, with applications on both the phone and desktop. As the technology matures, it will permit multi-channel interaction, giving people the ability to verbally request information and have it delivered back to them as a text response. The response could be delivered via a phone or in text format through a mobile device, e-mail, text pager, or even a fax machine. Imagine the ability to request customer data over your cell phone while driving to your customer's office and have it waiting in your pocket PC when you arrive!

Voice portals are one of the emerging components of the increasingly connected ecosystem. Voice information access provides direct interaction with databases and legacy systems for reading and writing content. While simple information requests are already available, voice-enabled commerce (v-commerce) is in the early stages.

Infrastructure Innovation

To prepare for a tidal wave of wireless data traffic, different aspects of the infrastructure need to be upgraded. These bandwidth improvements are taking place in three areas: in the network, in the home/office, and in your personal space. As a result, three major trends associated with the development of a wireless data infrastructure include:

- **Bandwidth Explosion—Extremely Connected.** Before a major increase in high-speed, always-on mobile Internet connectivity can occur, the infrastructure must be upgraded. 2.5G or 3G brings together high-speed radio access and critical IP-based services into one powerful environment. IP-based services are vital to mobile access. IP technology is packet-based, which in simple terms, means users can be "always on" at all times, without having to pay until they actually send or receive data.
- **Personalized Bandwidth—Extremely Productive.** Today, many people carry a variety of portable devices, such as laptops, mobile phones, PDAs, and MP3 players, for use in their professional and private lives. For the most part, these devices are used separately—that is, their applications do not interact. Imagine, however, the increased productivity if they could interact to create a personalized network. For example, as commuters enter a train, their laptops would remain online or incoming e-mail would be diverted to their PDAs by their personal network.
- **Network Convergence—Extremely Convenient.** In the past, we've relied on separate networks in the home or office to carry different forms of communication, e.g., cable TV, wireless, telephone, and Ethernet. Each was a specialized network for handling voice, video, or data. Installing and upgrading these networks was a nightmare. Finally, there is light at the end of the tunnel. Network convergence is finally becoming a reality.

Bandwidth Explosion: Third-Generation Networks

As mobile telephones began to appear everywhere in the early 1990s, their technology actually went through two major generations. First-generation (1G) mobile phones used analog transceivers designed purely for voice calls. These devices were far more advanced than two-way radios and brought users the first widespread wireless access to the traditional telephone network. Second-generation (2G) mobile phones used digital technology. Transmissions between the base station and the handset used one of several different types of digital radio frequency (RF) signaling. Digital voice compression made it possible to fit three or more users on an RF channel that previously could carry only one.

In order for the mobile infrastructure to reach a mass market, networks must first evolve from voice to data transmission and communication. Today, the mobile data infrastructure is made up of three generations of technology, called 2G, 2-1/2G (GPRS), and 3G. In the near-term, the focus is on GPRS, which solves problems such as better connect times, quicker downloads, and cheaper rollout. However, the debate is about the more glamorous 3G technologies that promise broadband Internet access. Depending on the geography, 3G is one to five years away. Japan and Asia lead, Europe follows, and the United States is last.

The United States is lagging because over the years, too many fragmented standards were adopted by various carriers, resulting in basic connectivity that isn't very good. It is quite normal to have dropped cell-phone calls, which require redialing. This intermittent connectivity simply would not do in a connected data environment. To improve infrastructure quality, U.S. companies will require a leapfrog effort, adopting new global standards and solving the base connectivity problem. Only then can they add next-generation services on top.

Why so much interest in 3G? Both the phones and the network were designed for voice traffic only. However, the widespread use of laptop computers and other mobile data devices created a demand for a high-capacity wireless network for data transmission. This high-capacity wireless network represents the third generation (3G) and the convergence of two powerful forces: wideband radio communications and Internet protocol (IP)-based services.

The market trend is to help operators migrate today's technologies to 3G systems, supporting higher bandwidth and greater functionality. The carriers have a vested interest in pursuing high-bandwith network infrastructure, since it will permit them to offer voice service for free while data service helps them to attract and retain new subscribers. The infrastructure firms—Motorola, Nokia, Ericsson, Qualcomm, and others—are actively transforming the wireless voice networks into Internet data-ready, always-on, always-connected networks.

3G wireless technology is not only about more data capacity and new kinds of digital signaling. Its other innovations include:

- Wireless packet switching instead of circuit switching. 3G systems break data up into self-contained packets similar to the

Internet instead of establishing a continuous connection that dedicates a circuit for each call. Each packet contains a destination address and a sequence number for independent routing and reassembly into a complete message.

- An always-on connection. Handsets will maintain constant contact with their networks but will exchange packets of information only when needed. This "always on" characteristic works well for intermittent data transmission and shortens the time required to set up a new connection.
- Bandwidth on demand. Data capacity that can be shared flexibly between users makes better use of the RF spectrum and the network infrastructure. With 3G systems, one user can send or receive several hundred thousand bits per second, while another may only exchange several hundred.

In many cases, the deployment of GPRS, the precursor to 3G, will allow operators to retain much of their existing investment in current 2G mobile technology. GPRS can also be deployed incrementally, permitting operators to control just how quickly—or slowly—the migration of subscribers takes place.

Personalized Bandwidth: Bluetooth

The ability to link a number of peripheral devices to a PC has existed for years. More recently, it's become possible to link peripherals to a cell phone. With both cell phones and PCs, the more peripherals that are connected, the more wires running everywhere, creating a cable jungle.

Bluetooth, an emerging innovation, attempts to solve the "cable jungle" problem.[9] Bluetooth is a low-cost, low-power, shortrange radio technology originally developed as a cable replacement to connect devices such as mobile phone handsets, headsets, and portable computers.

The main advantage of Bluetooth is that it will vastly simplify communications for consumers, taking mobility one step further into the home and office markets. Using Bluetooth, data can be transmitted without any wires or cables. By enabling standardized wireless communications between devices, Bluetooth has created a close-range wireless personal area network (PAN).

Bluetooth is suitable for short-range connections between a variety of mobile devices. These include mobile cellular phone to a notebook PC; mobile cellular phone to a headset; LAN access points for laptops or palmtops; and communication between laptops and palmtops.

Bluetooth-enabled devices work as follows: Using Bluetooth allows the cell phone to act as a modem. The laptop user opens an application requiring Bluetooth to dial up a network connection. The laptop scans the environment for any Bluetooth-enabled devices by transmitting a series of inquiry packets. The cell phone then replies with a frequency hop synchronization (FHS) packet. The FHS packet contains all the information the laptop needs to create a connection to the cell phone, including both major and minor cell phone device classes. The major device class tells the laptop that it has found a phone; the minor class says that the type of phone is cellular. Every Bluetooth-enabled device in the PAN that is scanning for inquiries will respond with an FHS packet. As a result, the laptop compiles a list of enabled devices. With the link established, information can flow freely over the connection.

Bluetooth technology can lead to increasingly beneficial scenarios. For example, the biggest disadvantage of today's digital camera technology is having to transfer images from expensive memory cards to a computer hard drive or other storage media before printing them. Bluetooth enables users to print the photos directly from a digital camera onto a Bluetooth-enabled printer, or transfer them for printing to a computer equipped with a Bluetooth player/recorder.

Bluetooth in conjunction with wireless LANs (WLANs) makes a potent combination. Most media reports seem to suggest that Bluetooth is a replacement for WLANs. On the contrary, more powerful scenarios can be visualized if they are seen as complements. A WLAN system uses radio links instead of cables, freeing users to access network services from many different locations with no plugs, no wires, and no hassles.

Why link Bluetooth to WLANs? As power requirements in handheld devices grow in complexity, systems and application designers have to carefully consider voltage requirements and power efficiency. As a result, it makes more sense to use the WLAN infrastructure than to use the battery-constrained cell phone as a modem.

However, the development of WLAN industry standards is a critical catalyst for the deployment of wireless networks and the continuing evolution of wireless devices that change the way we work, live, and play. Having standards in place decreases time to market for designers of wireless products and saves money for original equipment manufacturers. Consumers benefit from continuous product improvements and by having dependable wireless devices enabling seamless communications.

Unfortunately, there are too many WLAN standards fighting it out for market acceptance. The different standards are listed in Table 2.1. Until a standard is widely adopted, development of a WLAN marketplace is going to be spotty at best.

Multimedia Network Convergence: Wireless Home Networking

Imagine being able to control your home heating or cooling through your mobile device. Carrier and IBM have announced the development of a new wireless remote monitoring and control service called Myappliance.com. This service will provide Web-enabled air conditioners that communicate in real time with devices such as mobile phones and PCs. With the new service, Web-enabled air conditioner owners will be able to set temperatures or switch the units on or off using mobile devices.

Imagine your refrigerator seamlessly talking to your PC and to other Internet-enabled appliances, and keeping track of groceries and automatically ordering them when needed. Whirlpool, Maytag, GE, IBM, Cisco, and Sony are home networking's most enthusiastic proponents, building various prototypes of next-generation home scenarios.

For these scenarios to work, several things have to be in place, the primary one being a home networking infrastructure that lets smart appliances, PCs, Internet-capable game consoles, digital cameras, and mobile devices to network with one another. A central element of this vision is the residential gateway, an entry point to the burgeoning home network market that enables the sharing of Internet access.

Residential gateways (synonymous with service gateways and home

Table 2.1: Wireless Local Area Network (WLAN) Standards

WLAN Standards	Description
802.11a	The next generation version of 802.11 debuts in 2002. It increases the data throughput to 54Mbps (from 11Mbps) and moves to the less congested 5-GHz radio band. That could make it popular in homes that are cluttered with cordless phones and baby monitors. Backed by: 3Com, Apple, Cisco, Intel, Nortel.
802.11b (Wi-Fi)	The current wireless network standard designed for businesses. Operates on the 2.4-GHz frequency and moves data at speeds up to 11Mbps. Despite interference and security issues, its affordability and prominent backers have made it the standard to beat. Backed by: 3Com, Apple, Cisco, Intel, Nortel.
802.11g	An extension to 802.11b, it moves data at speeds of at least 20Mbps and perhaps as high as 54Mbps. Available at the end of 2002, it's likely to be the corporate choice, since it is compatible with existing 802.11b products. Backed by: 3Com, Apple, Cisco, Intel, Nortel.
802.11e	Improves streaming media performance for every flavor of 802.11. When it rolls out at the end of 2002, it will attempt to unify and offer seamless interoperability between business, home and public environments (airports, hotel). Backed by: AT&T, Cisco, Intel.
HomeRF	The current alternative to 802.11b. It stands for Home Radio Frequency. Also operates on the 2.4-GHz spectrum, but data moves at a slow 1.6Mbps. Less prone to interferences than 802.11b, but it has been hurt by decreasing prices for 802.11b products. HomeRF uses shared Wireless Access Protocol. Backed by: Compaq, Motorola, National Semiconductor, Proxim, Siemens.
HomeRF 2.0	Boosts to 10Mbps, but stays on the 2.4-GHz band, ensuring compatibility with existing HomeRF devices. Slower than 802.11, but voice and multi-media support could win consumers. Backed by: Compaq, Motorola, National Semiconductor, Proxim, Siemens.
HyperLan2	The emerging European standard, it operates on the 5-GHz band and boasts a 54Mbps data speed. Likely to be a contender at least in Europe. Backed by: Ericsson, Lucent, Xilink.

gateways) are a key part of the home networking solution. They provide a shared platform for integrating a myriad of broadband access, several wireless networking solutions, and new technologies such as personal video recorders (PVRs). As more homes obtain additional PCs and other Internet-capable devices, and as the rich media experiences offered by broadband become more widely available, sharing broadband connections will be a major motivation to purchase residential gateways. Residential gateways are sparking increased interest among a growing collection of service providers, set-top box and cable modem manufacturers, and venture capitalists.

Today's home network applications are a work-in-progress. They represent the first of three developmental phases:

- The current phase centers on connecting multiple PCs in the home and on providing the following four key benefits: (1) Internet access sharing, (2) peripheral sharing, (3) file sharing, and (4) multi-player gaming.
- The second phase of home networking applications will center on wireless in-home networks, and its adoption will be driven by the need to (1) eliminate wires; and (2) enable multi-device connectivity, such as set-top boxes to communicating with a wireless tablet on the refrigerator.
- The third phase will be characterized by digital multimedia content and service distribution over a home's wireless network. Wireless networking solutions will allow consumers to connect disparate devices and content sources.

There are numerous initiatives under way within the home networking industry that may help speed market acceptance. This includes improvements in ease of installation, "no new wires" technology, interoperability initiatives, and standards. Maximum bandwidth will increase over time. Higher bandwidth will enable better performance and support for multimedia—benefits that are important if mainstream consumers are to be attracted to home networking.

Several companies are jockeying for position in the race to own the entry point into the home. Take, for instance, Motorola's acquisition of General Instrument, which has over 70 percent market share in the cable set-top box market. This acquisition gives Motorola the ability to convert these set-top boxes into residential gateways. Another player who is taking a Trojan horse approach to the residential gateway market is Microsoft with its XBox gaming system and Ultimate TV personal video recorder. Once installed, the boxes can be configured to handle more challenging applications.

Gemstar and its partner, News Corp., are taking the most interesting approach to owning the residential gateway. Gemstar owns some of the prime real estate in the interactive TV market with TV-Guide, a programming guide. Gemstar's technology and patents play a significant role in Ultimate TV and AOL TV. The TV-Guide is a multi-faceted instrument. It can be a navigator to programming and help in recording content. It can also be a TV portal, which controls access to the advertising and e-commerce on it. If News Corp. gains ownership of Hughes Electronics, which owns DirecTV satellite service, the residential gateway market dynamics will get even more interesting.

Clearly, high-performance, multimedia in-home networks can easily extend the broadband experience anywhere in the home. In doing so, it makes consumer interaction with content and applications more enjoyable, convenient, and affordable. These networks also benefit service and equipment providers by reducing the cost and complexity of installing broadband customer-premises equipment and by enabling the delivery of new applications, such as video-on-demand and remote appliance management.

A Final Thought

The best way to predict the future is to invent it.

—Alan Kay

The trends that are creating the demand for new solutions are best understood as a series of transitions in which power is shifting from what has long been the basis of value creation toward something that is secondary or even tangential. Essentially these discontinuous transitions can be classified as follows: from wired to wireless, from customer loyalty to customer attention, from atoms to bits, from assets to information, and from rigid command and control structures to flexible configurations.

To stay on top of these transitions, a company's management is responsible for performing an ongoing analysis of market and demographic trends. This position provides management with a unique perspective on where new value can best be created and which innovations the firm should pursue. How an innovation gets selected and which innovations get implemented are often determined by the company's corporate culture. Firms typically select one of three approaches:

- **Trendsetter.** These companies are optimists. They take risks and chart new directions when selecting the technologies they will pursue.
- **Trendfollowers.** These companies are cautious. They follow a conservative selection process, often waiting to learn from others' mistakes.
- **Trendmakers**. These firms attempt to balance the wide-open innovative culture of the trendsetter with the risk-averse, overly pragmatic culture of the trendfollower.

Trendsetters are often oblivious to the uncertainties that characterize the marketplace and how the mass of consumers will respond to an innovation. They risk rushing headlong down a rigid path without carefully assessing a strategy's risk. Statistically, a few such firms will choose the right markets. Most, including some with smart people and established track records of success, will fail. The key to success as a trendsetter is to remain flexible, adjusting course as needed, and significantly increasing market options.

Trendmakers work quietly toward laying the groundwork for change. They see the unfolding landscape, and understand both its opportunities and risks. Above all else, they understand that high-quality technology alone isn't enough to ensure success. They must create a flexible corporate structure that allows the company to deal with rapid business change. *So, what approach does your company follow?*

Finally, because new trends represent a change from the status quo, they often fall prey to the problem of corporate inertia. Overcoming corporate inertia is a significant portion of any strategy exercise. Freud once wrote, "What a distressing contrast there is between the radiant curiosity of the child and the feeble mentality of the average adult." In a similar vein, the battle between old and new is a cultural quagmire. Innovative firms such as 3M, Corning, Nestlé, and Microsoft know how to nurture and foster a creative culture, while keeping the core business humming. *So, what kind of culture does your firm have?*

The M-Business Landscape

There is a certain "gee-whiz" wonderment as the mobile economy unfolds. It's easy to marvel at a specific technological achievement or become enthralled in assessing who'll win a major product battle. However, those who are seduced by these superficial aspects of the mobile revolution risk losing sight of something far more fundamental: What new business opportunities do these emerging technologies present? What is the scale and scope of these opportunities? Are they greater on the customer-facing, supply chain, hardware platform, or software application side?

Mobile solutions are shifting gears from "toys" to "tools." Determining mobility's practical real-world applications is difficult without an understanding of the changing business landscape. The first step toward a comprehensive understanding of the mobile environment is to look beneath its surface activity and apparent chaos for patterns. The next step is to categorize these patterns based on the appropriate analytic framework. For example, a pattern of competition among Microsoft, Palm, and Psion for dominance of the handheld operating system is obvious. This specific pattern can be classified under a broader framework of creating software for clients or devices. In fast-moving markets, where industry boundaries are frequently being drawn and redrawn, simple analytical frameworks are both essential and useful for mapping and explaining various competitive actions.

We will discuss six frameworks for assessing the mobile environment. A framework provides context for understanding the complex business landscape. This understanding is a prerequisite to taking the second key step in understanding the mobile environment—analyzing the business models that companies use to go to market. A sound business model is critical for understanding how revenues will be generated in the mobile environment.

Mobile business models are perhaps the least understood aspect of the mobile economy. As with e-commerce, m-commerce's endless growth potential excites the business community and, simultaneously, leaves it confused as to how to turn potential into profits. For example, market innovator eToys was an e-commerce leader. The company scored extremely well on understanding and meeting its customers' needs. eToy's failure was in translating the rich, positive customer experience into profits. eToys was not alone in this regard; many e-commerce start-ups failed for the same reason.

Analysts worldwide are seeking to understand who will profit in the emerging mobile landscape. M-business is in a period of business model experimentation, often through trial and error. The history of technology has proven again and again that it is difficult to figure out how to make an innovation profitable. Technological innovation, without a well-grounded business problem, will not ensure business success. To understand who is in a better position to exploit mobile innovations, it is necessary to know if mobility is core or an extension of the business.

Mobility—Core or Enabler

The question for senior executives is this: What do we do about mobile business? Faced with so few certainties, precedents, or comparables, the answers can only be broad. Determining how to take advantage of the opportunities of the mobile Internet requires first asking these questions:

- Is mobile, like the telephone, an enabler of your business? For financial institutions, manufacturers, and retailers, mobile is an enabler. It complements and makes the core business more efficient but does not radically change it.

- Is mobile, like telecom companies, your core business? For cellular operators, handset and handheld device manufacturers, and some segments of the hardware, software, and consulting industries, mobile is their business.

The answers to these questions dictate the urgency that is felt within your company. For companies like GE that see mobile as an enabler, the focus is on understanding its impact on the customer or employee value creation. On the other hand, for companies like Nokia that treat mobile as a core business, there is incredible pressure to move quickly and carve out a profitable niche. The companies for which mobile is core have a vested interest in convincing everyone around them that they should abandon their existing ways of doing things and migrate immediately to the new, new thing.

To figure out if mobile is right for their company, management must focus on three key issues:

- **Innovation and Customer Value**. Given the vastness of the mobile landscape, which opportunities should a firm pursue, which ones hold the greatest efficiency or value creation potential, and which complement core competencies and capacities the firm currently has? When Cisco Systems implemented its Customer Connection Online system in 1994, it was using the Web to do business in innovative ways that gave it a multi-year lead over competition.
- **Profitable Business Models**. Innovation without reasonable chance of margin improvement or profitability is an empty exercise. To meet the challenge of mobile technology, managers must ask: How can our company profit on a given innovation, and what capabilities are needed to ensure that we profit? For what innovations is the customer willing to pay?
- **Focus and Leadership**. What business issues must be confronted in order to bridge the gap between opportunity and execution? Cashing in on technological innovation is made difficult because there are more good ideas than companies have time and resources to implement. Companies need decisive leadership that can select the right innovations from those that are merely good. This leadership must then set a clear technological

direction based on its selection and have the courage to lead the firm in this direction.

Visionary leaders and their companies succeed by reacting to what customers say rather than blindly executing what they believe the markets should be doing. In emerging markets, leadership means balancing a culture that promotes innovation with one that builds a sustainable business. To explore this further, let's look at Nokia, a company for which mobile is a core business.

The Nokia Story: A Company Built on the Mobile Vision

For over a century, Nokia has consistently demonstrated the patience required to develop a compelling strategic vision based on an adaptable business model. The company was founded in 1865 with the establishment of a wood-pulp mill in southern Finland. By the early 1960s, the company had evolved from a broad-based manufacturing and distribution conglomerate encompassing paper, chemical, and rubber products to telecom. Nokia's electronics department, formed in 1967, entered the telecom market with PCM (pulse code modulation) transmission equipment. In the early 1970s, Nokia developed its first telecom switch, the DX 200, which still forms the basis of its network today.

Nokia entered the mobile market in 1981 behind the adoption of the analog NMT (Nordic Mobile Telephony) standard by many European countries. European communications standards gradually converged by the late 1980s and the GSM (Global System for Mobile Communications) standard emerged. In 1991, Nokia introduced its first mobile system and has since become the number two global supplier of GSM infrastructure, servicing over ninety-nine operators in forty-four countries. In 1994, Nokia became the first wireless manufacturer to launch a series of "handportable" phones for all major digital standards, including GSM and TDMA. Since then, Nokia experienced tremendous growth during the digital boom of the 1990s, and outdistanced its competitors such as Motorola and Ericsson.

Nokia has mastered the subtleties of consumer tastes dating back to the pre-technology days of wood-pulp production to, more recently, consumer electronics items ranging from TVs to computer monitors. The Nokia brand is a symbol of simplicity, style, and quality. It is the fifth-most-recognized brand name, ahead of Sony, Nike, and Mercedes-Benz.[1] Nokia's design capabilities have been instrumental in the company's mobile success. The company's products successfully integrate functionality and aesthetics, but its designs also helped pioneer new market categories and opportunities, such as the first mobile data "communicator."

Nokia is adept at developing robust product lines. The company uses only a few basic designs that share components. These include colorful facades, screens, keypads, batteries, and chips. Motorola, by contrast, grapples with a complex, hard-to-manage product line. In addition, Motorola's many different model platforms have little parts overlap, making it difficult to get economies of scale like those enjoyed by Nokia.

Nokia's current strategy assumes that the mobile Internet will dominate economic development in the coming years. The company has adopted an approach to the mobile Internet similar to that adopted by Gillette in the consumer products market. Simply put, selling razors enables Gillette to sell blades. Similarly, the mobile Internet will enable Nokia to transition from selling cell phones to selling high-margin infrastructure equipment and data services.

Nokia is moving to a strategy where the sale of the phone is simply step one in selling an ongoing set of services to the consumer. This approach alters the company's conventional pricing and revenue models by downplaying the importance of achieving profit on the sale of the physical product in favor of generating a revenue stream over a period of time through the sale of continuing services and content.

Nokia will face some considerable challenges in the years ahead. The drive to wireless broadband is forcing Nokia to develop new areas of skill and knowledge far different from the world of the cellular handset it knows so well. Even more, the push to 3G technology means Nokia must prepare to compete with Microsoft and Sony. In order to exploit the business opportunities the advent of the mobile Internet presents, Nokia must modify its business model and address two core strategic questions:

- How will the company bring the Web into the phone and tap the mobile commerce market?
- What must the infrastructure road map look like to facilitate information, communication, and commerce today, tomorrow, and in five years?

Nokia faces a difficult problem: be an innovator or a fast follower? History has shown that new business models can emerge quickly but are typically slow to evolve, coexisting with existing models for long periods before eventually displacing them. Why? As discussed earlier in the case of eToys, it is much easier to create a new technological innovation than it is to ensure its profitability. Xerox's technological creativity is legendary; its culture of innovation revolutionized the world with its development of the graphical user interface, the laser printer, and the local area network. However, the company never commercialized these innovations. Other firms did. Understanding Nokia's position in the evolving mobile landscape may shed further light on its strategy.

The Mobile Landscape

A sound m-business vision begins by clearly articulating what is possible. Figure 3.1 illustrates that the mobile landscape is composed of six general but distinct frameworks. These frameworks are mutually exclusive and exhaustive enough to capture literally every activity taking place in the mobile landscape.

These six frameworks are:

- **New Breakthrough Platforms.** Software and hardware companies have long known that the most lucrative position to hold in any market is as a platform for which other developers write their applications. Platform companies provide the tools and the foundation upon which others build their solutions. These include new operating systems (e.g., Palm OS), new device platforms (e.g., Handspring, Nokia), and new hardware platforms (e.g., Texas Instruments, Intel).
- **Mobile Application Infrastructure.** These companies enable, deliver, and manage mobile applications and services. They

include four different segments: mobile application platform providers (e.g., Openwave), mobile Internet service providers (GoAmerica, Palm.Net), mobile application service providers (e.g., Aether), and system integrators (e.g., Mobilicity).

- **New Innovation Opportunities.** Companies can use the extended Web to develop and deliver new products and services for customers. For example, a wireless portal operator could bypass retailers and distribute content directly to subscribers. A company, like DoCoMo, is using the mobile Internet to become the dominant player in the mobile channel, controlling access to customers and setting new business rules.
- **Customer Focus.** The mobile Internet needs to be put into the context of how technology integrates into everyday customer tasks and lifestyle. The mobile Internet will be an important new channel for commerce. But, for what tasks, activities and transactions? Companies can use the mobile Internet to establish direct links to customers to complete transactions more easily. This is one scenario, what about others?
- **Supply Chain Focus.** In many industries, business pace and velocity has accelerated so quickly that a company's fortunes can rise and fall on its ability to monitor and manage the supply chain. Mobile Internet technology enhances supply chain and distribution operations by improving the flow of information, orders, products, and payments among the various players.
- **Operational Focus.** Many enterprises share a common problem: They have made large investments in business applications that are inaccessible once their users leave their desks. As a result, companies are adding wireless access to existing applications in order to leverage their technology investments and increase the productivity of the mobile workforce. Productivity improvements will result when a company's employees, sales force, and business partners share and access information and perform transactions anytime, anywhere.

Using these frameworks, executives should systematically analyze their current operation to determine what new opportunities and risks a mobile strategy provides. At a minimum, these executives will understand the business opportunities mobility makes available to them and

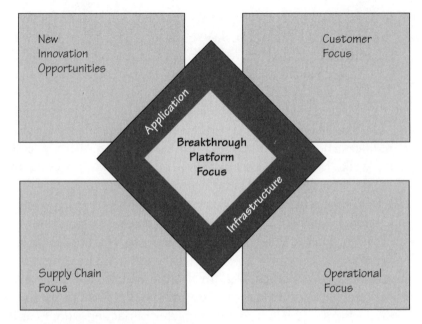

Figure 3.1: The M-Business Landscape

the risks associated with both pursuing these opportunities or not pursuing them. Based on this assessment, executives can realistically determine what, if any, mobile investments they should make. Use the framework in Figure 3.1 to clarify your company's focus.

Breakthrough Platform Leadership

At present, the underlying hardware and software platform of the mobile Internet is up for grabs, with a number of rival camps already in the running. Intense competitive conflict is under way between companies seeking to provide the standard platform upon which mobile applications will be built. The participants in this conflict seek nothing less than mobile hardware/software supremacy. The competition is being waged on four fronts:

- Hardware Platforms—Texas Instruments versus Intel
- Mobile Devices—Sony, Handspring, Nokia and Motorola

- Network Operating Systems and Programming Languages—Microsoft .NET, Sun J2ME, and Qualcomm BREW
- Handheld Operating Systems—Microsoft's Windows CE, Palm OS, Psion EPOC

Unlike the desktop browser competition between Microsoft and Netscape, the mobile rivalry won't be limited to two industry-dominating participants. So many firms—whether large, small, established, or start-up—are seeking early advantage in the mobile market that it makes the browser wars pale by comparison.

The stakes are high. Whichever company owns the dominant technology will earn billions of dollars from licensing fees for years to come. For example, the competition for chips in cell phones and handheld PCs between Intel and Texas Instruments (TI) is intense for a market worth tens of billions of dollars. It is estimated that the average cell phone has $60 worth of components. With an estimated 500 million handsets sold in 2001 alone, the market is worth $30 billion annually. Given the stakes, Intel has unveiled aggressive plans in the mobile arena:

- Personal Internet Client Architecture (PCA)—used by software developers to design next-generation mobile data products.
- XScale microarchitecture—enables hardware manufacturers to combine key components on a single chip, including a radio function, a processor, memory, and the speech processor.

These advancements take Intel deeper into the mobile device hardware and software arena. Furthermore, Intel's PCA, when developed over the XScale, will compete with Texas Instruments' Open Multimedia Application Platform, which is also used to design applications capable of operating over mobile networks. TI has already signed on much of the handset world as customers, including Nokia, Ericsson, and Sony. These companies will use the TI platform for their mobile handsets and computing products. As Intel encroaches on TI's space, the battle will be interesting to watch.[2]

The handset market, which has been dominated globally by a few large firms such as Nokia, Motorola, Ericsson, and Kyocera, is characterized by fierce competition. More recently, these established mobile phone manufacturers have ventured into the smart phone and multi-mode handset markets, the latter being capable of operating on multiple networks, including GSM, UTMS, and GPRS. Meanwhile, PDA manufacturers are enabling their products to link to wireless networks. In addition to competition from the PDA producers, the established handset manufacturers will experience strong competition from appliance and consumer electronics players, such as Sony, Panasonic, and NEC, who already have significant mobile Internet expertise through their NTT DoCoMo relationship.

Key handset issues that must be resolved include battery life, small-screen usability, and chip integration. Ensuring an adequate supply of components and manufacturing capacity will also be important factors in determining market dominance.

Palm Computing and Microsoft Windows CE are also engaged in "winner-take-all" competition. Each is striving to be the operating system standard for mobile devices and gain market dominance. On another front, Qualcomm and Sun Microsystems are vying for dominance in the virtual machine (VM) market. Qualcomm's BREW— Binary Runtime Environment for Wireless—software allows users to download programs to their mobile phones. These programs might include games, applications, music, or even video. Sun is marketing its mobile version of Java programming language—micro Java (J2ME), developed specifically for small devices with small screens. By providing richer functionality than those found in the text menus on current cell phones, micro Java and BREW could lead to more compelling and sophisticated feature-rich applications for mobile devices of all types.[3]

The mobile device is rapidly becoming a window into a range of network-based services. With conventional PC products and consumer electronics, the product's capabilities are hard-coded or built-in. In the future, many mobile device capabilities and services will actually reside on an Internet server or corporate network with which the handheld device communicates. In contrast to the conventional PC paradigm, where functions and capabilities are "frozen" at the time of purchase, network-based services will be organic, evolving over time. In this paradigm, the network is the computer. As a result, server-side operating systems, programming languages, and tools are being transformed. Microsoft's .NET platform supports this vision of an Internet resident service. The .NET platform includes the tools to build and operate a new generation of services, novel user experiences to enable rich clients, and device software to enable a new breed of smart Internet devices. In Chapter 4 we discuss breakthrough platform models in greater detail.

Mobile Application Infrastructure Focus

The focus of this framework is on creating a foundation on which mobile applications and services can be developed. In the e-business world, this is equivalent to the Web servers, Internet service providers, and application service providers who provide the foundation for building and deploying robust Web applications. There are four categories of mobile application infrastructure:

- **Mobile Application Platforms.** Carrier-class platforms and enterprise-class platforms
- **Mobile Application Service Providers (MASPs).** Infrastructure hosting (Aether) and application hosting (JP Mobile)
- **Mobile Internet Service Providers (MISPs).** General wireless carriers (AT&T) and specialized data carriers (GoAmerica, Palm.Net)
- **Mobile Application Enablers.** Data and transaction security, data synchronization, billing and payment service, systems and application integration providers

Mobile Application Platforms

Mobile application providers offer a software platform of prefabricated components for extending a company's business-critical applications to its mobile sales, service, and executive personnel. The complexity of extending e-business functionality to an increasing diversity of mobile devices has created the need for a single common application infrastructure or platform. For example, most applications are designed for viewing with a standard desktop PC. Small-screen wireless devices, such as mobile phones and PDAs, require optimizing the applications for quick viewing and data retrieval.

Information must often be completely reformatted for the best possible user experience.

Successful mobile application platforms will provide mobile users access to its business software with no loss in transaction capability and with a consistent user experience based on the type of device and connection speed. Mobile platform designs should include the following features:

- **Support multiple mobile devices.** The application platform should be capable of delivering Web-based content and applications to multiple mobile devices employing diverse technological platforms. It should also be capable of adapting Web-based content and applications to fit the variety of mobile device specifications, capabilities, and formats with their different screen sizes, colors, and markup languages.
- **Optimize content and applications based on varying connection speeds**. The application platform should optimize the amount and format of content for delivery based on the connection speed of the device requesting the information. It should also integrate effortlessly with the companies' existing Web infrastructures, reducing the need to re-create existing functionality and content solely for wireless delivery. Lastly, it should be compatible with existing Web infrastructure security standards.
- **Provide cost-effective support for increasing numbers of applications and capacity.** The application platform should be scalable to support additional applications and increased capacity as businesses expand the scope of wireless delivery to their mobile employees, customers, suppliers, and business affiliates.
- **Enable companies to develop, maintain, and manage wireless capabilities easily.** The application platform should be designed to enable programmers to develop, maintain, and manage wireless delivery capabilities easily as they introduce additional applications and devices or change the format of existing content and applications.

Take, for instance, JP Mobile. JP Mobile's Surewave Platform integrates with existing backend databases and business applications to deliver Wireless Application Protocol (WAP), Web Clipping, Voice XML or any one of a number of wireless protocols. Surewave provides broad functionality, permits efficient infrastructure management and has the following benefits:

- Optimizes application and content delivery to each interface
- Separates business logic from the presentation layer, allowing for integrated links to existing business applications and enterprise systems with minimal impact on existing infrastructure
- Allows cross-media functionality; for example, a user session may be started in voice and completed in Web Clipping for optimal end-user interaction and benefit

The mobile application platform's primary role is to provide middleware for mobile computing. Wireless capabilities do require specialized middleware, and middleware vendors, such as JP Mobile or ViaFone, are addressing the unique requirements. These include multiple radio protocols; multiple devices and their form factors; the inefficiency of TCP/IP in a wireless setting; and the security, compression, and disconnected nature of mobile sessions. As a result, these providers are best positioned to facilitate the extension of enterprise applications to the mobile Internet. A number of vendors currently provide specialized mobile middleware and target their platforms toward wireless carriers, portals, and Fortune 1000 enterprises with mobile initiatives.

Mobile Application Service Providers (MASPs)

Mobile application service providers play the role of intermediary between a Web portal and different wireless carriers and devices. This new class of outsourcer will be crucial to companies who are looking to "go mobile." MASPs will offer translation services for porting Web content to wireless networks, wireless application services, and infrastructure technology and services. Broadly speaking, MASP companies provide the piping (access or connectivity), data centers (hosting), and the hosted applications that together form the foundation on which business automation and productivity applications rest.

For example, Aether Systems provides its enterprise customers with an outsourced mobile data solution—a MASP service—packaged together with wireless connectivity—an ISP service. Charles Schwab uses Aether to enable wireless stock trading for handheld devices. Aether charges Schwab customers a monthly fee for unlimited wireless trading access and the service is branded by Charles Schwab. The actual service provided by Aether consists of (1) the retrieval of customer-level account information from Schwab's transactional processing system, which is then compressed and encrypted, and (2) the transmission of the data over a wireless connection through agreements with carriers such as AT&T and Verizon for use of their networks, as well as with Cingular for use of its Mobitex network.

The MASP model gives enterprises a fully outsourced solution, enabling rapid deployment and low up-front investment. Under the MASP model, enterprises benefit not only from a complete mobile middleware solution, including consulting services, but also from carrier contracts, security and network management. Furthermore, a MASP solution does not require an enterprise to make a substantial up-front investment before the firm's wireless strategy produces additional revenues or cost efficiencies. A company typically pays the MASP an initial consulting fee, followed by recurring hosting fees. These fees will likely be offset by the positive revenue or efficiency impacts resulting from the implementation.

Mobile Internet Service Providers (MISPs)

The MISP business model is similar to the traditional ISP model. Internet service providers (ISPs), such as AOL, MSN, and Earthlink, provide customers with access to the Internet over the public switched telephone network (PSTN) for a monthly fee. Essentially, mobile Internet service providers (MISPs) provide customers with access to the Internet over a wireless network.

Wireless carriers such as AT&T Wireless, Nextel, Sprint PCS, and Verizon are the MISPs for mobile phone Internet access. Mobile Internet access is provided over a dedicated circuit-switched wireless connection, similar to a regular wireless voice call (Sprint PCS and Verizon), or over a packet-based network, which sends data in packets (AT&T and Nextel). Circuit-switched network operators generally charge a basic fee of $10 per month and deduct wireless Internet minutes from a customer's monthly plan. Packet-based network operators generally charge customers a \$10–\$20 add-on monthly fee to a wireless voice plan for unlimited wireless Internet access. Packet-based operators have this flexibility because packet transmission is far more efficient than circuit-switched transmission, and puts much less strain on an operator's network.

Several network independent MISPs—GoAmerica, OmniSky, and Palm.net—provide wireless Internet access for handheld devices. These companies provide service over AT&T's and Verizon's networks, as well as Cingular's Mobitex packet data network, which covers roughly 80 percent of the U.S. population and offers transmission speeds up to 9.6 Kbps. MISP rate plans for handheld wireless Internet access cost anywhere from \$10 per month for limited Internet access (limited to a certain amount of kilobytes of information), to \$45–\$60 per month for unlimited access.

Mobile Application Enablers

This services category groups the diverse array of business firms dedicated to mobile strategy consulting, implementation, and integration. It also includes other ancillary services ranging from content conversion to project management. These firms run the gamut from full-service consultancies to niche service providers to the Big Five systems integrators.

Mobile computing requires a significant systems integration effort since there is no single development standard for mobile devices. For example, when a company's salespeople use PalmPilots, its production managers use RIM BlackBerry devices, and the firm's customers and partners use everything from Palms and BlackBerries to Pocket PCs, wireless cell phones, and more. The enterprise must find ways to communicate with them all.

In Chapter 5 we discuss in greater detail application infrastructure business models and the system integration they require.

New Innovation Opportunities

The mobile portals market is composed of a variety of companies, each with its own unique motivations, skills, and challenges. Many of these firms, such as established Internet portal AOL, and major brands, such as Virgin, are new to the mobile market. Their arrival is shifting the balance of power in a market dominated by the telecom carriers, as new players vie for market position and force the "old guard" to redefine their strategy.

The new services will emerge within a highly competitive business environment. Mobile portal partnerships will become increasingly vital, as no single player has all the skills to go it alone. Branding will become an important bargaining tool in defining these partnerships since the stronger the brand, the better positioned a company will be in negotiating an agreement.

There are four primary categories of mobile portals:

- Wireless operator
- Multi-purpose portals
- Commerce/transaction portals
- Pure play—niche portals

Wireless Operator Portals

Most carriers see the advent of the mobile Internet as a means of strengthening their hold over the customer. Each wants to become the AOL of the wireless world, deeply integrating their presence in the customer's everyday life through Web access and content. This strategy is nearly identical to that of the early Internet service providers (ISPs), such as AT&T WorldNet, where the goal was to generate e-commerce and advertising dollars beyond the core service of Internet access.

In the future, the carriers will serve two distinct markets—consumer and enterprise—characterized by two different business models. The consumer market will likely involve low hit rates and higher levels of pushed data and content and evolve into a more transaction-oriented medium. Its goal will be to support m-commerce, advertising, and subscription revenues.

As enterprises provide their sales network, inventory management, and logistics operations with wireless capabilities, the mission-critical applications need to be up and running all the time. In the enterprise market, the pricing model will center around bandwidth, reliability, and guaranteed levels of service.

Wireless operators can leverage their customer-access advantage and enter into partnership with newer companies to transform their traditional organization. Vivendi and Vodafone were the first to form such a partnership; they created a joint venture—Vizzavi—which holds both companies' wireless portal and service activities. The company will poll the wireless Internet resources from each of Vivendi's and Vodafone's subsidiaries in Europe. Similarly, T-Mobile's international alliances and joint ventures have followed suit by founding a new subsidiary—T-Motion—with T-Online, Deutsche Telekom's Internet subsidiary. T-Motion combines both companies' competencies to ensure success in the wireless Internet arena.

Multi-purpose: Information and Entertainment Portals

General information and entertainment portals, such as AOL, Yahoo!, Microsoft Mobile (MSM.com), and others, have emerged as the leading aggregators of Internet traffic. Each seeks to provide a unique blend of the six Cs—content, community, connectivity, communications, commerce, and context—in the emerging mobile environment.

The general portals will assist wireless operators in attracting customers by offering a suite of basic applications across the following categories:

- Messaging—electronic mail; unified messaging targeted to professionals to allow e-mail, voice mail, and fax-mail retrieval on any device; instant messaging for younger audiences
- Collaboration—conferencing for business meetings or face-to-face calls with family or friends
- Personalized and localized content—creating a personalized portal such as MyYahoo to give customers an opportunity to personalize and localize content such as news, stock reports, weather, and horoscopes
- Photo sharing—allowing customers to store photographs on the network and retrieve or share them using any device

- Gaming—downloading and playing games offline or in an online interactive mode

In addition to established players such as Yahoo! and AOL, newer entrants such as Nokia and Motorola are building their own mobile portals to attract customers and secure their loyalty. Nokia has established Club Nokia, which offers a number of exclusive services. These range from the Club Nokia Careline for instant call center support to an online magazine. A members-only Web service features the latest product information, contains picture message and ringing tone composers, and provides updates on advances in mobile technology. Club Nokia also includes third-party content, games, jokes, dictionaries, currency and language translation services. Nokia can easily customize Club Nokia to become a private branded portal for mobile operators who don't have resources to build their own.

Commerce/Transaction Portals

Mobile services are evolving from merely informational to transactional services. Commerce/transaction portals, or vertical portals, are destination sites where buyers and sellers come together to communicate, exchange ideas, advertise, bid in auctions, conduct transactions, and coordinate inventory and fulfillment activities. Similar to horizontal portals, vertical portals serve as channels for specific industries, such as retail, banking, chemicals, steel, and agriculture.

M-commerce sites use the mobile channel to provide a new experience for the user. Many of today's sites focus too much effort on attracting visitors rather than focusing equal effort on converting these visitors into repeat users and paying customers. The key to engaging a site visitor in the online purchase cycle is to offer services that first convert them into registered users, then into consumers, and finally into repeat customers. The challenge is to move visitors through the value chain by meeting their individual needs, and bringing them back to the site throughout their buying cycle. This approach effectively transforms a mobile portal from a one-stop instantaneous sell into an ongoing, round-the-clock sales process.

For example, the online auction site eBay has more than 2,000,000 items listed for sale on any given day. More than 250,000 items are added daily in a wide range of categories that include antiques, books, movies, music, coins, stamps, collectibles, computers, dolls, jewelry, photos, electronics, pottery, sports memorabilia, and toys. Users interested in specific items can conduct keyword searches or peruse eBay's 1,600 categories. Most auctions last an average of three to ten days, so unless people are on the site regularly, they may miss an item listing they care about.

In this extremely time-specific market, eBay's key priority is to provide users with the personalized features that enhance their onsite experience. One way the company enhanced the auction process was to provide a Personal Shopper application that automatically watches for user-specified items and price ranges during a requested time frame. In addition, users can track items using keywords or phrases within a specified price range, as well as choose to receive mobile notifications daily or once every three days. eBay's goal is to keep the user experience simple and exciting.

Niche or Pure-Play Portals

A significant number of start-ups have seized the opportunity to set up new wireless portals within specific industries. These include financial services, entertainment, information, and location services. These start-ups' value proposition is to establish a direct relationship with the customer, add a new interactive service dimension, and enhance the customer's experience. Niche or pure-play portals seek to enable improved customer experiences over multiple fronts and monetize the relationship over time. A number of these business models are capital-intensive and are characterized by low gross and negative operating margins. This is largely due to the costs associated with establishing first-mover advantage, scale, and branding.

For example, the niche wireless portal BarPoint is compiling a database of product information indexed to universal product codes (UPCs). You're in a record store, holding the latest Madonna CD. Since you are a price-conscious shopper, you pull out your cell phone, punch in the twelve-digit UPC on the back of the CD, and bingo— your cell phone displays detailed information about the recording, a short review, and even a price list showing what several online retailers charge for the same CD.

Rather than attempting to index every product in the world, BarPoint's initial focus is books, music, videos, and computer products. So far the company's product coverage is spotty, and sometimes all BarPoint can tell you about a product is the manufacturer's name. But BarPoint's potential benefit is clear: Shoppers will no longer be vulnerable to misleading product packaging information and less-than-knowledgeable salesclerks.

The niche portal Yodlee is creating a personalized portal. American Express, using Yodlee technology, has launched Account Profile, a free service that allows users to organize and track all their financial accounts and assets with almost any financial institution. During registration, American Express customers provide the user names and passwords for their financial accounts and then receive a single password to retrieve all of their financial information. Even more convenient, the display is on one page. In Chapter 5 we discuss mobile application infrastructure in more detail.

Customer Focus: Making It Easy for the Customer

Let's say you are an established company with customers, what can you do with mobile? Several dominant models for classifying the types of channel applications are emerging. They are described below:

- Channel presence—information-only channels
- Channel extension—transaction-capable channels
- M-commerce applications—new services available only in mobile channels
- Channel synchronization—fusion of a portfolio of channels into an integrated offering

Channel Presence—Information Only

Many companies will use their mobile channel to increase their customers' understanding of their products and services. This is primarily for marketing purposes—a brochureware solution. Other applications of channel presence include digital couponing and customer service and feedback.

These solutions use a transcoding process to make their Web site content accessible quickly from a mobile device. Transcoding essentially converts a company's HTML Web pages into WML (wireless markup language), a content format for the mobile world. Transcoders allow a company to have a quick brochureware channel presence by first reading the firm's Web site and then automating the content format for delivery to a portable device. The quality of transcoding services can vary significantly. Transcoding allows marketing groups to leverage existing Web site material without the time and expense incurred when creating additional content.

Channel Extension—Mobile Channels for Existing Customers

Instead of using the mobile channel to generate sales, some retailers and financial institutions use it as part of a channel extension strategy to support their existing offline and online channels. CDNow is an example of such a strategy. The firm offers Web site access for users of wireless-enabled Palm devices and cell phones. Customers can purchase compact discs from CDNow's Web site and also download additional content, such as reviews and news articles. Other popular Web sites, such as Amazon.com, Travelocity, and Yahoo!, are scrambling to deliver their content to young, Web-savvy consumers through Web-enabled cell phones, two-way pagers, and personal digital assistants.

M-Commerce Applications

M-commerce has been defined as providing the mobile consumer and businesses with an ability to purchase, track, and receive goods and services securely via mobile technology. As companies move from informational to transactional services, specialized m-commerce applications with unique mobile channel capabilities are being developed. These include:

- M-ticketing—for flights and other travel, as well as tickets to movies, concerts, and other performances
- M-shopping—"personalized shopping" that can be combined with location-based applications

- M-banking—allowing customers to check bank balances and transfer funds from anywhere and on any device
- M-trading—buying and selling stocks, bonds, and currencies while on the go and from the most convenient wireless device

For firms to succeed in each of these m-commerce areas, the top priority in application design must be creating an exceptional customer experience—one that is intuitive, informative, personalized, pleasant, secure, and reliable. We delve into creating a customer focus in more detail in Chapter 7.

Channel Synchronization—Integrating Offline, Online, and Mobile Worlds

Eventually, companies will need to integrate their mobile, brick, and Web business channels. With every channel innovation, there is an initial belief in the complete displacement of existing channels by the innovation. Over time, the new channels are seen as complementing existing ones. Since the existing channels will not be displaced, the company must begin the significant task of multi-channel integration.

Supply Chain Focus: Interenterprise Process Integration

In a business environment as fluid and information dependent as the supply chain, accurate information delivered in a timely fashion is critical to business success. Fast-moving companies must respond immediately to real-time business changes. Mobile solutions enable these organizations to respond faster to supply chain disruptions by proactively adjusting plans or alerting key personnel about critical supply chain events as they occur.

Mobile supply chain management applications include:

- Procurement—mobile ordering applications
- Supply chain execution—fulfillment and delivery management
- Supply chain measurement—asset tracking and visibility
- Service management—field force automation

Mobile Ordering Applications

Mobile ordering solutions basically extend e-procurement applications and enable orders to be taken using handheld devices. Nesco Distribution, a leading distributor of electrical products, uses mobility to transform its order-to-cash cycle. Nesco's customers are highly mobile and need to order supplies from remote locations. In partnership with Vignette, Nesco created a wireless application that lets customers order products from just about anywhere via a handheld device. A key business objective of the new application is to ease some of the pressure on Nesco's busy call center.[4]

The application helps customers save time, better manage their businesses, and eliminate order errors. These solutions also include retail reorder applications that use handheld devices to scan item information and either store it locally or transmit it to a central server where it is matched against a replenishment plan. If a certain threshold is met, orders are automatically placed to the suppliers. A number of vendors, including Symbol and Intermec, have been offering a variety of mobile reorder systems for years. Their offerings include simple portable bar code readers and more sophisticated PDTs (portable data terminals). These tools will read information from assorted devices and automatically transmit this information through wireless local area or wide area networks.

Fulfillment and Delivery Management

McKessonHBOC, Inc., the world's largest health care distributor, uses mobile technology to improve its delivery process and provide electronic confirmation of every delivery. Approximately 800 of the company's 2,800 truckers use Symbol handheld devices running Palm OS to save the company—and its customers—time and money. Every package is bar code imprinted and scanned before and upon delivery. McKessonHBOC is also providing these handhelds to customers, who use the scanners to place orders and obtain instant order confirmation and detailed order status.[5] The McKessonHBOC example illustrates how mobile solutions are rapidly becoming a major presence in the delivery side of the supply chain.

Delivery management is one of the critical functions in any supply chain and is one of the first business functions to use mobile technology. Everyone is familiar with the FedEx or UPS delivery person writing on a tablet. The tablet is a wireless delivery automation platform that integrates the field activities with the company's back office. These drivers use the latest handheld devices to capture critical information and make it immediately available over the Internet. As delivery information is collected, customers can track their order throughout the fulfillment cycle. This technology alone has helped improve productivity, shorten billing cycles, eliminate proof-of-delivery issues, and improve customer service—all by taking an error-prone, paper-based process that once spanned several days and reducing it to a few minutes.

Asset Tracking and Visibility

Imagine a supply chain where raw materials from China become component parts in Taiwan for a product made in Singapore, which is then shipped to San Francisco. The product goes through final assembly before being sent to the customer in New York. The manufacturing supply chain has been characterized by this kind of materials movement for decades.

As the world economy transitions to global outsourcing, monitoring highly mobile, geographically dispersed assets will take on increasing importance. It has also been defined by an inability to know where products and materials are at any given time along the chain. Such lack of supply chain visibility is costly. The issue of supply process delays and waste has taken on new urgency with the advent of real-time commerce and increased customer intolerance for fulfillment errors.

Field Force Automation

Mobile two-way radio communications have been used for many years and have been an effective way of giving out work to field technicians and resolving problems. Field force automation, also known as field service dispatch, is one of the most popular mobile computing applications. Traditional service dispatch methods receive requests at a central location where a supervisor decides which representative will take the call. This approach has numerous problems: It lacks responsiveness, it cannot handle schedule changes on the fly, and it creates delays when parts are ordered from the field electronically but the transaction must be completed at the office.

But now companies are embracing mobile data solutions to increase efficiency. Consider AT&T MediaOne, the broadband company, which replaced its 1,200 technicians' paper-based system for responding to service calls with a wireless system that included two-way messaging and a workforce management system, devised by Intermec. Time-critical activities, service requests, and up-to-the-minute work assignments can be automatically dispatched to field personnel to ensure timely responses and efficient scheduling. The system resulted in a 25 percent productivity gain by improving logistics and avoiding canceled appointments. In Chapter 8 we discuss a supply chain focus further.

Operational Focus: Enterprise Wireless Applications

Operational applications include software for managing mobile employee and contractor access to a business's information and applications. Operational applications can be broken down into four major segments:

- Messaging models
- Enterprise application extension models
- Business or enterprise information portals
- Legacy application extension models

Enterprise E-Mail and Personal Information Management (PIM)

Messaging applications, such as those pioneered by PalmPilot and the BlackBerry pager, give workers wireless access to corporate e-mail, calendars, and address books while providing a high level of security. A PIM and messaging application connects all leading mobile devices to existing enterprise messaging and information systems, such as Lotus Notes and Microsoft Exchange. The application enables users to access and respond to in-box messages, compose new messages, and access and modify contact, task, and scheduling information—from anywhere, at any time, and with any device.

Enterprise Application Extension

Consider the curbside check-in application from JetBlue Airways, a low-fare airline. The handheld system, which consists of a wireless local area network, portable data terminals, and portable receipt/ticket printer, allows JetBlue staff to access passenger and flight information via a real-time connection to the HP Open Skies reservation system. The "bust lines" application helps JetBlue staff to check in passengers, print boarding passes, and check luggage virtually anywhere inside or outside the terminal. The value of this solution is that it reduces the stress of flying during peak travel times like Christmas. For the company it improves on-time operational efficiency by allowing JetBlue to get passengers, especially late ones, checked in and to the plane without delay.[6]

Extending enterprise applications for easy access is a natural next step. Enterprise application extension models allow employees access to a company's mission-critical enterprise applications, such as enterprise resource planning (ERP), customer relationship management (CRM), and supply chain management (SCM). For example, field sales personnel need access to CRM applications to review customer data or to submit a sales order without returning to the office. Productivity and customer service improves because inventory can be committed in real time and the shipping process can begin immediately. Improved process cycle times can result in significant return on the company's application extension investment.

Business Portals

Business portals give employees a single entry point into their business applications. For example, time and expense entry applications are used by professional service firms whose consultants record information in the field and send it in electronically. All manual paper-based record entry processes are eliminated, saving time, reducing entry errors, and permitting faster billing and reimbursement. Business portals are designed to overcome such problems by aggregating information from a variety of sources. They compile information from the firm's e-mail systems, front-office applications, legacy applications, and Web-based content and deliver only the most relevant information to the user.

Legacy Extension Models

Most large firms have legacy applications and other focused applications that they have accumulated over the years. Providing access to these applications may become necessary in many industries. One way to do this is through middleware technology that unites disparate computer systems. Middleware addresses the inefficiencies resulting from the ad hoc buildup of legacy systems over time and distance. Left unchecked, incompatible systems can create "islands of data," with seriously limited ability to automate work processes and optimize business operations. As companies seek to capitalize on the potential of mobility, using middleware applications to integrate data, company business processes and legacy systems become critical.

A Final Thought

Each problem that I solved became a rule which served afterwards to solve other problems.

—René Descartes (1596–1650),
"Discours de la Methode"

The mobile Internet is in its infancy and no real frameworks are available that can provide a systematic way to think about opportunities or problems. Both the business models that support implementation and the competitive landscape are still in flux. By systematically approaching the problem, it becomes clear that the mobile landscape is a complex puzzle that accommodates the development of multiple business models.

As we developed the mobile framework, it became clear to us that mobile solutions build on top of the e-business investments. In one sense, the current transformation is simply the movement of e-business to a mobile environment. M-business is not yet a reality; it is still a developing concept, as are the business models that support it. In summary, mobile business models must take into account the following factors:

- **Key Enablers.** Advances in infrastructure, software, and hardware technologies
- **Source of Innovation.** New application concepts and designs
- **Arbitrators of Success.** Consumer preferences and marketplace dynamics

Business model innovations, while exciting in themselves, are significant mainly because they enable the creation of usable products. The relationship between a business model, the evolution of infrastructure, and the usefulness of an application, however, is not a simple one. Consumer preferences, corporate capabilities, and marketplace dynamics make mobility even more complex. However, it is marketplace dynamics that will ultimately determine which mobile product innovations achieve commercial success and which are relegated to the dustbin of history.

Historically, the most elegant and technologically advanced product designs are not necessarily those that come to dominate a market. Other economic forces, from manufacturing efficiency and financial staying power to the impact of branding, ultimately dictate a product's success. It is clear to us that the rapid growth in the number of mobile start-ups is suspect, as the business models are still in the formative state and as a result unstable. It would be safe to predict that in the long term, emergence of several large, established firms as key performers in the coming mobile Internet infrastructure and applications build-out is likely.

Breakthrough Platform Strategies

- Why is Sun Microsystems, a dominant leader in server operating systems, changing its strategic focus to secure a foothold in the emerging Web services arena?
- Why is Texas Instruments completely transforming its chipset—Digital Signal Processing (DSP)—into a hardware platform that anchors mobile multimedia?
- Why is Nokia transitioning from a market leader in the notoriously razor-thin-margin world of cell phones to a provider of 3G platforms?

Like other high-tech firms, these companies are positioning themselves as leading solution providers. As solution providers they must innovate and execute a broad-based platform strategy to ensure sustainable dominance in the emerging m-economy.

The success of Microsoft can be directly traced to its ability to provide comprehensive platforms in different computing environments. For example, Microsoft Windows is the operating systems platform for desktop computers, servers, and even handheld devices. Visual Studio is the development platform for creating applications. Commerce Server is the platform for several of their e-commerce products. Microsoft .Net is a platform strategy for providing services in a multi-device, multi-network environment. As each of these examples illustrates, the ability to systematically engineer multiple platforms and lock in a customer base is Microsoft's unique competency.

A platform strategy is quite different from a product strategy. If a company produces only a few simple products, it can successfully develop each independently of the others. However, as the number and complexity of a company's products increases, it becomes more efficient to move from a product-by-product to a platform approach built on a portfolio of products based on a common technology. A platform strategy can be defined as a coherent, generic technology that forms a common shared structure from which one or several derivative products can be efficiently created and manufactured. SAP, the enterprise application software provider, is another prominent example of a company whose success resulted directly from a well-crafted applications platform strategy.

Such strategies are not new. They have been used for decades to create shared design elements in diverse industries such as automotive, consumer electronics, and medical equipment. For example, Ford produced an automobile chassis that is common to several of its vehicles, whereas the suspension, brakes, and drive train were tailored to individual vehicles. Most models of Sony televisions and Kodak cameras have a few unique features and share a majority of components with other models in the product line. The medical equipment provider Medtronic used a platform strategy to transform itself from a cardiovascular-focused company to a broad-based medical-devices maker.

Companies focus on platform strategies for the following reasons:

- **Linking long-term direction with product strategy**. A platform road map means technology development is more focused and often reusable. For example, of the 4 million lines of code in Microsoft's Windows NT, 35 percent were reused from earlier versions, significantly reducing development cost.[1]
- **Presenting a solution to customer needs**. Too many discrete, stand-alone products can confuse the customer. To avoid this, present customers with cohesive well-integrated products and servic-

es. In the 1970s, Black and Decker redesigned several of its power tool groups in order to identify and standardize similarities among products. The result was phenomenal customer adoption of the redesigned products and increased speed to market. The company launched one new product every week for several years.[2]

- **Identifying business competencies to be developed or acquired.** Effective platform planning can spot gaps in product offerings that can result in considerable loss of revenue. Hewlett-Packard's success in the laser and inkjet printer market was due to a superior platform strategy that prevented holes in their product lineup.

Not identifying the platform components with greatest value can severely impact a firm's ability to capitalize on their value. For example, when IBM created the enormously successful PC platform in the early 1980s, it outsourced the development of the disk operating system and central processing unit (CPU) to Microsoft and Intel because it did not perceive these as being core platform technologies. In retrospect, this was a very costly mistake. Therefore, managing a platform strategy in an outsourced business model can be quite tricky. Companies must be conscious of which components within a platform family remain constant and which vary. Even more important, firms must also identify which components are core and which are peripheral to the platform's success.

Dimensions of Platform Thinking in M-Business

For many firms in the mobile space, the key concern is not what product to develop to meet the market's needs. The major issue is identifying which product can serve as a platform for additional products well into the future.

Platforms have significant economies of scale and scope, which bear important strategic implications. For example, Sun's Java environment is a platform for which multiple derivative products have been created. Sun's major competitor, Microsoft, has the objective of preventing Sun from achieving similar dominance on the cell phone or the PDA side of the industry. As more companies use Java, Sun's market position gets stronger.

A platform's strength is directly proportional to the size of its user community. History has shown that platforms that become de facto standards are very powerful in terms of version economics. Each version ensures a steady revenue stream from the replacement cycle and also ensures continued customer lock-in.

As Figure 4.1 suggests, m-business platform thinking can find expression along four important dimensions. Each of these four represents a long-term opportunity for growth and profits. They include client-side software, device platforms, hardware platforms, and the rapidly emerging Web services area.

Client-Side Software Platforms

The engineering and performance objectives of portable handheld software platforms are quite different from those of desktop platforms. Established operating systems such as Windows, UNIX, and Linux are designed for desktops with ever-increasing processing and storage capabilities. As a result, they are unsuitable for portable appliances, which require a smaller, lightweight, and flexible operat-

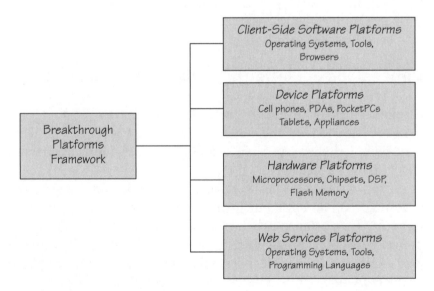

Figure 4.1: Breakthrough Platforms Framework

ing system. Therefore, new client-side software platforms must address the unique needs of portable devices and provide a variety of new features, such as connectivity with other devices.

The client-side software platform market is dominated by four entities: Palm Computing with its Palm OS, Microsoft Windows CE, Symbian EPOC, and, to a more limited degree, Research in Motion. Symbian is a consortium formed by Psion, Ericsson, Motorola, Matsushita, and Nokia.

The Palm OS has enjoyed significant success in the personal information management (PIM) arena. However, extending the Palm OS's functionality from its current PIM application focus to supporting m-business enterprise applications will be a serious challenge. Extending the PDA platform for the broader m-business application market means creating powerful new development tools. These tools would then be used to develop an integrated set of components and then seamlessly connect these components to the enterprise's applications with which they must interact.

In an example of history repeating itself, in 2001 Palm Computing was in the exact same position relative to the mobile device market as Netscape was to the browser market in 1995. Both instances are characterized by companies with a great product and considerable momentum but lacking a complete platform for business users.

Microsoft, on the other hand, is starting from a powerful market position, since its strategy already addresses the client, server, and network sides. The company is working hard to make its Windows CE platform attractive to a wide variety of markets, including mobile devices, information appliances, music players, game consoles, 3G phones, retail point of sale, industrial automation, and server appliances.

The history of Windows CE has been one of steady progress. The platform was first introduced in late 1996, with version 2.0 coming one year later. These early versions were characterized by extremely convoluted user interfaces, slow response times, and poor hardware. They offered little competition for Palm. Windows CE version 3.0 addressed several of these design problems. Today, Windows CE is one of three major components in Microsoft's Windows Embedded platform strategy: Windows CE, Windows NT, and Windows 2000. Significant complementarities characterize the relationships among these three platforms.

To broaden Windows CE's appeal, Microsoft is seeking to dominate key beachheads along the mobile value chain. The company's strategy appears to be to acquire, invest, and conquer. Microsoft began its quest for wireless dominance by investing $600 million in Nextel with plans to roll out Microsoft Network (MSN) to more than 2 million Nextel subscribers. Microsoft then acquired OmniBrowse, a wireless content delivery firm, and rebranded the service as MSN Mobile. Through MSN Mobile, users will be able to access Web content via any wireless device, including cellular phones, handheld devices, and interactive pagers. Microsoft also acquired the Swedish wireless Internet server company Sendit, and formed the Microsoft Mobile Internet business unit as part of the server applications group. The company then purchased STNC, a U.K. company developing a microbrowser to convert wired markup languages, like HTML and XML, to a wireless-friendly format such as WAP. The company also acquired Entropic, for its speech-recognition software. Microsoft has also formed alliances with many key wireless companies, such as NTT DoCoMo, Ericsson, Wireless Knowledge, Motorola, and Cingular. These alliances have resulted in many initiatives, ranging from the Mobile Information Server (MIS), which targets carriers and Fortune 1000 companies, to the Stinger screen phone.

With its army of experienced developers, Microsoft appears extremely difficult to compete against in the long run. Unless Microsoft makes a major faux pas or a disruptive event occurs, it is tough to see why it will not extend its desktop domination to the handheld marketplace.

Palm OS

By almost any criterion, the PalmPilot is wildly successful. PalmPilot sales have exceeded 15 million units in a short time and captured more than 65 percent of market share. Users purchase them faster than any other handheld. Product reviewers give them award after award.

Why is the PalmPilot handheld successful? The now-extinct Apple Newton had more features, the Rex is more compact, the Avigo is less expensive, the Psion has a keyboard, and the Windows CE–based Compaq iPaq functions as a mini-PC.

Some of the reasons for the Palm's success are obvious. It is truly portable, it is aimed at executives with an inexpensive price point, and it has a long battery life. It is a focused solution—addressing a specific need—rather than a general-purpose tool. However, the main reason the PalmPilot overshadows all the others is that it is easy to use, which is the primary expectation users have from a personal information management product.

History and Product Families

In 1992, inventor Jeff Hawkins and marketers Donna Dubinsky and Ed Colligan joined forces to form Palm Computing. Hawkins had worked at Intel and GRiD Systems, which brought the first pen-based computer to the market; Dubinsky had worked at Apple Computer and Claris; and Colligan had worked at Radius, a maker of Macintosh clones.

In 1993, Palm Computing's first software product appeared in a device called Zoomer, a Casio product with a Geoworks operating system. It was sold in Tandy retail outlets. Zoomer's shortcomings inspired further work on the key handheld functions users value today: handwriting recognition software, personal information management, and one-touch desktop synchronization software. With Zoomer's failure, Casio discontinued the product, leaving Palm's founders—Hawkins, Dubinsky, and Colligan—to start up their own vertically integrated device company. Palm partnered with U.S. Robotics to manufacture the original Pilot. U.S. Robotics subsequently acquired the company for $44 million in 1995. The following year, the firm unveiled its PalmPilot-connected organizer. More than a million Pilots were sold within the first eighteen months. When U.S. Robotics was bought by 3Com in 1997, Palm became a subsidiary of the networking giant. 3Com sold 1.2 million Palms in 1998. That same year, Palm's founders left to form rival Handspring, which launched its Visor product in 1999. In 1999, 3Com released the Internet-ready Palm VII and launched its Palm.Net Internet service for handheld devices. In 2000, Palm was spun off by 3COM, and it is now an independent company.

Today, there are four families of Palm handheld devices—Palm III, m500, Palm V, and Palm VII—all based on the same platform. Customers buying the Palm package receive a Palm handheld device, a cradle to connect the device to a PC, and personal information management and synchronization software. The software runs on a PC and serves as a conduit between the device and other personal computer applications. While all of these devices are designed to offer a combination of utility, simplicity, wearability, and mobility, Palm has differentiated its products to appeal to specific market segments. For example, Palm V appeals to users who value wearability. The device has a sleek, compact, and lightweight form factor. Similarly, the Palm VII, with a built-in wireless modem, appeals to mobile professionals and enterprise customers who want connectivity and mobility.

The Palm Platform

In addition to the Palm OS operating system, the Palm platform consists of several components and features:

- A simple user interface to interact with the Palm device and the application programming interfaces, which allows developers to write applications that run on multiple devices based on the Palm platform.
- Standard personal information management applications, including datebook, address book, to-do list, memo pad, calculator, and expense-management functions.
- Developer kits that enable third parties to write applications and kits that enable licensees to design devices around the Palm OS operating system.
- HotSync data synchronization technology, which enables a handheld device to synchronize information with personal computers or enterprise databases.
- Graffiti script recognition technology, which enables users to input script data directly through a pen-based user interface.
- Web Clipping, which is Palm's proprietary content presentation standard. The underlying assumption is that the most efficient way to deliver satisfying wireless applications in a thin-pipe, low-resolution world is to run applications locally while retrieving data remotely.
- Expansion slot support, including Secure Digital, Sony Memory-

Stick, Compact Flash, and Handspring's Springboard. While the Palm platform will support all of these technologies, Palm has announced plans to use Secure Digital in its own devices.

The Palm platform is designed to allow applications to run quickly and reliably. It minimizes power, processing, and memory requirements without sacrificing performance, which in turn reduces component costs for manufacturers. These attributes allow for a slim form factor and permit application designs that allocate greater processing resources to operating these applications rather than to running a complex operating system. However, as processor speeds increase and miniaturization of components continues, these advantages will pose only limited barriers to competition.

Palm Platform Licensing Model

Palm is seeking to make its platform the industry standard by expanding its use in a wide variety of handheld devices and information appliances. The company's strategy is to position itself at the center of a "Palm Economy," mirroring Microsoft's position as the center of the "PC Economy."

In the Palm Economy, the company envisions generating revenue via software licensing of its products, particularly the Palm operating system and related applications. Under this strategy, the company would license the Palm platform to other handheld device manufacturers, such as Sony, and other information appliance manufacturers. Nokia signed on to integrate the Palm platform into several of their mobile phone products. Palm also extended its license to Handspring, Symbol, and Kyocera. In spite of its remarkable growth, the company's major challenge remains Microsoft, with its considerable resources and capabilities.

Outsmart, Outwit, and Outplay—
Palm Needs to Get Aggressive

In the Microsoft-versus-Palm competition, Palm has won the first-to-market contest. But this conflict has just begun. Palm's success will depend on its ability to develop and introduce new products and enhance existing products to continue its emphasis on utility, wearability, mobility, style, and ease of use. However, in the long run, it is difficult for a product to achieve market dominance on features and functions alone. Forming key alliances with select firms while maintaining a clear focus on the company's strategic objectives is critical to a product's success.

It is extremely important for Palm's management team to focus on gaining client-side platform dominance. However, the company's management could easily be distracted from this primary goal by acquiring several companies and expanding the portfolio of products. The scotched acquisition of infrastructure software maker Extended Systems due to falling stock price is an example. Extended Systems would have given Palm a strong foothold in the enterprise market. If Palm fails to maintain and grow its platform dominance, it will follow in the footsteps of its former parent company, 3COM. 3COM, which had tremendous potential, could not compete against the innovation and resources of Cisco.

Handheld-Device Platforms

The handheld-device market is divided into five categories:

- **Feature phones.** Cell or mobile phones are optimized for voice traffic and can access limited amounts of data from the Web. They are also the smallest of the three devices. Microbrowsers for feature phones will play a leading role in this market as the platform for information access.
- **Smart phones.** Bigger than a feature phone, smaller than a Pocket PC, smart phones offer both voice and data capabilities, with color displays, in one device. An example is the Nokia Communicator running Symbian's EPOC operating system. Microsoft's Stinger, which is also aimed at this market, offers users scaled-down versions of Pocket Outlook and Internet Explorer.
- **Handheld organizers and pagers.** These devices are compact and optimized for personal information management (e.g., Handspring Visor) and e-mail/pagers (e.g., Research in Motion, BlackBerry). PIM handhelds, unlike the phones, can also be used offline without network connectivity.

- **Industrial handhelds.** These are specialized devices—for example, bar code scanners—serving industrial segments, including retail, transportation, parcel and postal delivery, manufacturing, and health care. Examples are Symbol Technologies and Intermec.
- **Pocket PCs.** These handheld devices are miniature PCs—for example, Compaq iPAQ. They have greater data capabilities and larger displays, and are equipped with a keypad or stylus for inputting data. They run not only Pocket Internet Explorer but also other Pocket Office applications.

The boundaries between these categories are rather tenuous, as the coming wave of new applications and capabilities is forcing the redesign of today's mobile and handheld computing platform. For instance, Palm began as a handheld organizer but has now morphed into a pocket PC equivalent. With increased bandwidth, these platforms must be able to deliver support for new, never-before-imagined screen sizes (also known as form factors) and sophisticated new services such as streaming media.

The trade press reflects industry confusion over which specific market and customer problems will be addressed by the emerging handheld device platforms. However, a deeper analysis of the various strategic moves clarifies the issues at hand. The strategic moves can be classified into two camps:

- **Multi-device integration platforms.** One platform that can support the information exchange between multiple devices—consumer electronics, personal computers, and handheld devices. The growing battle between Sony's PlayStation and Microsoft's Xbox is an example of this.
- **Multi-purpose device platforms.** One platform that can support a consistent experience across multiple tasks—PIM, phone calls, and e-mail. The conflict between Handspring's Springboard and Microsoft's Windows CE exemplifies the multi-purpose competition.

The competitive nuances in each of these cases can be best understood by taking a closer look at the strategies of incumbent firms such as Sony and the strategies of innovator firms such as Handspring.

Sony: Multi-Device Integration Strategy

The shift in market demand from stand-alone consumer electronics to integrated multi-device platforms radically changes the competitive landscape. Typically, as the environment becomes more complex, customers gravitate toward integrated solutions that address this increased complexity. For example, Microsoft Office has eliminated the need to shop for individual word processing, spreadsheet, and presentation packages. Customers love its integrated functionality.

The digital consumer electronics market has the same unmet integration need. Customers are simply bewildered by the device choices with which they are presented. For example, the simple act of moving pictures from a digital camera to a PC for manipulation often requires knowledge and skill that the average user just does not possess. This transferring of photographs to a PC would be much easier if there were a cradle on which to place the digital camera and the camera displays as an icon on the PC. If the same cradle could be used to synchronize a handheld and also to upload contacts into a cell phone, the cradle would suddenly become a multi-device platform.

Electronics firms have been attempting to create a multi-device platform for years. Sony is the leader in these efforts. The company not only has the consumer electronics expertise, it has tremendous computer expertise. With its VAIO product line, a 60 percent share of the video game market with PlayStation 2, tremendous knowledge of content through Sony Entertainment, and a deep understanding of wireless technology through its alliance with NTT DoCoMo, Sony's expertise is unparalleled. Then, of course, there is the company's brand recognition and brand loyalty.

In its electronics business, Sony has positioned four product categories as gateways to the networked world: digital TVs and set-top boxes, VAIO home-use PCs, PlayStation 2 game systems, and mobile devices. Based on the gateway concept, Sony will upgrade its various product lines, enabling them to link to Web-based content and services. Sony's future plans include introducing a host of new devices featuring "smart" picture frames with rotating electronic pictures, and a PDA called the CLIE, which is based on the Palm OS. (CLIE stands for "Communications Linkage for Information and Entertainment.") However, the VAIO line of PCs is the central platform upon which

Sony's future will depend. The VAIO line will allow diverse consumer electronics devices, such as digital cameras, digital jukeboxes, and MP3 players, to interconnect to one another, providing users with the optimum in entertainment and information experience.

Sony will design elements of its strategic VAIO platform into each of its devices to enable them to communicate with one another, connect to the Internet, and share content. Sony's current platform elements include their "Memory Stick" modules for storage and transferring information from one device to another and the PlayStation 2 game system as a home-based Internet platform connecting to all other devices via wires, Memory Sticks, infrared or Bluetooth.

The company is also introducing an integrated console with combined PC and home entertainment functionality. The console will include video recorder capabilities and numerous high-end stereo features. Sony's "Trojan horse" strategy embeds key technologies into the communication and entertainment devices customers already buy. For example, Sony digital cameras already include a Memory Stick. Soon these cameras will be able to communicate with a PlayStation to upload photos to the Internet, and PlayStations will work with cable TV and 3G networks to connect to the Internet.

Sony is systematically penetrating the household from various entry points. Most important, the company's strategy directly targets next-generation wireless Internet users—today's teenagers. These young users represent the largest group of consumers of video, music, and games. Just as the previous generation grew up with the Walkman brand of Sony tape player, today's teens will grow up with Sony brand Internet-capable devices. Meeting the needs of this teen market is critical to the success of companies competing in the wireless environment.

Sony is adept at introducing tasteful designs, easy-to-use functions, and new and exciting product concepts. By taking a long-term view, Sony is building both market and technology platforms, providing it with a foundation for meeting emerging customer needs.

Handspring: Multi-Purpose-Device Strategy

Some companies focus on a culture of continuous technological innovation. They understand how novel and creative responses to changing customer needs can ensure future success. Such firms aren't overly concerned with what their competitors are doing. They mainly seek to understand their customers' priorities and then adapt the firm's products and services to meet the customers' needs. Handspring exemplifies this culture of innovation and downplays the conventional wisdom that handhelds be smart devices loaded with every digital feature and wireless capability imaginable.

Handspring's goal is to create simple, practical, easy-to-use tools for the consumer. Its vision centers on the belief that the handheld is the foundation for mobile voice and data applications. To support this vision, Handspring was the first to create a hardware extension platform. Called Springboard, it is an expansion slot built into the top of the Visor—Handspring's entry into the handheld market. The Springboard platform gives the Visor greater extendability, similar to equipping a PC with a parallel port to which you can attach a variety of devices.

Springboard: Extending Functionality

Handspring's expansion slot has resulted in a second layer of usability on top of the Palm OS platform. Handspring's Springboard allows and encourages third-party development of software and hardware applications. The applications these third-party developers create are often in the form of plug-and-play modules that snap easily into the Visor's port. A number of these are now available, including games, modems, e-book readers, GPS add-ons, and a digital camera.

Handspring's Visor and Springboard platform are the foundation for the company's next transition. In addition to its current role as a competitor in the growing handheld-device market, Handspring will leverage its innovations to offer a platform for mobile Internet applications. The firm made this transition a reality by:

- **Converting the Visor into a mobile Internet and communications device.** Through product evolution and module enhancement, the Visor has the tools to become a leading mobile Internet appliance.
- **Developing a self-reinforcing business model.** The Springboard platform allows Handspring to attract and retain a market of

Visor-dependent users. The Springboard platform and its modules will thus foster loyalty to Handspring products.

But competition is not standing still. Microsoft and Palm quickly copied this innovation in their next generation of products.

Handspring's Strategy

Unlike Palm, which is very focused on the business market, Handspring is targeting the consumer market. The business drivers that should help Handspring maintain its momentum are the following:

- **Consumer-friendly pricing and relevance.** Consumer markets grow as a function of price and relevance. Lower prices allow more users to purchase an item or service. The more relevant a product is to users' needs, the more likely it is that they will buy it. With an entry-level price point of $149, the Handspring products are priced to sell. When Nintendo introduced the original GameBoy more than ten years ago, it cost $179. More than 100 million Gameboys have been shipped since.
- **Flexibility and vertical market potential.** The Springboard expansion slot makes the Visor the most flexible handheld on the market. The platform's ability to integrate hardware modules allows the Visor to tap into a number of markets. In addition, the Springboard platform will enable users to leverage existing applications as well as hardware developments. Potential markets for these new applications include the medical, educational, and scientific markets.
- **Efficiency by leveraged outsourcing model.** Handspring has created a lean operating model by outsourcing manufacturing, order fulfillment, and repair. Also, by licensing the Palm OS, they keep their development costs down.
- **Version economics.** Version economics occurs when a company's customers must upgrade the products they've purchased in order to get the latest in features and functionality. Microsoft utilized this business model quite effectively to gain total market dominance, and Handspring must now do the same in consumer markets to gain a foothold.

Handspring must be clear about their target customer. Trying to be all things for all customers is likely to cause execution problems. For instance, initially the company was aiming at consumers—women especially. As the consumer market developed more slowly than anticipated, the company switched its strategy to focus on the business consumer. The fact that the young company is public with a broad product line does not help matters, as it struggles to keep Wall Street happy. For Handspring to succeed, it must continue to do the following:

- **Keep it simple, affordable, and lifestyle enhancing**. Make the product more like a consumer electronics device, such as Game-Boy, than a PC. There is no reason for the company to lose its focus on the consumer market. Handspring must release products that push the accepted limits of innovation and design but that are eminently usable and affordable.
- **Develop multiple revenue sources**. Although Handspring's primary revenue is from Visor sales, it has additional revenue sources, including internally developed Springboard modules. Handspring is expanding this revenue footprint by licensing the Springboard platform to Symbol for use in industrial handheld computing products.
- **Offer high-end and low-end products**. Handspring should follow the mass consumer business model and develop handhelds that appeal to the broad spectrum of the market. Future high-end handheld devices will likely include new form factors, added communications features, and high-resolution color screens.

The company faces significant challenges in its quest to become a dominant leader. In the rapidly evolving consumer sector, Handspring must continue its heritage of successful, ongoing innovation in order to stay on top of trends and consumer expectations. However, to succeed, innovation isn't everything. Management counts. Handspring's management team has a good track record of executing any business strategy they undertake. As the visionaries that successfully built Palm Computing, this team has demonstrated the ability to deliver products to the mass market.

M-Business Hardware Platforms

Today's m-business environment is characterized by several hardware platforms competing for customer and industry attention. These range from communication protocol standards such as those provided by Qualcomm, design platforms from ARM Holdings, microprocessor platforms from Intel StrongARM and Motorola's Dragonball, and multimedia and speech recognition platforms from Texas Instruments' OMAP.

The increased demand for new hardware platforms correlates with the accelerated convergence of voice, data, and wireless technology. These platforms are prerequisites to the development of the next generation of mobile Internet-enabled wireless devices. In short, businesses and consumers are demanding a broad array of new and enhanced handheld products—PDAs, smart phones, Web tablets, e-books, telematics, and Internet appliances—that provide mobile Internet access for computing, communications, and entertainment applications.

Of all the participants in the hardware platform competition, Intel bears watching. The company is in the process of reinventing itself in order to stake out a key position in the mobile hardware platform space. As with Microsoft, there are so many technological initiatives and novel architectures being developed by Intel that it almost requires a Ph.D. in electrical engineering to understand which initiatives relate to which products. The scale and scope of Intel's mobile initiatives is astounding. The company's creative focus is on supplying new multimedia capable components for current and next-generation cellular technology. The list of components is comprehensive and ranges from high-performance, low-power processors to flash memory, chipsets, and software.

The mobile processor market has two sectors: compute-intensive processors and communications-intensive processors. Intel is seeking to attain dominance in the compute-intensive processor market by using its Xscale microprocessor architecture. Xscale consists of several core components, one of which is the high-performance RISC engine—the StrongARM microprocessor. Intel acquired the StrongARM processor architecture with its 1998 purchase of Digital Equipment IC operations.

Intel plans to use XScale as its application processor and a combination of the XScale and Micro Signal Architecture (MSA) that DSP, codeveloped with Analog Devices for its communications processor. Intel acquired DSP Communications in 1999. This combined solution represents Intel's Personal Client Architecture (PCA). The goal of PCA is to enable different computing and communications equipment to work together seamlessly.

The major challenge facing companies seeking to implement the mobile Internet is delivering services to the customer across multiple devices. The only feasible way to provide the same consistency of content across a variety of devices is by relying on standard technological platforms and architectures. Current mobile applications are based on a model that requires applications to be written for each specific device and wireless network. This makes it difficult for handheld devices to share information with each other and slows the development of new applications. Since the PCA architecture consists of interchangeable hardware and software building blocks, it can support a wide range of services across devices, networks, and platforms.

Motorola Inc.'s Semiconductor Products Sector (SPS) is also using a variety of approaches to address mobile processor market needs. In 2001, Motorola processors could be found in more than 75 percent of handheld computers. To innovate and protect its market share, Motorola is embarking on a two-prong strategy. One, enhance existing processors such as the Dragonball VZ, which is inside all major handhelds that use the Palm operating system, with the next-generation Super VZ processor. The Super VZ will run at 66 MHz, more than twice as fast as the current VZ processors, and is estimated to cost $14 each in volume. Two, build a new line of advanced processors called MX1, using technology licensed from ARM Holdings. The MX1 will run at 140 MHz to 200 MHz and is expected to cost $19 each in volume. Motorola's goal is to provide 3G handset components that combine an ARM processor with the StarCore DSP.[3]

The lines of hardware platform competition have been defined, with individual firms forming strategic alliances in hopes of ensuring their success. At stake is a dominant share of the mobile market and the profits accruing from an almost monopolistic stranglehold on the technology. A careful analysis of the various application processors on the market reveals a striking pattern of control over hardware platform development by one firm. The major firms in the hardware platform competition are licensing their designs from a relatively unknown company, ARM Holdings, which has silently become the major power in the mobile processor business.

ARM Holdings: The Intellectual Property Business Model

Intellectual property (IP) creation and licensing is an established business model in the electronics industry. For example, Qualcomm owns the patents to all CDMA wireless telecommunications standards. These standards have been adopted internationally. Qualcomm has licensed this essential CDMA patent portfolio to more than a hundred telecommunications equipment manufacturers worldwide.

IP licensing is also practiced in the chip design sector. Having the intellectual capability to design the chips that power the microprocessor is the best competitive position a firm can occupy. For example, Intel produces the StrongARM chip for powering mobile devices. Motorola produces the Dragonball chip that powers Palm devices. The actual inventor of both of these microprocessors is ARM Holdings, headquartered in Cambridge, England.

ARM Holdings—The Company

ARM, formerly Advanced RISC Machines, is a leading "knowledge provider" of embedded microprocessor technology to semiconductor and consumer electronics manufacturers. The firm's customers include Sony, Intel, Nokia, and Motorola. Its tagline "the architecture for the digital world" sums up ARM's role in shaping the future of mobile commerce.

Almost every wireless and mobile information appliance requires an affordable processing solution with both high-performance computing power and low power consumption. The ARM platform meets this industry requirement—a feat that none of their competitors have matched to date. Their success has secured their position as the industry leader in the microprocessor market segment.

ARM began as a PDA company. Apple Computer and the British

firm Acorn Computer set up ARM Holdings in 1990 to develop and sell the ARM chip. Apple's interest was in securing a new chip to power its Newton handheld. A decade later, both the Newton and Acorn Computers no longer exist. Although it created the PDA as a product category, the Newton was a commercial failure and Apple stopped production in 1998. In 2000, Acorn Computer changed its name to Element 14 and its focus to developing broadband communications chips. In that same year, Broadcom acquired it.

In order to survive, ARM changed its business focus from manufacturing to licensing its intellectual property (IP). ARM licenses its IP—high-performance, low-cost, power-efficient RISC processors and system-chip designs—to leading electronics companies. Its designs use less power and are thus ideal for mobile phones, handheld computers, digital music players, digital cameras, and in-car computers.

ARM's designs are rapidly becoming the standard in mobile communications, handheld computing, digital signal processing (DSP), and other technology markets. The company believes that once it has established its architecture as an industry standard, it will be able to derive significant revenue growth through new and repeat licensing, royalty payments, and consulting fees.

Business Model and Growth Strategy

ARM's strategy is based on structuring the company around a semiconductor intellectual property (SIP) business model. In this model the company's primary source of revenue will be through the licensing of its architecture, consulting, and maintenance support to a worldwide network of multi-national semiconductor partners.

In other words, ARM is a "chipless chipmaker." Its business model is based on the view that ideas are worth more than physical assets. ARM's strategy is to develop and design microprocessors and then license the technology to other manufacturers in exchange for a royalty or a flat fee. The manufacturers do most of the cost-intensive work, from handling the manufacturing to marketing.

For the SIP business model to work, a company must sell its licenses at high volumes, since royalty payments are often small. High sales volumes are needed to create enough of a revenue stream to sustain business. The mass market of handheld devices is the best position for an IP firm such as ARM to occupy. More than two-thirds of ARM's revenues come from licenses and royalties. Moreover, as ARM's technology becomes the industry de facto standard, its royalty revenues will increase dramatically. ARM's SIP business model has significant operating leverage.

As discussed above, the model generates revenues in several different ways. Apart from its licensing fees, ARM earns income by assisting clients with layout and implementation. ARM also receives maintenance and support income for software and hardware updates. Finally, ARM offers a consulting service to help with software and to design complete chips or specific parts of chips.

ARM's Partnership Ecosystem

ARM's strategy is to position the ARM architecture as the global embedded RISC standard in the microprocessor market, similar to Intel's positioning as the standard architecture in the PC computing market. ARM's success depends on a well-developed partnership model. The company's partnership model currently involves four areas: Semiconductor and Systems, Development Tools, Systems Software, and Specialized Design.

ARM's Semiconductor and Systems partners form the core competence of the company's business model. They take ARM's concepts and innovations and develop them into digital electronics products for the mass market. In return, ARM works closely with these firms to ensure that its products satisfy real-life consumer needs. Such close cooperation means that the high cost of research and development is shared across the partnership. ARM also has partnerships with third-party operating system, software, and hardware tool vendors. ARM is not simply an intellectual property firm. It provides its partners with a broad range of services, from support tools to design consulting.

ARM's success is attributable to a partnership model that has not only leveraged the company's strengths but that has differentiated the company's offerings through partnership diversification. For example, ARM's partnership network extends into the wireless area through its relationship with VLSI Technology, into the automotive market through partners like Texas Instruments and OKI, and into the LCD products market through its relationship with Sharp.

The Future of ARM Holdings

ARM is well positioned to benefit from the trend of licensing intellectual property for system-on-a-chip solutions. System-on-a-chip solutions are critical to the successful implementation of next-generation electronic and embedded applications. However, ARM must develop new designs every eighteen to twenty-four months; maintaining this level of performance is necessary for attracting new licensees as well as for keeping current ones. Licensee acquisition and retention are key to ARM's ability to protect its software investments.

Corporate efforts to dominate the microprocessor market are made more interesting by the convergence of mobile phone and PDA technology. Intel and Analog Devices are jointly developing digital signal processor chip design, which will be combined with Intel's ARM-based Xscale chip. Motorola, which also makes DSP chips, will have an ARM chip of its own that can be used both inside its own mobile phones and in those made by others. As mobile markets continue to develop, ARM will occupy a strategic position in each.

Web Services Platforms

In the late 1980s, Sun Microsystems first expressed the vision "The Network Is the Computer." Microsoft's "Software as a Service" captured its vision of the technology industry of the late 1990s. Hosted software services are currently enjoying considerable popularity in server-side development. Companies increasingly use hosted services to develop distributed, robust, and scalable Web-based applications.

The transition toward distributed systems requires the development of an entirely new software infrastructure to support the Web services model. It is the software infrastructure arena where major competitive conflicts are currently taking place. At stake is nothing less than control of the most valuable software asset in existence today: the network.

In reality, however, there is no "one" network. The "Network Is the Computer" vision, when translated into the day-to-day realities of digital communications and processing, references a network of interconnected Internet-based networks. There are currently six possible network configurations:

- **Desktop Information Web**. The Internet's first configuration has been based on a narrow-band dial-up implementation designed to take advantage of desktop computers. Despite a proliferation of other devices, desktop computers maintain clear advantages that new devices will never have.
- **Broadband Media Web**. The Internet's second configuration is characterized by a broadband always-on DSL or cable modem connection. It is rich with on-demand services and requires major broadband infrastructure upgrades. The broadband media web provides a much fatter "pipe" from the home to the external world. This enables the enriched environment mentioned above and realistic two-way interaction between content providers and users.
- **Interactive Appliance Web**. The third configuration is the smart home network. This configuration is perhaps the most fascinating of all. For example, it will allow your refrigerator, television, home security system, and personal computer to communicate with a central information hub inside your house. This hub—a single point of contact—is your connection to the external world.
- **Mobile Handheld Web**. The fourth configuration is the mobile web, which enables support for the mobile user. The movement from a fixed-location model (desktop) to a more uncertain random-movement model (wireless device) is driving this new network configuration. The mobile handheld configuration also includes the use of mobile broadband technology to permit users a desktop experience via a handheld device.
- **Voice Web**. The network's fifth configuration is the voice web, characterized by telephone and voice services such as speech-to-text and text-to-speech conversion. The ability to use your voice to interact with browsers and with search, e-mail, and transaction engines requires sophisticated software services. Companies such as Cisco, Nortel, and Intel are racing to create the voice web infrastructure. A number of companies are beginning to create voice browsers incorporating technology to perform speech- and text-conversion functions. Other firms, such as TellMe Networks, are creating new application-enabled voice Web services.
- **Supply Chain Web**. The sixth Internet configuration is the enhanced business-to-business version, where machines will

communicate directly with each other over value-added networks (VAN) using EDI and XML standards. This configuration facilitates the smooth execution of intercompany transactions and is essential for efficiency and productivity. The current infrastructure can support only limited aspects of this configuration. However, as the world moves toward more real-time supply chain activities, a new generation of software will be required to support the supply chain revolution.

These six networks are no longer discrete, isolated entities. They are increasingly interconnected, enabling a seamless, end-to-end flow of information across the unified network they form. The next step in their evolution involves more than just sharing information across their communications' boundaries; it means developing the ability to run the same software applications regardless of the network you access.

For example, you begin a PowerPoint presentation on your office computer and later edit this same file on your home TV. For this scenario to work, the TV must be capable of running PowerPoint. Moreover, it needs to be the same PowerPoint your office PC runs, not PowerPoint for TV. Otherwise, each network will require specialized applications. For such interconnection and interoperability to occur, the current communications hardware and software infrastructure must undergo considerable innovation.

Fully integrated communications is but the initial step in interconnecting the web's multiple configurations. Software vendors, such as Microsoft with its .NET strategy, are currently developing the applications required to make sophisticated services possible over these distributed networks. A major factor in interconnecting these six environments will be the development of common application design standards applicable to each. Such standards will ensure that an application's functionality is consistent regardless of the web accessed.

Microsoft .NET

.NET embodies Microsoft's vision of "software as a service." .NET is a development environment for Web services, and its goals are critical to software development success in the mobile environment. Since mobile devices tend to have extremely limited storage capabilities, only a minimal number of functions can run on the actual client handheld or cell phone device. Thus, the future success of mobile computing will depend on using client-side devices primarily as network access tools. The network is where most of the actual software will reside. The mobile device will be used to access, download, and run these network-based applications.

The Web Service Philosophy

Web services are reusable application components capable of being shared across the Internet. Historically, software applications were designed and developed as the need arose. Web services, however, permit software functionality reuse. Microsoft is currently in the process of rewriting all of its major flagship products from Visual Studio to Office XP to incorporate Web services standards. The company's goal is to decompose the complex functionality of, say, Microsoft Word into a Web services format. For example, a user at the airport opens a Word document using her Compaq iPaq with Windows CE operating system. She needs to make changes to this document e-mailed to her by a client. She can download a Word Web service customized for the iPaq and use it to make the changes she needs. On-the-go access and use of software functions comparable to what currently exist in the desktop environment is central to the successful adoption of mobile computing.

The Web services business model is analogous to the outsourcing model. The Microsoft .NET vision assumes a market of developers, each building sophisticated LEGO-like application building blocks in whatever programming language—C, C++, Visual Basic—they are comfortable. By subscribing to various "plug-and-play" building blocks, such as voice and text messaging, and signature authentication, developers can create new applications more quickly. Web services is the outsourcing of common development tasks comparable to a corporation outsourcing its payroll processing. As with the outsourcing model, the Web services approach is intended to permit a business to focus on its core competencies. The company's noncore business activities should be performed by vendors and partners with the appropriate expertise. For example, many companies have outsourced their shipping function to third parties such as UPS and FedEx.

Web services are designed to enable a programmer to "shop" for the Web service they need, whether it is finding a catalog, credit-card authorization, or a billing/accounting function. Each of these components has been written and distributed by other programmers. Then you are responsible for bringing these components together, combining them with a bit of XML "glue code" of your own, and creating a new business logic.

The Web services philosophy is this: assemble—seldom build from scratch. Application assembly using modular components saves development time and helps create more consistent software products. Currently, most organizations start new when developing service components such as messaging and notification. A Web services approach permits a company to leverage the IT talent it has to focus on its mission-critical application needs and not on technology peripheral to the firm's core success.

For example, HailStorm Web Services, an authentication and instant messaging service available over the Web, saves programmers time since they no longer must write these services themselves—they simply reuse the appropriate code. Another example: a calculator Web service used in conjunction with a mortgage or tax program running on another Web site. Another common e-commerce Web service is credit-card processing. A company that wants to allow credit-card transactions must address the issue of the differences between how AMEX, Visa, and other credit cards allow access to their services. By downloading a credit-card processing Web service designed to interface with the different card companies, programmers no longer need to develop the application itself; they need only code the Web service interface.

The .NET Strategy

To help .NET adoption in the mobile space, Microsoft has alliances with a number of mobile operators, handset manufacturers, and systems integrators. What is the strategy behind these efforts? One, understand the mobile business. Microsoft is working with mobile carriers to understand their business and help deliver new mobile data services to their customers. Two, get customer penetration. Microsoft has developed some key pieces of mobility technology, but it will take an industrywide effort to get adoption. Microsoft is working closely with partners to bring devices, servers, and services to customers. A key piece of the strategy is making the right business investments and building strong relationships that will enable the development and deployment of new mobile data services and solutions, both today and in the future.

It will be years before Microsoft's .NET strategy is rolled out in its entirety. It will take even longer to gauge its success in the m-business marketplace. The scale of the .NET rollout is immense and not without significant challenges. The only other historical parallel to Microsoft's .NET initiative is IBM's Systems Application Architecture strategy, introduced in the 1980s. Similar in scale to Microsoft's strategy, IBM attempted the integration of diverse systems and applications in large enterprises. IBM's strategy was a complete failure due to software limitations and unanticipated shifts in technology owing largely to the introduction and dominance of the personal computer.

Similar risks await Microsoft. In order for the .NET strategy to succeed, its execution must be nearly flawless, its timing impeccable, and it will require constant monitoring of disruptive changes in the technological landscape. However, no other blueprint currently exists that may present Microsoft with competition. In the absence of substantive competitive pressures, Microsoft may very well have the time it needs to implement this radical vision of software development and implementation.

Microsoft's retooling of its own software offerings to use a common set of Web services further minimizes the company's competitive risks. In addition, their strategic acquisition of Great Plains Software provides them with several of the most frequently used Web services components—accounting, billing, and record keeping. Their next step will be to convince their enterprise clients to use the Web services Microsoft provides. If they are successful, it will mean a continuous license revenue stream for Microsoft and an end to any serious competitive threat.

A Final Thought

All truth passes through three stages. First, it is ridiculed. Second, it is violently opposed. Third, it is accepted as being self-evident.
—Arthur Schopenhauer

Every decade of computing has had its epic platform conflicts. In the 1960s, IBM competed against Sperry. In the 1970s, it was IBM versus Digital Equipment Corporation. Early in the 1980s, it was IBM versus Apple Computer; in the late eighties, Apple competed against Microsoft for desktop dominance. In the early 1990s, Microsoft challenged Novell in the local area network market, Oracle competed against Sybase in the database market, Microsoft confronted Lotus in the desktop application market, and AOL competed against CompuServe. In the mid-1990s, "browser wars" emerged and Microsoft vied for dominance over Netscape. In the late 1990s, SAP, PeopleSoft, Baan, Siebel, and J. D. Edwards competed for the enterprise application space.

The current decade will be no different. Competition for market dominance will continue on the same grand scale that has characterized the past forty years. The intersection of wireless communications, mobile computing, and the Internet is driving the need for new mobile platforms. In this chapter, we described how some companies have used platform management to their competitive advantage. This fact cannot be emphasized enough. Many companies are transforming their strategies from ones focused on creating products to ones focused on creating technology platforms that serve as launchpads for future growth. Managers and strategists must reflect on how the transition from product-focused to platform-focused strategies will impact their businesses by asking the following questions:

- What is the product or service platform of choice for your m-business and how does the platform evolve over time?
- How do robust platforms and the product, process, and service innovations embodied in those platforms drive business growth?

Developing a robust platform strategy could mean the difference between success and failure. Many managers tend to ignore the importance of determining which technology platform is appropriate for their business and which platform will provide their firm with the greatest opportunities for long-term product development and security. Most managers focus almost exclusively on the development of specific products, with minimal consideration given to the platform used. However, a clearly thought out, long-term platform strategy, leveraged to create multiple products, is the key to success in the rapidly changing mobile marketplace.

5

Mobile Application Infrastructure

Companies seeking to implement a mobile solution face numerous application infrastructure challenges. First, they must assess the current state of their IT capabilities to determine the likelihood of leveraging their existing information systems' investments. Second, they must determine whether to build, buy, or lease capabilities that extend their existing systems for access and use by their customers, suppliers, and employees. In addition, they must figure out how to deliver new functionality without spending millions on consultants, contractors, and redesign costs.

For companies just coming off e-business implementations, call it the applications nightmare, part deux. Most executives understand that technological and process innovations are only minimally useful if businesses cannot properly align the software applications and infrastructure on which these innovations depend. They also understand the business value of implementing a low cost of ownership mobile infrastructure to serve as a foundation for introducing sophisticated applications in the future. The big unknown is navigating the uncharted waters of mobile application infrastructure to get from the current state to the mobile vision.

To help companies build mobile solutions, an entirely new category of companies is emerging. The purpose of this category is to facilitate the creation of a new class of mobile, yet scalable, secure, mission-critical enterprise applications. The goal of this software category is to provide the building blocks that take the magic and cost out of building mobile applications. In the past, Fortune 50 companies such as Pepsi, UPS, and FedEx developed mobile applications in-house at a cost of hundreds of million of dollars. Companies such as these can now buy third-party products and roll out a complete mobile solution in months, not years.

What Is the Customer's Pain?

For telecommunications carriers like Verizon Wireless to build new mobile applications—messaging, portals, or m-commerce—on top of their legacy infrastructure will take years of effort and millions of dollars. So they turn to companies such as Openwave Systems that provide an application platform with prepackaged components. The carriers then use this platform to develop customized applications.

Before application platforms, telecom companies had to either build everything from scratch or assemble multiple technologies in order to deliver mobile solutions such as messaging. This approach meant devoting significant resources to the integration and testing of wireless connectivity, mobile databases, synchronization packages, middleware, and application management software.

The resulting custom-built infrastructure possessed an inherent fragility. A minor change by any of the underlying components meant spending additional time, money, and effort on reassembling and retesting the entire application infrastructure. As a result, a constant challenge was stabilizing the custom infrastructure instead of delivering new mobile applications that addressed new customer needs.

The telecommunications companies are not unique. Similar problems exist in other industries. In order to deploy mobile applications, enterprises have to invest in mobile application platforms capable of bridging three constituencies: legacy/existing enterprise software, multiple network operators, and Web-enabled mobile devices. Also, these mobility platforms must bridge multiple networks, operating systems, and coding protocols—not an easy task.

Given this scenario, most corporate IT departments simply lack the resources or expertise needed to navigate the new and treacherous waters of mobility solutions. IT managers are looking to determine which application platforms, business models, and vendors are the ones to invest in for the long haul. In effect, they are struggling to define a mobile infrastructure roadmap.

In order to cut through the fog and define the problem better, we will break down the application infrastructure broad landscape into value-added types. By defining these types, we can classify companies by the segment on which they focus. In addition, this approach clarifies where the conventional software providers are vulnerable to competition from mobile companies and whether the value proposition of these mobile-only companies is defensible.

M-Business Application Infrastructure Types

To deliver a mobile solution, a large firm needs to first build an infrastructure. An infrastructure is made up of several different types of interrelated pieces. Figure 5.1 captures the different types of pieces—or, to use the industry jargon, enablers—that make up a typical mobile infrastructure. We believe that this categorization gives you a good sense of the mobile application infrastructure market today and where it is going.

At a very high level, mobile application infrastructure enablers can be segmented into four types:

- **Application Gateway/Platform Providers**. These provide user management services such as secure access, directories, and administration; communication services such as e-mail, messaging, and scheduling; portal services such as knowledge management, content aggregation, and personalization; and e-commerce services such as catalogs, transactions, and billing. Examples include Openwave and EveryPath.
- **Mobile Application Service Providers (MASPs)**. These provide data center and infrastructure hosting services. Also called colocators, these companies rent equipment, space, and bandwidth to companies that don't want the hassle of creating the plumbing needed to host their own mobile sites. Hosting companies,

called managed services providers (MSPs), take this a step further and maintain the infrastructure for large corporations. Examples include Aether and JP Mobile.

- **Mobile Internet Service Providers (MISPs)**. These provide connectivity to link the devices to the Internet. Examples include general wireless carriers such as AT&T, specialized data carriers such as GoAmerica and Palm.Net, and resellers such as OmniSky.

- **Mobile Application Enablers**. These provide data and transaction security services such as Verisign, data synchronization services such as Synchrologic, and micro-database providers such as Sybase. This group also includes service, systems, and application integration providers.

In the sections that follow, we delve into each market segment. Our goal is not to predict the future but rather to look at the existing established players today and to try to understand directionally where the market is headed. Our conclusions are less about winners and losers and more about how one should think about and evaluate each segment as a function of addressable market potential, economics, and technology.

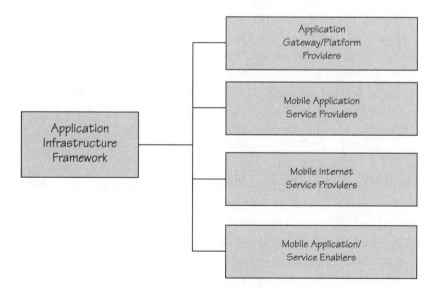

Figure 5.1: Application Infrastructure Framework

Application Gateways/Platform Providers

A plethora of disparate mobile devices, closed networks, language disconnects, differing protocols, and point solutions characterize today's wireless landscape.

Mobile application servers, mobility platforms, and mobile application gateways are comprehensive platforms that mask the complexity of the underlying technology and speed development of innovative solutions. These platforms can be further classified based on the customer base they target: carriers or enterprises.

- **Carrier Class.** With the convergence of voice and data networking technology, communication service providers (CSPs)—including wireless and wireline carriers, portals, and broadband providers— seek a standard platform capable of supporting a wide range of applications as well as the growing and changing demands of consumer and business subscribers. Carrier-class mobile platforms provide CSPs with complete communications, personal productivity, and commercial application solutions. Vendors such as Comverse, InfoSpace, and Openwave provide carrier-class platforms.
- **Enterprise Class.** Enterprise class mobile platforms provide enterprises with the opportunity to leverage their existing Web infrastructure investments. They enable companies to extend the reach of their Web-based content and applications to their mobile customers, employees, suppliers, and business affiliates. A growing number of vendors, such as 724 Solutions, Everypath, Brience, JP Mobile, and ViaFone, provide enterprise-class solutions to connect the company's internal business applications to the outside mobile world.

Carrier-Class Application Platforms: Openwave Systems

Openwave Systems, formed in November 2000, was the result of a merger between Phone.com and Software.com. Openwave combines the wireless data platform of Phone.com with the messaging platform of Software.com into one offering. The combined company provides an end-to-end software solution to large carrier customers.

Business Description

Openwave is also a supplier of carrier-scale Internet infrastructure software for communication service providers (CSP) worldwide. These include wireless network operators, wireline carriers, Internet service providers (ISPs), portals, and broadband network providers. The company's products enable CSPs to implement an Internet business model by offering more services to consumers with the goal of increasing the average revenue per user (ARPU). Openwave serves over 150 CSPs, with more than 500 million subscribers.

Openwave's software, applications, and services enable the delivery of Internet-based information to mass-market wireless telephones. Wireless subscribers use the company's products and services to access the Internet and corporate intranets for e-mail, news, stocks, weather, travel, and sports.

Products

Openwave offers a scalable platform for service providers to use when deploying next-generation business and consumer Internet services. Each of the company's product offerings can be assigned to one of the following groups:

- **Applications** that enable end users to exchange instant messages, electronic mail, facsimile, voice mail, and multimedia messages from PCs, wireline telephones and mobile devices. In addition, these software applications include a personal information manager (PIM) with address book, task lists, and calendar.
- **Infrastructure software** is the software carriers need to enable Internet connectivity to mobile devices. It includes communications gateways to connect wireless devices to the Internet using a variety of protocols. Infrastructure software provides mobile location information as well as a directory that serves as a standards-based repository of information about users and devices in the network. In addition, the software permits Internet connectivity, Web browsing, and synchronization of information among networks, mobile devices, and PCs.

Openwave and Wireless Application Protocol (WAP)

Openwave pioneered the convergence of Internet and mobile telephony. In June 1997, under the name Unwired Planet, it founded the Wireless Application Protocol (WAP) Forum. Its goal was to produce a standard for wireless Internet transmission to mobile phones. The company's vision was to promote WAP specification compliance to phone manufacturers, network operators, content providers, and application developers as a way of making mobile products and services interoperable.

WAP specifications were designed to address wireless Internet transmission issues. These issues included (1) transport related issues, such as limited bandwidth and intermittent network coverage where the transmission of wireless data is hindered; (2) presentation issues, such as the small screens on mobile phones and other hand-held devices; (3) data input issues, such as the lack of QWERTY keyboards and point-and-click mouse functionality in the majority of wireless devices; and (4) wireless-device limited memory and power resource issues.

WAP specifications are based on WML (Wireless Markup Language), which is a scaled-down version of HTML designed for wireless Internet content. WML is itself based on XML (eXtensible Markup Language), which is a programming language that enables the description and exchange of data in an open format. WML addresses the issues of limited wireless network bandwidth—limited to 9.6 to 19.2 Kbps in most markets—as well as the small screens and data input limitations of wireless devices.

WAP was designed to be independent of wireless networks and operating systems. It is compatible with most digital wireless technologies, including CDMA, GSM, and TDMA. In addition, WAP works with most operating systems, including Palm OS, Windows CE, and Java OS.

WAP has made initial headway with mobile phone manufacturers, network operators, and developers. At present, more than thirty phone manufacturers have deployed WAP-based microbrowsers in mobile phones and more than sixty wireless carriers worldwide have implemented WAP "gateways" in their networks, which optimize the exchange of data between the Internet and WAP-based mobile phones. But WAP is going through some growing pains, as first-generation applications were overhyped. As a result, disillusioned users are reporting unsatisfactory experiences—with the level of effort required to obtain information exceeding the threshold for perceived value.[1]

WAP has been under fire for proving too slow and cumbersome for most subscribers and because few worthwhile services were made available. As a result, competition is mounting. Japanese wireless operator NTT DoCoMo has deployed its wireless Internet service, i-mode, based on its own proprietary cHTML technology. DoCoMo's adoption rate success dwarfs the number of customers using WAP-based mobile phones. Still, it is far too early to predict which standard will dominate the wireless application market.

To deflect the WAP criticism and blunt competition, the GSM Association and phone companies, including Telecom Italia, France Telecom, Nokia, and Motorola, have created a new standard called M-Services. M-Services provides mobile operators a common standard for data services as they battle to increase revenue per user in the face of slowing subscriber growth. To ensure better customer adoption of the next generation of mobile phones, which will use always-on GPRS, the GSM Association has produced a set of standards in an attempt to ensure that music downloading, graphics, video streaming, and messaging will be ubiquitous throughout new handsets.

This standard will be based on a software platform made available on a no-royalty basis from Openwave. This is a huge win for Openwave, as these guidelines do not replace WAP—they complement and include WAP. Openwave does not receive any money when its browser is installed on a handset. Instead, it makes the vast majority of its revenues from software that resides on servers behind the wireless network.

In the long term, the need for optimized standards such as WAP or cHTML should abate as advances in technology increase the amount of bandwidth available. Moreover, as companies eliminate gaps in their coverage, problems with intermittent network access should be minimized. Higher transmission speeds and better coverage should reduce problems with bandwidth limits and latency. However, these advances do not address issues related to small screen sizes, data entry, and wireless-devices' limited computing power. Therefore, the need for a language beyond standard HTML for developing content intended for wireless devices will persist. One language, xHTML, represents the convergence of WML and HTML, and potentially could mean the convergence of WAP and i-mode technologies.

Business Strategy

Originally, Openwave's core business was providing data links between network operators and handsets. Their offerings included a server housed by the network operator, a browser stored on the phone, and the WAP protocol to facilitate data transfer between the server and the browser. These elements are roughly analogous to major components of the wired Internet arena—the Web server, the Web browser, and HTML, respectively.

Clearly, Openwave hopes that mobile carriers will find its platform strategy more compelling than the traditional approach. With Openwave, the carrier purchases the platform and adds applications on top of it. In the traditional approach, the carrier purchases applications individually. Openwave will leverage its installed base of gateways to sell its application suite.

We believe that success for Openwave will be more execution-specific than technology-specific. History has shown that the best technology seldom wins. So in the long run, Openwave's strategy should be to provide mobile carriers with better software tools to have more control over their subscribers and enhance the breadth of their customer relationships.

Enterprise-Class Gateway: 724 Solutions

724 Solutions provides an enterprise platform to financial services such as Citibank, Bank of America, Wells Fargo, and Bank of Montreal. The platform allows the company's clients to offer secure, personalized online banking, brokerage, and e-commerce services across a wide range of Internet-enabled wireless and consumer electronic devices.

The Financial Services Platform provides consumers access to online banking and brokerage services through network service providers using digital mobile phones, PDAs, and two-way pagers.

The company's software resides on the financial institution's network and extracts customer data from the institution's legacy systems. It then makes this data available through wired or wireless access.

Current Approaches to Enterprise Solutions

Most companies have attempted the delivery of Web-based content and applications to mobile devices using one of the following two methods:

- **Transcoding or Screen Scraping**. A process used to excerpt Web-based content and applications for presentation on mobile devices by copying and converting the content of a Web page. The actual content is converted, as opposed to accessing the original data source.
- **Custom Developed System**. This method duplicates Web-based content, infrastructure, business logic, and data to create custom content accessible by particular mobile devices.

Screen scraping offers an easy way for delivering Web-based content and applications to mobile devices. However, it lacks certain features needed to support wireless delivery of Web-based content and applications for enterprise companies. The screen-scraping process is not a scalable solution because it converts the content of actual Web pages, and any changes to the underlying content typically requires reprogramming. In addition, because the screen-scraping process does not link to the template that generates the page, it limits the extent to which content can be optimized for delivery to smaller displays and thus limits the functionality.

Custom developed systems are generally used when existing software solutions are either unavailable or insufficient. This method tailors a solution to meet the exact specifications of existing applications and devices. It therefore may not be flexible enough to easily adapt to future advances in technology. A custom solution may require duplicating application code and content in order to support additional applications, new devices, and increased capacity.

Mobile Internet Delivery Platform

724 Solutions provides a platform that is device-, operating system-, and wireless network-agnostic. 724 Solutions platform ensures a consistent user experience regardless of mobile device type or connection speed. The platform offering also goes beyond simple translation/transcoding solutions by providing the following functionality:

- Supports multiple mobile devices by employing diverse technology platforms. In order to do so, the software must be capable of adapting the content and applications to work with the variety of mobile device specifications, including different formats, screen sizes, color support, and markup languages.
- Optimizes content, format, and the applications being accessed to work with varying connection speeds of the devices requesting the information.
- Integrates with existing corporate Web infrastructures to minimize the need to re-create existing functionality and content solely for purposes of wireless delivery. All mobile functionality must comply with current corporate security standards.
- Increases the ease with which enterprise companies develop, maintain, and manage new capabilities. Optimizing a company's wireless development process is critical to the firm's ability to introduce new applications and devices or change the format of existing content and applications.

Revenue Model

724 Solutions has four primary revenue streams: license fees, hosting fees, implementation fees, and maintenance fees.

- **License fee**. 724 Solutions charges its financial institution customers a per-user, per-month license fee. The initial stages of the company's revenue model requires customers to pay their license fees according to an agreed-upon quarterly minimum. In other words, customers must pay a fixed fee regardless of the services they adopt. 724 Solutions recognizes the revenue from these quarterly agreements once service has been delivered and accepted by the customer.

These minimum license contracts are important because they (1) help protect the company in its early phases of growth when its adoption rates are still low, and (2) encourage the aggressive marketing of 724's service by the company's financial institution customers in order to minimize their expense. As 724's adoptions rates increase, the minimum quarterly agreement revenue model will give way to a variable user fee–based model.

- **Hosting fee**. 724 Solutions charges an additional per-user, per-month fee of approximately $2 plus appropriate volume discounts to customers choosing the company's hosting service. The monthly revenues derived from the hosting offering are applied to service and maintenance revenue.
- **Implementation and customer service fee.** Implementation and customer service revenue includes fees from implementation, consulting, and training services, and are charged on a time and expense basis.
- **Maintenance fee**. The company's maintenance fee is in addition to its license fee. The maintenance fee is approximately 18 percent of the license fee and is realized monthly, as is the license revenue.

Business Strategy

The banking industry is 724 Solutions' primary market. However, the company is extending its core competency into other financial arenas, including bill payment and presentment, stock trading, investment services, cash management, and multi-lingual/multi-currency capabilities. To ensure its future success, 724 Solutions must continue to look ahead to the possibilities of wireless and seek out how best to make mobile commerce "possibilities" a reality.

Mobile Application Service Providers

A large Fortune 50 company wants to provide its employees "always connected, always online" access to corporate information on a variety of mobile devices. However, getting up to speed on wireless Web technologies and keeping up with the rapid changes in wireless protocols, devices, and markup languages would require a major investment. It is an investment that the Fortune 50 company is not quite ready to make. Instead of building the capabilities internally, they would rather outsource it to a specialist. Fortunately, help is on the way for corporate IT departments that wish to outsource their mobile solutions.

Mobile application service providers (MASPs) help corporate IT departments extend Internet applications to mobile devices. Many businesses have already made or are in the midst of making significant investments in their application infrastructures. These firms must now face the challenge of integrating their existing systems with hundreds of thousands of potential mobile device, application, and connectivity options and combinations. MASPs provide support for a broad range of devices and applications and help their clients avoid restructuring their enterprise applications to meet the needs of specific devices. MASP software and services assist their clients with the complex challenges associated with extending desktop applications to employees, customers, and business partners.

The Value Proposition

The MASP is an intermediary between an increasingly varied and intricate technological environment and firms seeking to implement a mobile strategy. Outsourcing to a MASP can free up a company's IT staff to focus on tasks related to the firm's core competency rather than focusing on implementing a technology based on constantly changing standards in which they have limited expertise. Companies can avoid making additional IT infrastructure investments in equipment, with the associated maintenance and upgrade costs, and in the training and hiring of staff. The MASP model enables the enterprise to rent or, in effect, subscribe to a complete or partial wireless solution.

Hosting is the core service a MASP offers. Hosting services involve both core and value-added offerings. Core offerings are scalable middleware solutions for wireless connectivity, wireless data service connectivity, and a secure network operations center. Value-added offerings include customer support and service, and fulfillment.

Another value provided by MASP are the relationships with the multiple data networks that connect end users to the information no matter where they are. Although several major carriers offer wireless data networks, not a single one offers 100 percent coverage while roaming. Layered on top of the coverage issue are concerns about the pricing plans and limitations on what devices can be used on a network. Some MASPs assume responsibility for negotiating wireless data carrier contracts and ensure that their customers have the coverage they need. The outsourcing of coverage issues and the implied assurance that the enterprise will receive the lowest possible rates are very compelling reasons for working with a MASP.

Another value is the network operations center with security and 24/7 monitoring capability. However, due to the wireless data environment's unique needs, a MASP's network operation center must also perform the following functions:

- It must have explicit procedures for how customer accounts are designed, deployed, and monitored. Potential connectivity, capacity, scalability, and data recovery problems must be identified, and whenever possible resolved, before they inhibit the flow of information.
- It must employ a highly trained and qualified staff to ensure the timely monitoring and maintenance of network operations center processes. Although application data is not stored locally at the operations center, the staff should also be well versed in security issues.

The introduction of any mobile application into a company brings unique technological challenges. A key challenge is how to address the incompatibilities resulting from the diverse array of operating systems, transmission protocols, and end-user devices. It is often recommended that any company considering deploying a wireless data strategy should have at least thought through the issues listed in Table 5.1.

Table 5.1: Wireless Data Implementation Issues

Technology	Issues
Wireless Carrier Management	Contract Negotiations, Multiple Bills, Telecommunications Infrastructure Connectivity
Wireless Data Support (Circuit Switched or Packet Switched)	Geographic Coverage, Airtime Pricing, Multiple Carriers, Device/Modem Availability, Speed, Interoperability, Roaming Cost
Wireless Security and Network Management	Security Monitoring, Wireless , Gateways, Interface Servers, and Network Connections
End-User Device Support	Usability Issues, Processing Capacity, Battery Life
End-User Support	Solve User Issues with Wireless Applications, Devices, Networks, Intercarrier Relationships
Growth Path and Technology Obsolescence	Integrate New Devices and Wireless Networks as Required Without Affecting Current Systems

Aether Systems: Mobile ASP

Founded in January 1996 as the wireless data consulting firm Aeros LLC, Aether quickly became a significant presence in the wireless trading arena. The release of its "Wireless Wall Street" set of applications completely redefined the company's mission as a leading provider of wireless data services and systems.

The financial services industry has been one of the first to incorporate wireless data access with its service offerings, since it views the real-time transfer of financial information as a logical offering. Aether anticipated the industry's strategy early on and positioned itself to capitalize on the growing demand for wireless data solutions. In 1997, it introduced AirBroker, which provided real-time stock quotes, alerts, and news through wireless phones. Aether followed up on the product's release by building a strong financial services customer base offering online trading and financial data for

Charles Schwab, Morgan Stanley Dean Witter Online, Merrill Lynch, Bear Stearns, and others.

Aether went public in 1999 based on their results in the financial services market. With the money raised from the IPO, Aether rapidly grew the business and through a number of acquisitions broadened their focus beyond just financial services into mobile software products, as well as other vertical markets such as mobile government, transportation logistics, and health care.

The opportunity Aether is targeting is enabling enterprise customers to extend their existing information or their existing investment in business information systems to a mobile workforce. Large enterprises have invested hundreds of millions and, in some cases, even billions of dollars in information technology, and yet when the users get up from their desks, they lose the value of that investment. So Aether is targeting the mobile workforce as one of the first areas for deployment.[2]

The Aether Full-Service Approach

As mentioned earlier, companies seeking to deploy a wireless data strategy must address several key issues before the technology can be implemented and successfully adopted. These include carrier selection and management, network management, and flexible wireless technology selection to minimize the risk of obsolescence. Also, the number of ways in which mobile devices, user interfaces, and operating systems can be combined is an extremely complex issue, as are technology selection, activation, inventory management, and device maintenance.

Confronted with such a maddening range of issues, executives at many firms have serious doubts as to their company's ability to successfully embrace mobile technology even though they clearly recognize the need for "anytime, anywhere" access to information.

Aether's full-service approach recognizes how this matrix of issues could very well delay or prolong the economy's transition to m-business. To address the needs of companies, Aether has three products:

- The Technology Foundation offering is a comprehensive family of software products used to construct a variety of mobile systems for businesses. It includes wireless integration, mobile data management, and wireless infrastructure products.

- The hosting service has three main components: core services, including the network operations center, carrier connectivity, and messaging middleware; value-added services, including product fulfillment and customer support; and general horizontal services, including wireless Internet messaging and vertical services for financial services, transportation, manufacturing, and health care.
- The consulting offering provides engineering services to complement Aether's software products and hosting services, and is offered on a stand-alone basis as well.

Revenue Model

Aether Systems has three primary revenue streams: recurring subscriptions, software licensing, and engineering services.

- Subscription is the core component of Aether's revenue model. It encompasses the services, software, and applications hosted for customers for whom Aether charges a recurring monthly fee per end user. Subscription revenue is derived from two drivers: the number of subscribing end users and the average monthly revenue earned per end user.
- Software licensing involves applications or platforms that are delivered to an enterprise customer instead of being hosted from Aether's network operations center. Aether intends to move more of its software licensing arrangements to recurring hosted arrangements.
- Engineering services are consulting-type arrangements with clients such as Merrill Lynch and Reuters. Once the core of Aether's focus, engineering services is now the least significant component of Aether's revenue model. Engineering service assignments are now taken primarily to penetrate new vertical markets, develop new technologies, or satisfy a major client.

Get Big Fast: Acquisition, Investment, and Partnership Strategy

Aether's goal is to be the leading supplier of mobile solutions. However, in order to outposition their competition, Aether must expand and grow quickly. The company has a three-pronged strategy for achieving rapid growth in a short amount of time:

- **Acquisitions.** Aether has built or acquired the key technologies it needed to create what could become the leading mobile hosting and transaction platform on the market. The company's acquisition strategy lets it enter new high-growth markets quickly.
- **Partnerships.** Aether has developed a partnership-dependent business model rather than focus on head-to-head competition. This aspect of their strategy creates a broad "ecosystem" of products, services, and channels.
- **Investments.** Aether has formed a venture capital division to focus its investments on emerging companies with product and service offerings complementary to its own. The company's goal is to encourage market adoption of specific technology standards and platforms as well as promote the company brand.

Where possible, Aether acquires the assets and competencies it needs to succeed. For example, in 1998 it acquired Mobeo, Inc., a provider of wireless foreign exchange and commodity information services. This acquisition allowed Aether to expand its service offering, subscriber base, and relationships with financial institutions. Mobeo's flagship service F/X Alert delivers real-time price quotes, news, and alert service that track over 150 financial instruments, including foreign exchange, fixed income, futures/derivatives, and commodities.

When acquisition is not feasible, the company forms partnerships, mainly with device manufacturers and wireless carriers. Aether's arrangements with the largest U.S. wireless carriers provide customers with virtually nationwide coverage at minimal airtime costs. The firm's wireless carrier partners include Ameritech, AT&T Wireless, Bell Atlantic Mobile, BellSouth Wireless Data, and GTE Corp. Aether has also joined with device manufacturers 3Com and

Microsoft to develop applications for the Palm and Windows CE units, respectively.

Through its wholly owned subsidiary, Aether Capital, LLC, the company also invests in developing new services offering compatible technologies. Doing so helps to (1) provide a window on new technologies and business models, and (2) fill critical gaps in the parent company's own product line and business ecosystem. Since 1999, Aether has invested about $150 million in twenty companies. For example, Aether invested about $9 million in OmniSky, formerly OpenSky, to pursue opportunities in the emerging consumer and business mass markets for e-mail and Internet access.

Where Is Aether Heading?

It would seem the company is well positioned in the wireless market given its first-mover advantage and full-service approach. However, a major issue currently confronting Aether's management is the company's long-term strategy. Aether's leadership must determine if its future success will be found in maintaining its diverse portfolio of products, services, and investments or in focusing more on its core competency.

Currently, Aether's strategic focus is on maintaining its broad portfolio approach. This strategy assumes that customers will gravitate toward a full-service, comprehensive solution provider due to mobile technology's complexity. Many m-business companies are faced with the same key strategic problem as the one faced by Aether. They, too, must assess whether the corporate customer is better served by focusing on the company's core competencies or by developing a broad portfolio of comprehensive services. Traditional management theory has always argued in favor of companies staying focused on what they do best—their core capabilities. However, traditional management theory assumes stable markets, and adhering to it can put businesses at risk in a marketplace where the technology, processes, and customer needs are in constant flux.

The challenge for Aether's management is similar to the portfolio problem facing investors who have to decide whether to put all their money on one stock or spread the investment around. Today, Aether's approach clearly emphasizes diversification of its offerings. It is not an approach without risk, as recent history illustrates. For example, Amazon.com took a similar diversified approach to Internet retailing and is struggling to make a profit. The key to a successful diversification strategy is maintaining a singular focus on profitability in whatever market you chose to participate in. If Aether can achieve sustained profitability quickly, then its future success seems fairly secure.

Mobile Internet Service Providers

Mobile Internet service providers (MISPs) are critical components of the emerging mobile application infrastructure since they provide users with wireless Internet access. Examples of MISPs include network operators, such as AT&T, Sprint, and Verizon, and pure-play participants such as Palm.Net, GoAmerica, and OmniSky. These companies offer mobile users continuous wireless Internet or corporate intranet access regardless of location.

The MISPs' focus is on making the customer's wireless experience useful and reliable. They do so by providing a simple-to-use service that offers a comprehensive mobile Internet experience. Typical MISP services include sending and receiving corporate and personal e-mail, instant messaging, navigating the Internet, accessing Internet content optimized for mobile devices, and securely conducting m-commerce transactions.

While the service may be simple for customers to use, it is based on an extremely intricate technology. Consequently, several key issues have affected the evolution of this market in the U.S., including:

- Complex system configurations and poor customer service
- The high and often unpredictable costs associated with using wireless data networks, including roaming charges that are typically assessed when users are outside of their home area
- Limited-coverage areas and disparate wireless networks that do not always work well together, leading to disconnections and other service problems
- Device-dependent wireless service providers, e.g., different providers are needed for accessing the Web, depending on if a cell phone or a Palm is being used

Companies such as GoAmerica, OmniSky, and others are in business to solve many of these problems. For example, GoAmerica provides its subscribers with wireless ISP services across a number of wireless networks, including AT&T and BellSouth. It also provides wireless ISP service to a variety of mobile device platforms, including Palm OS–based computing devices, Research in Motion's interactive pagers, laptop computers, Windows CE–based computers, and WAP-enabled smart phones. The wireless ISP market is becoming increasingly competitive with the widespread adoption of wireless data industry standards, making it easier for new market entrants and existing competitors to introduce services that compete against the market's incumbents.

OmniSky

OmniSky, Inc., is an example of the MISP business model. The company is headquartered in Palo Alto, California, and was formed as OpenSky in June 1999. Its business plan focused on pursuing wireless opportunities—e-mail, Internet access, and transaction applications—in the emerging consumer and business mass markets. In November 1999, the company launched the public beta trial of its service for thousands of Palm V's. Its service became commercially available in May 2000 and the company completed its initial public offering on September 21, 2000. OmniSky literally went from cradle to IPO in a span of fourteen months, partly due to extreme speculation surrounding wireless companies.

The OmniSky Service

OmniSky provides unlimited usage of its wireless e-mail and Internet service for handheld mobile devices. Subscribers to the company's service purchase a wireless modem from OmniSky to attach to their handheld device. The device is then enabled to access a broad range of Internet content and data, as well as to manage e-mail accounts and conduct e-commerce transactions. Much of the Internet information available to subscribers is modified for viewing and use on mobile devices, but the system allows viewing of unmodified sites as well.

At the core of OmniSky's service is its wireless portal that offers subscribers access to public Web sites from all supported devices. The portal organizes information into categories such as finance, shopping, news, and sports. In addition, the portal supports certain customized features. For example, it can be configured to speed up e-mail downloads through advanced compression; perform e-mail management; and allow the forwarding of e-mail messages to a mobile phone, fax, or pager directly from the handheld device. OmniSky's OneTap service can be used to download Web data directly into a user's address book, date book, or memo pad. The OneTap service also includes the ability to download directions and maps after completing a directory search.

OmniSky also provides access to corporate networks. Business customers often require secure connections to the enterprise systems with which they interact, but do not want to alter the way their systems are configured. OmniSky's virtual private network permits business users secure access to their corporate databases. OmniSky's standard interfaces let the company's corporate subscribers access enterprise messaging systems such as Microsoft Exchange and Lotus Notes or use value-added services such as sales force automation, customer retention management, and Web dispatch offerings. OmniSky also provides instant messaging, paging, and operator services.

The Revenue Model

OmniSky derives revenue from flat-rate service fees for unlimited use of its wireless service. Customers purchase service directly from OmniSky through the firm's Web site, by calling the customer service center or by visiting a retailer of OmniSky modems. Service can be purchased on a month-to-month basis or at a discount rate under an annual prepayment contract.

The company's service revenues also include content revenue from sponsorships and slotting fees. OmniSky receives these fees for positioning Web sites a customer requests in agreed-upon locations in the wireless interface. Future service revenues may include fees for advertisements delivered through the network and mobile e-commerce fees for transactions conducted through the network. The firm's equipment revenues include fees charged for OmniSky's wireless modem users and for related accessories such as power adaptors.

In any revenue model, the costs are an important factor to watch. OmniSky's costs include its activation fees, the airtime and network operations costs incurred to provide the wireless service, as well as the cost of providing technical support. OmniSky's costs also include fees it pays to content providers for information carried on the network service.

The company's revenues are proportional to the number of devices and locations serviced by its network. OmniSky's service is available for a variety of devices, including the HP Jornada, Handspring Visor, the Palm PDAs, and the Compaq iPAQ Pocket PC. The service is available in most metropolitan areas within the United States. The company's joint venture with News Corporation, called OmniSky International, was expected to expand its offering into several European countries, but was shut down due to lack of customers.

The OmniSky Value Chain

The OmniSky service is a good example of the "leveraging partners and sharing risks" paradigm. Its business model is effective during periods of economic transition and change when technology is evolving rapidly and new competitors with more innovative solutions appear almost daily.

OmniSky has a perpetual license to Palm's proprietary Web Clipping technology. This technology is key to mobile applications since it condenses Web content into a viewable format for a handheld device. Aether Systems has signed an agreement with OmniSky to provide its engineering services. As part of the agreement, Aether will resell OmniSky services for a period of five years. It can bundle OmniSky's services with its own enterprise offerings at a cost of approximately $3 per customer; OmniSky's service plans cost around $39.99 per month per customer.

The Minstrel V, manufactured by Novatel Wireless, is the wireless modem OmniSky sells with its service. OmniSky's portal uses Avant-Go software to provide subscribers access to over 300 "channels" of content as well as Web browsing. JP Mobile provides the company's customers with an e-mail program that supports access to almost any

POP3 e-mail account. OmniSky has also partnered with AT&T Wireless to utilize its CDPD network, where AT&T will co-brand the service and contribute $10 million to the marketing effort.

OmniSky's services are offered through a number of distribution channels. The company leverages the brand recognition and marketing capabilities of wireless carriers and Internet content providers by co-marketing its services through those channels. It also sells through major retailers—including CompUSA, Staples, and Amazon.com—that carry devices bundled with OmniSky services. The firm also markets to enterprise customers through Aether Systems, wireless carrier partners, and system integrators.

The Future Outlook

OmniSky "assembles" technology; it selects products from different vendors to create an ISP service. Unfortunately, since OmniSky has no proprietary technology of its own, its business model does not present any significant barriers to competitive entry, particularly to some of its major partners. It is possible some of these partners could turn into predators. It would not be a surprise if OmniSky's partners, such as AT&T Wireless, began offering ISP services themselves.

For OmniSky, attaining profitability will take many years. Its quest will be exacerbated by the lack of control over the costs of goods sold and mounting expenses associated with developing a brand. OmniSky's partnership model is complex. Effectively managing such an enormous number of relationships while staying abreast of technological advances and constantly improving service will be difficult. Should OmniSky's partners decide to compete with the company, a price and marketing war will likely result, further affecting the company's margins.

As the wireless market matures, competition between OmniSky and the network operators will increase. The key to this competition is whether Web access or content is the greater differentiator of value. The history of ISPs provides interesting examples of how these differentiators work. For example, AOL was quite successful at finding the right formula between an ISP and a content provider in the wired world. Similarly, NTT DoCoMo's transformation from a carrier into a content-focused MISP (through its i-mode strategy) has also been a success. OmniSky will likely focus less on "commodity" services such as e-mail and Internet access and more on unique content provision.

For OmniSky to succeed in the long term, it must build and keep a subscriber base at the lowest cost per additional subscriber while paying the least amount possible to the network operators. It must enable access to future wireless networks for new subscribers and ease the transition to new networks for current subscribers. At the same time, it must be easy for OmniSky's customers to do business with the company. Customers hate dealing with the technological intricacies of mobile communications and Web access. They want simplicity, convenience, and low cost.

Mobile Infrastructure Enablers

There are three types of mobile infrastructure enablers: development enablers, content enablers, and application enablers.

- Development enablers include systems integrators and consultants
- Content enablers include specialized content for the mobile platforms such as games and micro-content
- Application enablers include synchronization software providers, security software providers, and content providers

Development enablers were discussed in Chapter 3. Content enablers will be discussed in detail in Chapter 6. This section focuses on application enablers, the technological platforms that are prerequisites to an application's successful functioning.

There are two primary application enablers: synchronization and embedded databases.

Synchronization

Synchronization is the process of making two different sets of data appear to be identical. Synchronization solutions are critical in mobile offline scenarios where the user has only an "as needed," not continuous, connection to the Internet. A good example is PalmPilot e-mail, where the user can read and reply to a message without being connected. The act of writing into the PalmPilot results in two dissimilar versions of the data residing on the handheld and the server. Hence the need for synchronization to match the two sets of data.

Businesses have a critical need for data synchronization solutions. In the near term, synchronization technology must address increasing numbers of devices, data stores, information categories, and transmission mediums/networks. Next-generation synchronization technology must be able to manage the flow of corporate information both within and outside the firewall. Synchronization vendors capable of providing the secure and authenticated delivery of mission-critical business information to and from professional users will be in increasing demand.

First-generation vendors such as PUMATECH, Xcellnet, and Aether Software have created network platforms to help IT managers securely monitor the wide array of mobile users, devices, and network transactions. Wireless applications like field sales, fleet management, and supply chain management software use sophisticated next-generation synchronization solutions to map complex data transmissions between SAP and Oracle databases and professionals using mobile devices. Next-generation synchronization providers convert multiple database images into the same image even when multiple mobile users are simultaneously accessing and altering database information. An emerging concern for enterprise IT managers is how to manage the "leaking" of sensitive corporate data onto wireless devices.

Data synchronization has taken on new importance as users access enterprise applications when away from the desktop. In this role, synchronization solutions provide data translation, data mapping, data presentation, and session and information security management. With each of these offerings, the differences between enterprise-oriented mobile data solutions, such as mobile application servers, and next-generation synchronization solutions begin to blur. For example, companies such as fusionOne, PointBase, Solid Technologies, Steltor, Synchrologic, and Visto offer next-generation synchronization and data-management capabilities. In addition, traditional enterprise software and database vendors, including SAP and Sybase, are entering the market as advanced data management becomes a core component of any synchronization service.

Embedded Databases

Mobile users will demand more local computation capabilities as they transition from simple to more complex mobile applications. For example, a pharmaceutical salesperson wants to browse a catalog offline while sitting in a doctor's office without having to dial into the corporate network. Or you are visiting a new city and want to browse through the local restaurant guide without having to connect to your mobile Internet service provider, who may not have good service in the area you are visiting.

Both of these scenarios illustrates the need for local, handheld-device resident databases. The requirements of these databases include:

- Ability to be in sync with server-level databases
- Offline operation support to minimize the impact of inevitable "out-of-area" disruptions
- Internet and synchronization support for cost-effective, standardized, and coordinated communication within and across organizations
- Database support providing useful "historical" and corporate information to end users

The mobile database market is quite large. The primary competitors in this market are Oracle Lite, Sybase Anywhere Ultralite, Microsoft Access, and IBM DB/2. The strategic objective of these firms is to combine a strong database engine with superior platform support (from handhelds to servers) and highly flexible replication to support remote and disconnected sites. Watch the micro-database space for some key positioning battles.

A Final Thought

In these times you have to be an optimist to open your eyes when you wake in the morning.

—Carl Sandburg

The novel characteristics of the mobile Internet have created an uncharted territory for mobile infrastructure software. Some of these characteristics are open access to the network; the lack of standards; the multipurpose nature of the content; data latency problems; the uneven and unpredictable performance of the network; and the numerous types of communities it links together.

These qualities reflect the youth of the application infrastructure market, which continues to mature at a rapid pace. As in any fast-moving market, the different pieces are falling into place to create an explosive period of growth. But sorting out all of the options and requirements certainly is a daunting task. Designing the right mobile infrastructure roadmap takes thorough understanding of the benefits and trade-offs of the existing companies, as well as informed predictions about innovations or consolidations around the corner.

But one thing is clear: For companies to participate in the mobile economy, they must set up an application infrastructure that allows innovative processes to be developed and deployed. For example, customers must be able to interact with the firm's applications effortlessly before ordering, tracking, or paying for products. Similarly, to achieve optimal efficiencies, companies must enable employees to access this data anytime, from anywhere. It is the different elements of the application infrastructure that make all the mobile strategies possible.

6

New Innovation Opportunities: Mobile Portals

- American Express is creating a mobile portal to give cardholders a real-time, comprehensive picture of their finances. The account aggregation service consolidates a customer's financial information and lets them view it. Information is gathered from any number of cardholder relationships, including banks, brokerages, mutual fund companies, and others—and accessed through a single mobile portal.
- GM expanded its business focus from a major car manufacturer to becoming a mobile portal provider with Virtual Advisor. This portal offers voice-activated traffic information, news, e-mail messages, and stock quotes over the Web. The portal is built on Hughes Electronics' OnStar, a cellular and satellite based communications service. GM anticipates profits from selling mobile services to individual drivers and resellers like Honda and Lexus.
- Boeing "Connexion" and Tenzing Communications are competing to bring Web browsing and e-mail to airline passengers in their seats. The goal is to provide the portal-in-the-sky capability for business travelers to work on airline flights. Several air-

lines, including Air Canada, Cathay Pacific, and Singapore Airlines, are implementing these mobile portals. Boeing projects that the in-flight Internet market will grow to $45 billion a year in the next decade and hopes to grab a 10 percent share, or $4.5 billion in annual revenues.[1]

- AT&T Wireless, etrieve, BeVocal, and TellMe are creating voice portals where customers speak instead of click to obtain the information and services they need. These portals provide customers with shortcut access to Web-based content and services, voice-activated dialing, and e-mail by phone. To use a voice portal, you call a toll-free number and, using simple voice commands, select from a range of information services: driving directions, weather, stock quotes, news, sports, lottery results, or favorite TV dramas.

- Starbucks is enabling customers to be productive even while on their coffee break. The company is constructing high-speed mobile portals in 3,000 of its coffeehouses so customers can browse the Net using their own wireless notebooks, smart phones, and PDAs.[2]

Mobile technology is enabling the creation of new specialized service channels. As a result, firms are innovating their offerings to better serve their customers. These emerging mobile relationship opportunities can be broadly categorized as mobile portals.

Mobile Portals: What Are They?

A mobile portal is a customer interaction channel optimized for mobility. The term *portal* essentially describes an entry point for accessing Internet content and services. A portal aggregates large numbers of users and/or subscribers around specific types of service. They provide a context for Web-based interaction, communications services, information content, and software application access from a remote or wireless location. Mobile portals are comparable to fixed Internet portals, such as Yahoo!, which provide a gateway to content and transaction-based services.

As customer needs and preferences change, new mobile portal opportunities become important. These new channels have direct contact with the buyers and also have access to how customer preferences are changing. Also, the new portals can identify unmet customer needs, develop new types of value-added services, and interpose themselves between suppliers and customers in creative ways. The result is a profusion of new ways to bring content, information, community, and commerce to customers.

Currently, the mobile portal business is characterized by rapid, chaotic change. This will continue for several years, stimulating the emergence of radically different types of companies. New portal companies whose services add value to their customers' lives are poised for significant growth. Consider, for example, the astounding penetration of the i-mode portal of NTT DoCoMo. However, for every one success there seems to be hundreds of failures. As in any new market, new portal players will see their power and importance rise, fall, and rise again as the market dynamics of the m-economy fluctuate.

Mobile Portal Market Structure

Mobile portals represent an increasingly popular business strategy with many companies moving quickly to secure a place in the market. Take, for instance, cellular operators such as Vodafone who can no longer rely on voice services alone to grow revenues and market share. As a result, they are developing value-added services (VAS) to generate new revenue streams, reduce churn, and differentiate their businesses from their competitors. In mature mobile markets such as Finland, with 64 percent penetration, there is a real need to differentiate with VAS in order to sustain and grow the business. The new breed of VAS that operators are turning to is mobile portals. And they are not the only ones: Content providers, fixed Internet portals, hardware developers, and start-ups are all developing mobile portal strategies. All these firms are fighting for customer control.

To clearly understand the positioning of various players in the marketplace, it is necessary to look at the differences in approach, applications, technology, market development scenarios, and business models.

As Figure 6.1 illustrates, there are four main types of new portals in the market—wireless operator portals, multi-purpose Web portals, commerce portals, and pure-play portals. Each type possesses unique advantages for gaining primary ownership of the electronic relationship with consumers, and each type has its own strengths and weaknesses.

For example, mobile cellular operators, such as NTT, Sprint PCS, and Vodafone, already have an existing service relationship with mobile users. They can analyze customer billing and support data to learn valuable information about their customers' preferences, sites they frequent, and other specific profiling information. However, cellular firms do not typically have the Internet skills and experience necessary to develop user-friendly portals. Web portal developers have such skill and experience in abundance. On the other hand, although Web portals such as AOL, Yahoo!, and MSN have an established customer base and a network of content providers, they will face significant challenges adapting their business model to the mobile marketplace.

M-commerce portals, such as eBay, share the advantage of being able to port their existing business model from the Web to the mobile device. As a result, these firms may have a head start in the actual generation of revenues from the mobile portal channel. Some portals may choose to stay within the consumer arena but focus on a niche market. Start-up companies, such as Tellme, Yodlee, BeVocal, and AirFlash, since they focus solely on the mobile portal business, are more technologically advanced. However, these start-ups lack the important brand and content alliances of the major Web portals and may therefore be susceptible to cash-flow difficulties.

Choosing the right strategy, right value-added services, and right partners becomes extremely critical. Consider the case of NTT DoCoMo, a wireless operator that has created a very successful portal offering called i-mode.

NTT DoCoMo: I-mode Portal

In 1992, Nippon Telegraph and Telephone Corporation (NTT), Japan's phone monopoly, spun off its DoCoMo wireless division.

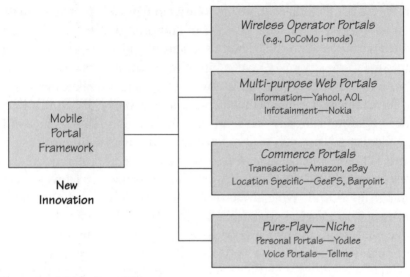

Figure 6.1: Mobile Portal Patterns

DoCoMo—which stands for Do (Japanese for "everywhere") Communications over the Mobile Network—has brought Japan to the forefront of the wireless revolution. DoCoMo's success has been due largely to i-mode, its popular mobile Internet service.

What Do Consumers Get with I-mode?

I-mode is an always-on mobile Internet service with more than 25,000 content sites. I-mode is sold as a subscription and is turned on when the customer signs up. As many as 80 percent of all new NTT mobile phone subscribers in Japan want i-mode as part of their voice subscription package.

I-mode is a "walled garden," which is essentially a closed portal where the company does not allow its customers to '"surf" outside its portal. The advantage of a walled garden is the considerable control gained from the company's intimate knowledge of their customers' profiles. This knowledge can be used to offer relevant services and content through the operator's portal. The success of this model is evident in the market-penetration statistics. Since i-mode's beginning in August 1999, the company has signed up an astonishing 25 million subscribers—slightly more than 20 percent of Japan's population of 120 million.

How does it work? Customers access i-mode by pressing the "i" button that comes on every DoCoMo cell phone. Pressing the "i" button connects the phone directly to the Internet through an i-mode gateway. A menu is displayed, with an English-Japanese choice button plus additional choices, including a bookmark list. The user can also type in a URL to visit various Web sites. The i-mode screen's display is colorful. Rich audio tones ring from the phone when it is called and sounds from sites customers visit are equally resonant.

I-mode Web sites are frequently used to check information or to interact with a site for short periods, often only one to two minutes. A customer can quickly check an e-mail, stock quote, or travel schedule, or play a short game. Entertainment is easily i-mode's most popular Web-based attraction. Entertainment represents 53 percent of the service's usage and includes activities such as downloading music, playing games, reading cartoons, telling fortunes, and betting.

The games i-mode makes available are also indicative of its simple, easy-to-understand, mass-market approach. For example, in the fishing game the subscriber picks a location, enters the type of lure, and sets the phone down to wait. At some later time the phone rings or vibrates and the player can look on the screen to see what kind of fish has been caught. There is even an option to bet on the type of fish you'll catch online.

Another primary i-mode use is for database inquiries to access content such as a dictionary, restaurant guide, or travel guide and general information such as business news, sports scores, and stock quotes. I-mode also supports transactions such as personal banking, online shopping, and ticket reservations. The portal's success is due to its ease of use and the ease with which content can be created for it.

DoCoMo's Architecture

There are four components to DoCoMo's i-mode portal: the network, the middleware software, the business model, and the i-mode brand. Both the network and middleware components are proprietary to NTT DoCoMo. The i-mode network is based on Personal Digital Cellular technology. The middleware software is based on cHTML, which is architecturally identical to WAP. I-mode's business model requires Web developers to pay for the service's content, for which the carrier then bills. The i-mode brand is a valuable differentiator, as cellular carriers worldwide attempt to replicate NTT DoCoMo's success in creating compelling mobile content for its end users.

Technically, i-mode is an always-on packet data service running at 9.6 Kbps out of a possible maximum speed of 28.8 Kbps. Rather than use a proprietary language that would require Web designers to recode their sites for i-mode, the programmers at DoCoMo developed a markup language—compact HTML (cHTML), which is a subset of HTML. The development of cHTML allowed users with HTML-capable phones to access a myriad of content sites via the i-mode portal. cHTML uses minimalist functionality, allows neither JPEG files nor frames. Web pages larger than a certain size are truncated. By using cHTML, i-mode has overcome usability problems plaguing other mobile portals using WAP. WAP-based portal customers often complain that getting information through mobile phones is too slow, expensive, and confusing.

Prior to the advent of i-mode, most analysts believed consumers would reject a mobile device incapable of providing the same level of graphic intensity as that found on the traditional Web. Furthermore, most believed it would be impossible to encode a Web page with true functionality and keep it small enough to be readily accessible via a wireless device. I-mode has proven both of these assumptions wrong. Its home page is 2 Kb and i-mode mail is limited to 500 bytes, which helps with rapid transmission and retrieval. Although the handsets used to access i-mode have color screens, they are tiny. Few users want to write lengthy e-mail messages using a small keypad. I-mode e-mail is basically text messaging; most messages are only several words long and are often selected from predefined responses.

The handset is a critical part of the experience. To find the right form factor, DoCoMo spent time analyzing what consumers wanted in an ideal handset. They found the following: The weight cannot be more than 100 grams, the screen must have at least 256-color resolution, and the battery life must be more than 300 hours standby and have at least 4 to 5 hours talk time. NTT's handset business is flourishing in the Japanese market, where the average handset retention period is less than three months, versus about seventeen months in the

United States. The only handset manufacturer anywhere near a competitive position against NTT in the Japanese market is Nokia. By all accounts, Nokia is a distant second and having a difficult time.

What Is the Business Model?

In developing the business model for i-mode, DoCoMo's management looked at some of the most successful business models on the Internet. The one company that stood out was America Online. AOL used proprietary content and charged advertising and promotional fees for the immense number of eyeballs it has amassed. Above all, however, AOL's success can be attributed to the fact that it was able to build a profitable ecosystem where various players are able to make money. Like AOL, the strength of DoCoMo's business model comes from three things:

- Network externality effects that generate more users. When a new user joins the network, his action creates incremental benefits for all users in the network. After a critical mass is reached, there is added incentive for new consumers to come in, and thus the network continues to grow.
- High customer-retention rates. DoCoMo incurred massive upfront investment and customer acquisition costs. Its success depends on its ability to create effective barriers for customers to switch. This creates a sticky business model where the trouble of switching to a competitor is greater than the value gained.
- Economies of scale. The cost of supporting new content providers, users, and new technology diminishes and the size of the network grows.

DoCoMo built onto AOL's business model with a prepackaged, menu-driven system positioned as a value-added service to the voice offerings. DoCoMo developed the guidelines for this system with enough incentives for content partners to work hard on developing innovative applications and services. To get scale, DoCoMo partnered with some powerful content aggregators, like Cybird, Mediaseek, Index, and Cyberbiz, instead of cultivating individual content providers.

How does the revenue model work? NTT DoCoMo retains 9 percent of collected subscriber fees. It distributes the remaining 91 percent to the content aggregators. The aggregators also retain a percentage of the fees and distribute the balance to the content owners. For example, Cybird is an emerging content aggregation leader that provides its services to more than sixty companies. Cybird keeps up to 70 percent of the fees before distributing the remainder to the content owners.

DoCoMo also learned from AOL that e-commerce success is based on effective marketing and not on technological prowess. NTT management consciously chose not to refer to the Internet or Web in its promotional campaign for the service during the entire first year of i-mode's development. Thus, no unrealistic expectations were created by the promotion of i-mode, in stark contrast to the recent history of WAP, which was marketed quite differently.

To appeal to the mainstream consumer market, i-mode is touted as simple, usable, and fun. Customers sign up for i-mode as an ancillary service to their mobile phone subscription. They are billed separately for the service based on usage or, more accurately, on the number of information "packets" transmitted. Users can easily relate the cost of service to actual usage—for example, the number of e-mails sent.

The Future of DoCoMo

NTT is rolling out an upgrade to i-mode in WCDMA, or Wideband CDMA, an early version of 3G that will run at 128–384 Kbps. The company said it will spend 1 trillion yen (US $8.19 billion) over the next three years on infrastructure for its 3G service, and it expects to turn a profit within four years of launch. This upgrade should enable the next-generation phones to display streaming video and run Java applications. This should allow a more complete desktop experience for users. DoCoMo needs to be careful as they move from low-cost, simple-to-use services to new services for which there is no proven demand, as with streaming video.

DoCoMo has found an untapped market in Japan and reaped the rewards of its discovery with loyal users and fabulous revenues. Yet DoCoMo is not resting on its laurels.

- DoCoMo signed a formal agreement with Dutch wireless operator KPN Mobile to accelerate its expansion into the European market by developing wireless applications and services based on its i-mode specification for this market.
- In 2001, DoCoMo paid an estimated $9.8 billion to acquire a 16 percent stake in AT&T Wireless. It is too early to tell if DoCoMo's i-mode solution can be reverse-engineered to replicate its phenomenal success in Japan to the European and U.S. markets.

With its customer base of nearly 25 million subscribers, DoCoMo is by far the leading success story of the mobile Internet market. Its i-mode technology has overshadowed the much-anticipated WAP, which has experienced drastically lower-than-expected adoption rates. Whether other cellular companies can realistically emulate the i-mode experience and whether DoCoMo's strategy can be directly applied to other global markets remains to be seen. For most cellular companies, mobile Internet and m-commerce strategies are still in their infancy. Few can predict, with any real conviction, which services and applications their subscribers will use and, more importantly, are willing to pay for.

The Portal Value Chain

As we analyzed the new business opportunities presented by the mobile Internet in the course of writing this book, we were surprised to find many different companies in the portal space, each with a slightly different approach. In order to simplify this complexity, we have grouped the different value-chain participants into several categories across a broad continuum from creators, aggregators, and distributors to portals and customers.

Participants in the value chain perform a well-defined role, taking inputs from upstream participants, adding value, and then delivering their output to a downstream contributor. This section discusses each value-chain participant's role in detail, their revenue strategies, and the value of their contribution. As mentioned earlier, the following groups participate in the wireless portal value chain:

- **Content creators**. News, database information sources, products, and entertainment
- **Content aggregators**. Content syndication and enhancement, content development, and hosting
- **Content distributors**. Content fulfillment and optimization services, synchronization services, assurance, and security services
- **Access portals**. Network operators, wireless Internet service providers, portal operators, and pure-play mobile portals

Content creators, such as CNN, develop new content, products, or services. Aggregators, such as Infospace, package the work of creators into packages or bundles for distribution. Distributors, such as Yahoo!, then take the content packages or bundles and deliver them to buyers. Access portals, such as AOL, are where the buyers and sellers actually conduct their transactions. Each of these definitions is rather fluid in the sense that some extremely large players—like AOL Time Warner—may actually have divisions that perform several of these functions.

Content Creators

Web content comes in many forms: news, entertainment, transactions, and database information. Content originators own copyrights to the material they create and license and distribute it either directly to carriers and portal companies themselves or in partnership with a middleman.

CNN Mobile exemplifies news content creation. It features breaking news, world news, and regional news stories, weather temperatures and forecasts, market updates, currency rates, world sports news and scores, entertainment news, and city travel guides. CNN Interactive commercially licenses and markets CNN Mobile. Cellular operators can customize the service based on their market and their subscribers' interests. Operators in the United States, Europe, and Asia Pacific can offer CNN Mobile services to their customers. CNN Interactive worked closely with Nokia to develop the platforms needed for accessing the content using multiple devices and formats.

Entertainment content must also be accessible across device types. Companies such as Indiqu create wireless content, and in some cases, take content developed for other media and make it wireless-ready. Music content is a typical media conversion example. Transaction content ranges from stock quotes to auction bids. For example, at eBay, users can track auction progress and change their bid wherever they are. Database content typically includes reference materials such as restaurant guides like Zagat.com, maps like those provided by MapQuest, and white pages.

Content Aggregators

Content aggregators function as middlemen between the content originators and the distributors. Aggregators license local, regional, national, and global content from its creators, then package, house, and format it for use by specific devices and networks. Aggregators provide value to the content originators by negotiating intricate and time-consuming distribution deals with individual carriers, resulting in wider content distribution. For the carriers, content aggregators create turnkey mobile data applications by combining content from numerous sources and integrating it into a single interface.

For example, i3 Mobile takes information from approximately sixty-five different content providers and uses its proprietary XML-based servers to pull out and format the personalized content subscribers have requested. It then distributes this content to the subscriber's mobile device through a carrier's network. Currently, the company works with twenty-seven carriers. While aggregators such as i3 Mobile emphasize the broad availability of content, other aggregators such as SmartServ Online bundle content together solely to drive transaction processing.

Content Distributors

To generate revenue, content aggregators must deliver the content they provide through new distribution channels. Content distributors provide the aggregators with the ability to publish their content on different networks, devices, and operating systems. Distributors support and develop applications for a wide variety of wireless protocols. Examples include cHTML and WAP applications, which use different programming standards to enable mobile devices to display Internet-based information.

The content distributor InfoSpace provides the aggregator companies with access to the wireless network operators and portals it uses to distribute content. Infospace has direct relationships with a number of leading wireless network operators representing more than 50 percent of the market for wireless phone users in North America. In addition, their technology can also provide digital content providers with the means to repackage their content for delivery through a wide variety of wireless data protocols such as SMS applications, WAP, microbrowser applications, and various voice applications.

Content distributors also offer content delivery services, which help to enrich the end user's wireless experience. Content delivery capabilities include:

- Synchronization services that enable data transfers over unreliable networks
- Optimization services, which compress data and thus speed the delivery to users in a bandwidth-constrained environment
- Security services that encrypt information as it travels over the network and authenticates users before granting them permission to access various content assets

Access Portals

Access portals are the windows into the mobile world. They are the windows through which the customers access the content. Access portals are of three types: wireless operators like Verizon Wireless, Internet service providers like AOL Time Warner and MSN, and hybrid operators such as Yahoo!.

Most access portals give away basic services as an enticement to get customers to pay for premium services. This model often results in very exorbitant customer-acquisition costs. As result, the access portal landscape is littered with companies that are spending too much money developing services that not enough customers are willing to pay for. Perhaps many failures can be averted if companies slow down and get a better understanding of their customers.

So who is doing it right? We examined the different players and came to this conclusion: The company that is taking the right approach to the access portal marketplace is AOL Anywhere.

AOL Anywhere: The Mobile Access Portal

Today's communications companies envision a future where each customer will be assigned a single telephone number for the home, office, and cell phone. The emergence of the e-economy makes the same objective logical for online identities and e-mail addresses as well. AOL Time Warner's "AOL Anywhere" strategy is based on the desire of its millions of users to simplify their lives.

AOL has one crucial advantage over their competitors—a revenue stream comprising 25 million customers paying monthly subscription fees. These revenues allow AOL Anywhere to experiment with providing wireless applications to this immense user community without financial risk. The AOL Anywhere strategy makes AOL services universally available on a variety of mobile devices, including handhelds, mobile communicators, cell phones, and TVs. The service frees users from worrying about managing multiple Internet identities, formulating multiple buddy lists, and having to learn and use complex technologies to port their online identities from platform to platform. AOL Anywhere is about convenience. The strategy allows AOL to combine service, ease of use, and universal availability and to craft a compelling wireless experience for users in all mobile and stationary venues.

AOL Anywhere has several products aimed at different market segments. For example, the AOL product Mobile Communicator basically performs two functions: e-mail and instant messaging. The Communicator is a customized version of Research in Motion's two-way pager, which uses Cingular's (Mobitex) network. The product is aimed at professionals who want real-time access to crucial information and the ability to respond to e-mail when they are out of the office or write a quick message when phoning might be inappropriate. This product is not designed for surfing the Internet, since it displays only a couple of dozen characters at a time. AOL customers who want to surf the Internet can subscribe to the AOL Handheld offering, which is more useful than Communicator for shopping or checking news, stock quotes, and sports scores.

Over time, AOL mobile offerings will evolve and provide many of the capabilities shown in Figure 6.2. This figure illustrates four different product categories that mobile users seem to want: entertainment, information, communication, and commerce. AOL has long demonstrated the leverage possible when a company functions as both an aggregator and a distributor. By first building a strong user base and attracting sponsors for whom AOL served as a broker/dealer, the company has proven its value to each constituency.

Apart from access fees, AOL plans to make money through target advertising. For example, an AOL subscriber, Wendy, stores her grocery list online. She asks AOL to inform her of deals on certain items at each of her local Kroger, Safeway, and Publix grocers. Before she leaves for the grocery store, she pulls up her grocery list on her cell phone and notices an alert from AOL telling her that a certain store is running a special on several items and that she can actually save more money by shopping there. If Wendy needs directions to the store, she can easily use her cell phone to access AOL MapQuest. AOL plans to charge a premium for ads that reach targeted customers and that prompt impulse purchases just as the customer is making an initial buying decision.

AOL is positioning itself to become a mobile portal leader. In the past, AOL's strength has come from the variety of integrated services it provides. The company is more than just an Internet service provider; it also provides both its own and others' content. In an effort to expand its service offerings and keep these services easy to use, AOL has acquired MovieFone, MapQuest, Quack, and Tegic Communications. It has also entered into a series of agreements that ensure consumer access to AOL services via cell phone, Palm unit, or any other mobile device. The company's early mover advantage, precise initial segment targeting, and content and partner lineup focus on customer ease of use. Clearly, innovative services are the core drivers behind AOL's marketing strategy.

Entertainment		Information	
• Games • Music • Video • Entertainment Info • Gambling • Lotteries	*On-the-go entertainment that can absorb time will dominate*	• General News • Sports News • Weather • Maps • Directory Listings	*Time-critical and location-specific information is useful*
• Instant Messaging • E-mail • Personal Information Management • Video Telephony	*Ability to be in touch and connected is useful*	• Shopping • Payment • Ticketing • Reservations • Auctions • Advertising • Stock Trading	*Impulse buying, location and time specific products will dominate*
Communication		Commerce	

Figure 6.2: AOL Mobile Capability Framework

Portal Revenue Models

A successful mobile business model must address the following questions: Does our portal offer the right content? Are we using an appropriate revenue model? Is our Web content appropriately priced? Attractive content and customer acceptance do not guarantee a mobile service offering's profitability.

Confusion as to the appropriate revenue model for mobile portals is a major obstacle in determining the initiative's profitability. This confusion largely results from not knowing which mobile services customers truly want and will pay for. A number of mobile services have been introduced with little or no understanding of how they will make money.

To plan a portal venture successfully, careful analysis of the revenue models and customer adoption trends is essential. Make a mistake and you are liable to lose millions of dollars. So, what are the different revenue models? There are five basic portal revenue models: access revenues, advertising revenues, subscription revenues, transaction revenues, and micro-transaction revenues.

Access Revenues

In the face of slowing subscriber growth, mobile operators are concentrating on data services. Revenue for network operators will increasingly be derived from data access. The major operators—NTT DoCoMo, Sprint, Vodafone, New Orange, and Deutsche Telekom—want to increase the data revenue per user. As a result, they are attempting to gain and to maintain their control over the data services customers will access. The network operators either are developing their own versions of these services or partnering with other firms to acquire them. The data-dependent nature of future mobile device revenues reduces the operator's role to little more than that of a bit pipe. Thus, the operators are positioning themselves as gatekeepers, charging customers an access fee to connect with their service and content providers.

For example, NTT DoCoMo's access revenues are based on roughly $3 per month for a basic subscription, plus usage charges at .003 cents per packet. The average communications charge runs about $10 per month. Total monthly fees average about $13 per subscriber. Multiply these figures by 12 months and 25 million subscribers and you have NTT's basic data access revenue per annum. NTT has also found that users' preoccupation with i-mode has increased their voice call spending, which, when billed separately, provides an estimated $2 billion additional revenue annually. Neither of these revenue sources includes the revenue NTT garners from its data web services or from the commissions it levies on its service providers.

One of the things mobile portals have a hard time dealing with is the concept of near-, mid-, and long-term pricing. Depending on the maturity of the market, different pricing strategies need to be created. For example, America Online moved from variable-rate pricing to flat-rate pricing in 1996. In some markets, the flat-rate access model is being threatened by the growth of "free" Internet access, where the Internet service provider takes a share of the telephony access charge and builds other revenue streams based on advertising and commerce. But it is becoming clear that the free-access model is unsustainable. The cost associated with the network infrastructure required to deliver data-rich applications must be passed on to the customer.

Access pricing has always been a sore issue for customers who hate being nickel-and-dimed. History has shown that single-rate pricing simplifies customer choice and drives consolidation. For example, AT&T Wireless has led the industry in simplifying customer choice through its pricing plans. In May 1998, AT&T Wireless changed the industry's dynamics by offering AT&T Digital One Rate service. This was the first time a provider charged a single rate with no roaming or long-distance fees for a specified number of minutes for calls made within the United States. AT&T Digital One Rate and similar plans by other service providers have increased wireless market penetration in the United States. The introduction of other simplified, targeted rate plans will increase mobile adoption.

Advertising and Sponsorship Revenues

Advertising and sponsorship revenues are derived from companies paying a fee to advertise their products on a portal site. In the Web portal space, Yahoo!, Lycos, and Excite are advertising/direct marketing funded. On the surface, the content appears to come at a bargain price, but deeper analysis reveals that the price is sustained by advertising. Internet advertising is more than the selling of visual-impact ads; it is also the sale of direct links from highly used portals such as Yahoo! to transactional sites.

Advertising-supported content is rich and varied. It ranges from annoying pop-up boxes to banner advertisements to complex blends of links, icons, messages, and backlinks that pay commissions to the referring site. Variations of this model include the sale of keywords, such as "airline," in search hit listings, giving a particular Web site top ranking on the list and in the banner advertisements.

Mobile sponsorship, or advertiser-funded programming, is being considered as a revenue model. It is expected that advertisers will use this model to convey brand values through association with programs that fit the company's product or corporate image. Similar to the sponsorship advertising used on television soap operas of the 1950s, mobile sponsorship is driven largely by modern market conditions and recognition of spot advertising's limitations in the attempt to meet positioning and branding objectives.

Advertising is the basis for many mobile portal business models.

Many of these models are making the common mistake of overestimating the size of the market and the amount of money advertisers would be willing to pay to acquire new mobile customers. Also, as competition builds among portals, the volume and price of advertising usually slumps. Hence, it is hard to visualize a sustainable mobile business model that is based on advertising alone.

Subscription Revenues

The most popular mobile revenue models are based on subscription and usage, with time as the common parameter. These models are basically designed to obtain up-front payments from customers for access to specific services or content. In contrast to this approach, some mobile portals use free trial subscriptions to get a customer's attention. For example, Air Canada has installed the Tenzing Communications portal-in-the-sky system on five planes and had 2,000 registered users quickly signed up. Tenzing's service enables airline passengers to surf the Web and send e-mail, using satellites to transmit data between the air and the ground. Depending on the results of its free test program, Air Canada might install the system on additional aircrafts. The subscription fee is expected to be between $10 and $15 per flight, with an alternative pricing model of $200 per year for frequent flyers.

Pure mobile portals that charge subscription fees include Palm.Net, which has three pricing models: a basic plan ($9.99), an expanded plan ($24.99), and an unlimited volume plan ($44.99). Subscription fees are usually billed monthly. Delinquent accounts can be canceled immediately. However, a customer who wants to cancel an online subscription often finds that the process takes considerable effort. Many subscription services consider the monthly payment more important than a simplified cancellation process, since cancellations mean churn. Adding new subscribers is more expensive and time-consuming than retaining current ones.

The subscription model attracts customers with services that enable them to maintain continuous contact with the company. Mobile subscription models will likely evolve into multi-tiered or premium service models to more closely match consumer preferences.

Tiered models have also been a mainstay for cable and satellite television companies, even with the recent offerings of free broadcast alternatives.

Transaction Revenue

Mobile services are rapidly transitioning from informational to transaction enabled. There are two types of transaction revenue models: match-maker (transaction fee) and distribution (margin).

In the match-maker model, the supplier, not the intermediary, owns the product. The portal revenues are based on the net revenue or the commission it receives from the product's sale. Under this approach, the portal extracts a toll from each transaction. In some cases, the fee is levied to both the supplier and the buyer, and is typically .05–3.0 percent. The complexity of the transaction typically determines the fee. Commercial transaction–based sites range from eBay (online consumer auctions) to Priceline (consumers bidding for travel). Many B2B portals also use this model. The definition of "transaction" differs from firm to firm in B2B models. For example, in some cases a company will define the line item in a purchase order as a transaction, and in others it is the purchase order itself.

In the distributor model, the intermediary takes ownership of the product. As a result, it realizes the total revenue it gets off the product's sale. For example, a supplier purchases a product for $1.00 and resells it for $2.00. The $1.00 is the supplier's margin before costs. Once cost is factored in, however, the gross margin can be substantially less. Amazon.com is a typical example of this model.

Transaction models look simple in theory but are notoriously difficult to profitably execute. This is especially the case in situations where the margins are low (less than 10 percent). Here, it would take significant transaction volume to build a sustainable business.

Pay-Per-Use Micro-Transactions

Micro-transaction revenues are based on a simple pay-as-you-go service and are essentially one-time pay-per-use transactions ranging from a few cents to several dollars. A typical example is pay-per-view television. A number of gaming, online information and entertainment portals are implementing micro-transaction revenue models in the mobile environment.

The Finland-based company Sonera is the leader in experimenting with many micro-transaction scenarios. For example, a thirsty Sonera wireless customer can call a Sonera switch number posted on a vending machine. The switch sends a command to the machine, which dispenses the beverage. The micro-transaction's cost is added to the customer's phone bill. The same technology can be used with a laundry machine, a car wash, or a movie ticket dispenser.

A flexible billing system is essential to making micro-transaction point-of-sale services feasible. For example, Sonera allows its customers, by dialing the appropriate code, to choose whether to bill an m-commerce transaction to a credit card or to a wireless phone bill. However, for a company to be able to add 10 cents to a customer's phone bill or credit card requires a significant billing infrastructure modification—a change in the way sophisticated real-time transaction-processing capabilities between multiple parties are handled. The next section discusses billing and revenue enablers in greater detail.

Revenue Enablers: Elements of a Wireless Portal

Revenue-enabling services are becoming important as Web portals increase in sophistication and prevalence. Revenue enablers provide critical value-added enhancements to mobile portals, which otherwise would be simply stripped-down versions of their traditional Web counterparts.

Figure 6.3 illustrates the unique features that form the underpinnings of a mobile portal: usability, personalization, messaging capability, real-time interactions, location-based services, and billing.

Usability: Making the User Experience Better

To generate revenue, the product or service has to be usable. As with traditional Web portals, usability is critical to the successful adoption and use of a mobile portal by customers. Usability issues are of partic-

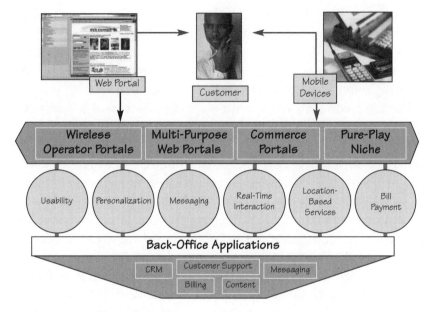

Figure 6.3: Portal Framework

ular concern given the small screens and keypads on cell phones. Their miniature size imposes extreme demands for simplicity, brevity, and clarity on m-commerce application developers.

"Don't shrink applications—rethink them" is a central theme of mobile usability design. Nielsen Norman Group, a consulting firm that specializes in user interface research, did an experiment in which they gave twenty subjects in London a WAP phone capable of browsing the Internet and asked them to do a series of tasks such as buying books, stock trading, and retrieving information. It then asked the users whether or not they would use a WAP phone within one year. Seventy percent of the surveyed users said they would not. Jakob Nielsen, who coauthored the study, wrote, "Unless the usability of mobile Internet services and devices improves considerably, people will simply not use them and billions of dollars will be wasted." Nielsen went on to say, "In my opinion, WAP stands for 'Wrong Approach to Portability.' Companies shouldn't waste money fielding WAP services that nobody will use while WAP usability remains so poor. Instead, they should sit out the current generation of WAP while planning their mobile Internet strategy."[3]

In the race to make new technology work, the issues of interface/ process usability—reducing confusion or creating better user experiences through improved process design—are often ignored. Business success, both now and in the future, will increasingly depend on a company's ability to improve users' experience first.

There are currently three main ways of enhancing a wireless customer's experience:

- **More portability**. Customers don't want continuous technological change that forces them to learn something new every couple of months. They don't have time. America Online has shown it understands this need by keeping their customers' experiences consistent and simple. AOL has mastered the art of experience portability. This issue more than any other affects user acceptance of new technologies and services. Mobile experiences should be consistent and simple and involve limited learning time.
- **Increased ease of use**. Customers want tools that are extremely easy to use. In any design activity, the top priority must be the user's experience, needs, and wants. For example, many programmers, in their zeal to present as much information as possible, overload screens with too much content. They often don't consider designing the application's navigation to be intuitive. Not surprisingly, users can easily get lost in the screen clutter. Mobile programmers must pay greater heed to what the system should do, what its features should be, and how the users' tasks can best be supported.
- **No latency or delays**. Mobile access should be fast and simple. The number-one priority for any Web surfer is speed. Internet users' biggest complaints involve frustrating navigation schemes that require multiple clicks to get somewhere or long waits to view pages. The content may be great, but if it takes too long to download or is difficult to navigate, users will skip to another site in a nanosecond and the company loses credibility and loyalty.

It is widely expected that speech recognition technology may improve a user's experience immensely. Speech recognition technology has particular advantages over the keyboard. The cell phone keypad is a simple user interface. However, it is useful only for entering numbers, not text. Entering text with the lettered buttons of a cell phone's keypad is laborious, time-consuming, and annoying. Companies such as Tellme, BeVocal, and Quack intend to use the human voice as their primary interface. These companies use automated voice recognition and speech-to-text technologies to respond to callers' requests. Voice recognition technology is already quite effective with short, simple commands. Whether the technology can evolve rapidly enough to address the usability issues discussed above remains to be seen.

Personalization: Profiling Customers and Their Preferences

Mobile portals offer a greater degree of personalization than can be found on Web portals. First-generation mobile portals used fixed menus. When you turned an Internet-enabled phone on, the operator provided a menu of preselected wireless sites and applications. These menus are currently considered invaluable assets and are highly coveted by m-commerce companies interested in being in front of the customer. The ability of today's mobile applications to personalize the content they deliver is nominal at best. Services amount to "picking and mixing" options from a limited portfolio of services. Mobile portal operators are not even close to meeting customer expectations of how the mobile interface should operate or how mobile content should be targeted and packaged.

Fixed menus lack the customization and personalization most users seek. Services such as MyAladdin, Visto, Yodlee, and many others allow users to design and build their own mobile portals. Personalization software vendors, such as Broadvision and Vignette, are also addressing the challenges personalization services must face in the mobile Internet environment. The range of potential personal portal services is vast and will one day include diary and information management, entertainment services, advertising, deals notification, banking, and personalized links to other sites. Competition for the user-made portal market will be intense in the years to come.

How does a personalized portal work? Users who wish to build their own portals submit their profile information to the personalized service provider. Profile information includes the user's name, address, location, and billing details (the number of a credit card or a bank account), and even—because screen size affects the kind of information that can be viewed—the type of device used. They also pick the different information elements that they want to look at. These information elements can come from many companies. For example, Yodlee, which is the personalization engine behind many financial institutions, lets users monitor all their bank or credit-card accounts in one place. Once customers overcome their fear of some-one having a 360-degree view of their information, companies providing personalization capabilities will gain an important competitive position in the value chain. However, personalization and privacy issues often conflict and remain a topic of debate.

Messaging and Real-Time Interaction

The incredible success of the short messaging service (SMS) caught many by surprise. In Japan, one of the most popular uses for NTT DoCoMo's i-mode service is sending text messages from person to person. Teenagers and executives alike use it to stay in touch with friends and colleagues. Similar services are heavily used in Europe as well. In both Japan and Europe, a single network standard makes SMS possible, convenient—and cheap.

For instant messaging to gain in popularity, it must work across multiple wireless-carrier platforms so that, say, a Sprint PCS user can send a text message to someone on an AT&T Wireless phone. Unfortunately, American mobile operators use a mix of incompatible messaging technologies, making it difficult to send text to someone using a different wireless carrier. Ideally, wireless chat services also should be able to communicate with similar PC-based systems, such as AOL Instant Messenger and MSN Messenger.

Real-time messaging must also be able to cross-connect channels. For example, in the foreseeable future, travelers will still most likely book flights through a travel agent or Web site. However, if their flight is canceled, they can be notified on their cell phone and have the option to access a m-commerce application to pick an alternative flight. As this example illustrates, isolated mobile applications can provide limited value in an increasingly integrated environment, especially when used in conjunction with real-world or Web-based commerce.

Location-Based Services

Location-based applications offer companies the opportunity to create new customer interactions. The following scenario illustrates how location-based technology works: You're driving through town when suddenly a row of red lights on a Gap ad displayed on the side of a building begins to rapidly blink. You point your cell phone at the ad and within seconds you're retrieving information about gift ideas and the locations of nearby stores. It's not as far-fetched as it sounds.

Or consider this: To avoid standing out in the rain or snow waiting for a delayed bus, you check the bus' status using your cell phone. Instead of wasting time waiting, you use the extra time shopping nearby, stopping for a cup of coffee, or even staying an additional ten minutes at work—with the confidence that you won't miss your bus.[4]

And, finally. You want to see a play at the last minute and need to know which theater has perishable inventory. It is quite possible that retailers will offer perishable and location-based inventory—such as hotel rooms, product "specials," and tickets to events—at discount prices to local mobile shoppers in real time and allow them to instantly purchase items via their cell phone.

Location-based applications capitalize on the mobile network operator's knowledge of where the customer is at any given time. In addition, the operator has the capacity to develop a detailed profile of customer preferences over time. Currently, location-based applications are fairly rudimentary and based on zip code. Next-generation location-based service will use GPS technology to pinpoint your location within a few feet. In the near future, cell phone carriers will know a caller's location within approximately 125 meters of where the call or wireless Web transaction occurred. Emergency service dispatchers will have the ability to locate people in distress who dial 911 from a mobile phone, which is a reason location-based technology has the support of the Federal Communications Commission (FCC).

In June 1996, the FCC requested two sets of improvements to the wireless 911 system. Phase I requires carriers to provide emergency dispatchers with the cell phone number from which the 911 call was made and to obtain the general location of the call. To meet these requirements, carriers will use either triangulation technology, which calculates a cell phone's location by examining signals from three different cell phone towers, or GPS receivers, or a combination of the two. Whichever approach the carriers implement will require upgrading their networks. Phase II of the FCC mandate goes further: It requires carriers to provide 911 operators with specific location coordinates within a few meters using automatic location identification (ALI). If carriers can provide exact user location data to 911 operators, they will most likely sell the same information to m-commerce companies.[5]

The network operators anticipate that many m-commerce firms will use location-specific information to target their services, promotions, and advertising at their mobile consumers. For example, when merchants know a potential customer is in close proximity to their stores, they can offer the customer a wireless coupon, based on the customer's known preferences, to encourage him to come in and shop. However, while the vision is being promoted aggressively, it is not clear how realistic or useful location-based services will be in the future. Until the potential uses and benefits are better understood, it will be difficult to determine the profit potential.

Billing, Payment, and Settlement

On the surface, using a wireless phone to purchase a movie ticket seems like a simple transaction, but in reality it is very complex. Billing is a key requirement for a mobile portal's success. Many wireless services will require some form of payment—whether to the service provider for the purchase of a product or from the service provider to the customer for refunds or a customer reward program. Traditional payment methods such as credit and debit cards must be supported by the technology. Credit and debit cards have the drawback of requiring subscribers to enter card information into a mobile device. In addition, security concerns related to sending card information over a wireless network must be addressed.

To avoid these issues, mobile portals can offer subscribers the option of charging or crediting a transaction to their account. Given the choice of entering card information manually and dealing with security concerns or simply charging a transaction to a mobile account, most users will likely prefer the latter. The mobile operators benefit from having wireless transactions billed to an already existing account. They already have the customer information they need to charge a subscriber for m-commerce transactions, and these charges can be easily integrated with existing account fees. Ease of billing will be a key factor in differentiating the value each portal provider gives its customers.

Micro-payment scenarios are also emerging enablers of mobile commerce. For example, a mobile user wants to view the latest news from *Business Week*. They access the *Business Week* site and are charged 20 cents for the transaction. Such micro-transactions require a significantly different payment infrastructure than those of other payment methods. Instead of using a credit card for a purchase, customers simply provide their telephone number. They then receive an on-screen message asking for approval via a password. Once the password is authenticated, the money is billed to the customer's account at the network operator, such as Sprint or AT&T Wireless.

Micro-payments using M-wallets are becoming quite popular. For example, X.com is a provider of a M-Wallet PayPal service. With a customer base of more than 3.3 million, X.com is the largest payment network. X.com's concept is a simple one: First, the purchaser and vendor each set up accounts with PayPal. The purchaser buys a $3.00 item from the vendor at a flea market. The vendor can charge any amount a customer owes to the PayPal account, which extracts the money from the purchaser's credit card account. The vendor then specifies the PayPal account number to which the money is to be credited. As money accumulates in the vendor's PayPal account, it receives periodic payments of the full account balance via check or direct deposit. A small fee is charged on the balance forwarded. PayPal is extremely popular in person-to-person commerce. Companies such as eBay offer PayPal as an authorized way of settling up accounts after an auction.

Today's mobile operators are the best positioned to leverage their existing payment-processing systems while they extend their billing expertise into the wireless and value-added service arenas. Mobile operators are also well positioned in the prepaid and invoice micro-payment areas. They can use their expertise to address the full value chain—from authentication, identification, and authorization to end-user risk management, payment processing, and fund clearing. For other types of payments, however, the operators' role across the value chain will vary from just providing customers with database access to identity verification. They will continue to play an intermediary role with credit-card payment methods but will have a lesser degree of influence on transaction processing for direct debit. To support a full range of payment options, several mobile operators have partnered with banking and other transaction-processing agents.

A Final Thought

The architecture of our future is not only unfinished; the scaffolding has hardly gone up.

—George Lamming

The original vision of the mobile portal is the Internet in your palm. To make this vision real, handset technology, the wireless infrastructure, and Web content are converging to create an environment where mobile transactions will become widespread. Integrating each of these components into a cohesive and easy-to-use package is already under way in the form of new mobile portals.

Portals, both consumer and business, have received tremendous attention over the past five years. Aggregating consumers on one side and providing products, services, and content on the other, portals are creating new roles in the digital value chain that challenge the supremacy of powerful legacy companies. The ability to form successful partnerships based on innovative portal models, such as those developed by AOL and DoCoMo, will be critical to attracting and keeping customers.

Mobile portal model experiments are in progress in all sectors of the economy. However, most of them are failing because they underestimated the amount of time it would take for consumers to adopt a new way of doing business. In most of the mobile portals, the "aha" is that new customer experiences can be delivered far more easily and efficiently. The problem is not so much whether companies can create new experiences but market penetration and economics. Although the customers who use the portals are happy, they don't draw in enough of their friends to cover the portal company's overhead.

It is far too early to speculate as to which portal models will ensure long-term success. Evidence of the market's immaturity can be found in the daunting technological challenges it faces. These challenges range from confusion over protocols, competition among wireless networks, and devices with differing capabilities to issues of uneven operator performance and consumer apathy. These challenges cause many analysts to question the viability of m-commerce. However, it is important to remember that in 1993 many of these same commentators questioned the value of the Web and online portals. It took a simple portal application providing instant market value—Yahoo!— to awaken us all to the Web's potential. It is likely that DoCoMo will play a similar catalytic role in the mobile revolution.

The portal models will look less daunting with every new customer in the mobile solutions arena. Mobile portals' biggest problem is their immaturity, but as Samuel Johnson, the British writer and lexicographer, once said when a woman told him he was too young, "'Tis a defect, ma'am, that time will cure."

Satisfying the Mobile Customer

Customers. That's the singular focus of companies everywhere. To really understand what mobility can do for customers, it is important to experience products and services through their eyes, and understand their pain. Being customer-driven is hardly an epiphany. Every business book in the last decade has preached the doctrine of customer-centricity. However, theory and reality don't seem to be in sync, as a majority of today's mobile initiatives are being rolled out with very little in-depth knowledge of customer priorities.

The term *customer-driven* is more convenient than precise. It means different things in the technology phase as opposed to the applications phase. In the technology phase, companies make products based on inventions, which are very focused on a nebulous idea of what the market might need. Then companies go to customers and say, "Voilà, look at this amazing thing we have," and the customer says, "That's great, but it isn't what I wanted." So the company goes back and fine-tunes it.

However, this model does not work in the same way in the applications phase. The speed of business doesn't allow for too much trial and error. Customer requirements just move too fast and competition is much more intense. Missteps result in lost market share. As a result, leading companies get into the marketplace very early, work with customers to isolate their specific priorities, and develop the applications suited to their particular needs. Another motivation for having customers shape applications is that cutting-edge applications create competitive advantage. Simply look at Dell and Cisco, with their pioneering customer-facing Web applications.

So, what are the customer priorities that are driving mobile applications? Today's consumers are acutely aware of how little discretionary time they have in their daily lives. As a result, they constantly look for more efficient ways to do simple everyday activities. Consumers already use the mobile channel as a timesaver for practical activities such as mobile banking, trading, shopping, making airline reservations, and buying tickets. Other examples are simple "line-busting" smart-card applications, such as highway and bridge toll payment.

However, customer preferences and needs change constantly. As consumers ascend the mobile learning curve and gain familiarity with mobile technology, they will demand more innovative experiences. Accurately anticipating this change in demand to coincide with new product and service design is the key to success in the mobile market. Companies have to continuously adjust their strategies to remain one step—but only one step—ahead of the customer. To paraphrase a quote from hockey great Wayne Gretzky, "I skate to where the puck is going to be, not where it has been."

History has taught us many times that there's a fine line between anticipating customer needs and reacting to them. Firms often act too aggressively when responding to changes in their customers' preferences. They develop business plans based on the assumption of rapid, mass customer adoption of the technology. This unrealistic expectation was seen with e-commerce, and we all know how that movie ended. The lesson learned is that macro-level changes, which require behavioral modifications, always take longer than expected. Serving mobile customers will be no different.

Focus on Customer Pain

In-depth customer knowledge—context, processes, and pain points—fuels successful business applications. Take, for instance, women. A woman's middle name should be mobile—she is constantly on the go. Easy-to-use mobile applications will be perfect for the hard-working businesswoman or mother who needs information at her fingertips and convenience that makes her life easier. We all know the juggling, scheduling, and details that most women deal with each day. Simplify this and you will have a loyal customer. Yet few applications exist to service this segment of the market.

Clearly, m-business needs to spawn new nimble companies with a different mind-set about what customers really want. Some fundamental questions in customer "diagnosis": What pain does the customer suffer from? What kind of experience is the customer looking for in the mobile environment? What activity style—ultrabusy, busy, or active—does the customer need support with? What features is the customer looking for? What is the customer willing to pay for alleviating the pain?

The advent of m-business will spawn a new breed of responsive companies with a different—and often novel—understanding of what today's customers want. For example, the retailer Babies-R-Us used wireless point-of-sales (POS) applications to provide its customers with new in-store experiences. Lynn wants to build a baby registry and checks in at the Baby Registry desk. Instead of reviewing a series of product catalogs to create a list of potential gifts, the store assistant gives Lynn a handheld optical scanner. Lynn walks around the store zapping the bar code on any product that interests her. The device's small screen displays specific item information for Lynn's confirmation. The scanner communicates with the store's database via a wireless network.

When Lynn gets back to the Baby Registry desk, the store assistant uploads the scanned data into a PC and helps Lynn edit the registry. The revised list is then uploaded onto the server and can be accessed from any Babies-R-Us store or over the Internet. "Have scanner, will shop" is a new in-store experience aimed at shoppers who dread the typical department store's byzantine registry processes. It is widely believed that the effortless registry-building program drove a significant amount of the Babies-R-Us sales.

As technology becomes affordable, it facilitates new customer experiences. Products such as handheld scanners, which used to cost thousands of dollars, are now available for a few hundred dollars. As technology prices drop further with volume production, the market will center less on high-end applications serving business customers.

Instead, the market will shift its service focus to mainstream consumers. Timing this market move with precision will be a major issue for strategists.

Designing New Customer Experiences

Like all revolutions, the mobile revolution will begin not in the boardroom but with customers. Customer demand will determine the specific path mobile innovations follow and which products and services succeed. In a sense, mobility will function as both a new channel and as a powerful enhancer of existing business relationships. In such an environment, companies will feel the pressure to ensure the loyalty of existing customers while building relationships with new ones.

Every company entering the mobile space has the same goal: leveraging this channel to create customer value. This value comes in two forms: "value for your money" and "value for your time." Location-based m-commerce illustrates the latter form. A mobile operator determines which street you are currently on and uses—like it or not—push technology to send you the ads or offers from stores in your immediate vicinity. If you read the incoming offers and respond to them using instant messaging, you receive an additional discount on any purchase you make. In the near future, many retail firms will make significant investments to bring their customers the most unique retail experiences possible and then compensate them for their willingness to experience the services offered.

Designing distinctive consumer experiences is as much an art as it is a science. Science is the technology, the tools, and the infrastructure and is the more tangible ingredient of a solution. But a solution is not achieved with technology alone. Creativity is required to pull all the parts together and make them work seamlessly. Creativity requires focus on subjective issues—consumer likes and dislikes, usability, processes, preferences, and needs. For example, Howard Shultz didn't invent the coffee shop when he launched Starbucks. He crafted an incomparable experience. Both Singapore Airlines and Cathay Pacific began as small, regional air transport companies. To compete with the major carriers, they redefined their customers' experience by focusing on airborne hospitality.

Similarly, mobile experiences cannot afford to just mimic those of the desktop. They must evolve differently, taking into consideration mobility's technological limitations. Mobility currently faces many of the same challenges confronting personal computer technology in its early days. Two decades ago, PC displays were extremely limited and text-driven, their applications were menu-driven, and concepts such as usability and personalization were unheard of. Déjà vu—sounds like the mobile devices of today. Developers working in the mobile arena must feel like they have taken the time machine and gone back to the 1970s. They now have to figure out how to design their applications to conform to the limitations of the medium while making sure the design is flexible enough to accommodate future technological changes. This is a central paradox of mobile application development. Its resolution lies in maintaining a strict focus on creating value-laden solutions for customers.

Over the past half-century, the focus of business has undergone a major shift as customers have gained increasing freedom of choice. In the early 1950s, when customers could purchase only what was offered by a limited number of manufacturers, companies such as General Motors and RCA enjoyed tremendous leverage over their markets. This advantage then shifted as retail distributors, such as Sears and Carrefour, offered customers an array of products from various manufacturers. Now, in the digital age, customer needs increasingly determine which goods and services companies produce. Accelerating this shift will be one of the central themes of the mobile economy. This is unsettling for many companies who are not trained to think in terms of digital solutions.[1]

Focus on Business Models, Not Simply Ideas

It is easier to set up a mobile presence to prove that an idea can work than to prove that there is a profitable business venture behind it. One lesson that was clear from e-commerce was that strong business models must support innovative customer solutions. One without the other is a recipe for failure. The mobile industry is searching for realistic applications that customers are willing to adopt and pay for. Much of the public discussion about mobility focuses on its futuristic, cutting-edge image. The challenge for managers and entrepreneurs is to turn customer-facing ideas and business concepts into fundable opportunities that create a return on investment.

To develop mobile applications with a strong mass-market and mainstream appeal, managers must narrow their focus. For instance, they must identify the target customer segments within the customer-facing applications market. Once these segments have been identified, a company can better analyze profitability or target application development. By focusing on a specific customer segment in which to introduce their mobile offering, companies minimize the risk of wasting valuable marketing and development resources on customers who are not interested in the product or service.

A key ingredient of a business model is that the mobile solutions be aligned with new, existing, and preferred distribution channels. Creating distinctive experiences is not enough; how they're delivered is equally important. The Mobile Customer Framework (Figure 7.1) illustrates how mobile experiences can be delivered via four channel strategies.

The strategies reflect whether the customer experiences that an organization seeks to provide have an inside-out (fixed -> mobile) or an outside-in (mobile -> fixed) orientation. The reason for dividing the framework this way is that the implementation and execution behind these models is quite different, as are the channel-conflict and change-management issues.

Inside-out experiences are delivered through the channel augmentation or channel extension models. The focus of an inside-out approach is primarily to improve efficiency and reduce cost. Under this approach, companies focus on how mobile technology can lower the firm's operating costs. Examples of an inside-out strategy include the Gap sending coupons to mobile customers and UPS providing its customers with parcel tracking capability to reduce the company's call-center traffic.

Outside-in experiences are delivered through new m-commerce channels or multi-channel integration models. The focus of an outside-in approach is on providing new customer-oriented solutions and revenue growth opportunities. Under this approach, companies focus on how to use mobile technology to provide the customer with exceptionally rich service experiences and greater satisfaction. Exam-

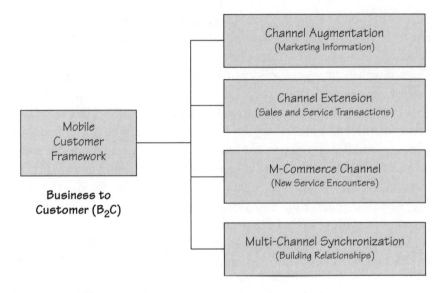

Figure 7.1: Mobile Customer Framework

ples of outside-in strategy include banks offering customers a mobile channel to increase the ease of conducting business with the bank, and retailers selling products customized for the mobile customer.

Creating multi-channel, multi-technology solutions in the fast-moving and technologically fluid mobile environment is difficult and extremely risky. First-generation technology-driven solutions tend to always start off as single channel. Early e-commerce pioneer Schwab is a typical example. The company prospered by creating stand-alone channels that offered a creative and innovative way to do business while lowering cost. In the early years, Schwab viewed the Internet as a stand-alone channel solution in order to perfect the experience. As they matured and understood the dynamics of the channel better, Schwab's perspective evolved. Today, the company uses a multi-channel approach in a potent click-and-mortar mixture. Many other Internet pioneers have also changed their e-strategy to support their customers' multi-channel behavior. This pattern will hold true in the mobile economy as well. Established companies will begin by launching stand-alone m-business initiatives and later realize their success will come from integrating old channels with the new.

Channel Augmentation

Channel augmentation solutions are information-only channels. Their purpose is to complement existing business channels such as stores or branches. Companies use these to provide marketing related information to customers and prospects. Channel augmentation solutions do the following:

- Enhance the brand presence
- Reduce sales costs by using technology to link and integrate lower-cost information channels into traditional face-to-face selling cycles

Channel augmentation efforts cover a broad and diverse array of marketing and information-distribution activities, from targeted e-mail campaigns and digital coupons to new approaches for collecting the "voice of the customer."

Mobile Marketing

Mobile marketing is the distribution of any type of message or promotion that adds value to the customer while enhancing revenue for the firm. It is a comprehensive process that supports each phase of the customer life cycle: acquisition, relationship enhancement, and retention.

The mobile dialogue between the customer and the company has the potential to generate impulse sales and optimize customer relationships by offering value-added services and loyalty incentives. Take, for instance, Travelocity, an online travel site. Travelocity frequently taps a database of information on its 19 million customers to develop special "limited-time" travel offers that are e-mailed to segments of the customer base. Travelocity performs business analysis, segmentation, and prediction so that special deals can be customized to member profiles.

Feedback and lead collection is another marketing application well-suited for mobile implementation. Consider the following experience at the SAP AG annual conference, which is called SAPPHIRE. SAP is using mobile applications to collect leads aimed at identifying attendee purchase intent, event satisfaction, and interest in post-event activities. How does this work? Every attendee, more than 7,000 in all, receives a Palm VIIx at registration, equipped with wireless service for thirty days, compliments of SAP. The attendees use the handheld to keep track of their SAPPHIRE experience—which sessions they attend, which demos they participate in, which keynotes or presentations they liked, and other feedback about conferences and facilities. This information is then used by SAP to customize their post-event Web experience, e-mail selected presentations, or provide follow-on product information. The value proposition: more targeted lead collection.

The concept of mobile marketing has received considerable media attention and is commonly perceived as a revenue generator for next-generation networks. Mobile marketing invokes images of SMS (Short Message Service) and ads scrolling across the screens of the users' cell phones or handheld computers. These capabilities can potentially allow companies to:

- Generate alternative income based on time-sensitive or location-sensitive content and services
- Reach new and existing customers with highly targeted, one-to-one promotions, especially for gift-oriented products and categories with frequently changing prices
- Build brand and increase user mindshare, driving traffic to both retail stores and Web sites

Many early mobile marketing efforts have failed due largely to a lack of appreciation for the technological limits of mobile devices. Marketing on a mobile device is different than on a PC. Only a small amount of information can be displayed on a typical device. This limitation means that the message must be small, to the point, and meaningful. Wireless customers tend to complete transactions more quickly and therefore need information at their fingertips. For example, there are users who take the Zagat guide on their handhelds while traveling to find a good restaurant.

Mobile marketing strategies must address a number of public policy concerns, such as privacy and confidentiality, before their full potential can be realized. For example, you are having a romantic dinner and receive a message on your cell phone. It is an advertisement from a local mortgage company introducing new interest rates. Not only has your "candlelight moment" been interrupted, but the charge for the call shows up on your phone bill. Customers are accustomed to junk mail, whether physical or virtual, and will soon be seeing it on their wireless devices. Spam can easily be sent to cell phones using the text-messaging services now offered as a standard feature. And because the e-mail address for most cell phones is usually a combination of the phone number and carrier's name, spam allows advertisers to target a specific audience by geographic location. Both the mobile industry and the government are scrambling to figure out how best to deal with privacy issues.

Coupons on the Go

Using the Internet to conduct one-to-one marketing began in the late 1990s. Corporate marketers lauded the benefits of personalization, and Internet advertising soared as a result. Soon, however, companies learned that most customers were visiting Web sites to window-shop. So we are now in the second inning of the game: digital advertising with mobile coupons. Mobile coupons provide companies with the opportunity to target their advertising to deliver time-sensitive and location-sensitive promotions. Promotions of perishable inventory and rapidly depreciating product lines are also ideal for mobile coupons.

Mobile coupons are not simply one-dimensional advertisements that push a particular brand; they are two-way interactive vehicles. Customers interact differently with mobile coupons than they do with other forms of advertising. In the mobile environment, a typical customer retrieves information using a handheld device by simply logging on, getting what he needs, and logging off. Customers don't usually surf the Web. In fact, the efficient way in which most customers use mobile devices may be the biggest obstacle to their taking the time to even read coupons, much less act on them. However, consumers who are waiting in line or waiting to meet someone will likely browse coupons to kill time.

How does it work? Distribution of mobile coupons is not random marketing. Users must elect to receive the marketing content and are guaranteed anonymity. Consumers can choose to receive digital coupons only for those products or services in which they are interested, such as repriced aged inventory, popular movies, or dinners. The theater chain General Cinema used PlanetHopper, a wireless marketing company, to promote awareness of its "Discount Days" program, which offered discounted movie tickets for films shown on traditionally slow days. CompUSA uses mobile coupons to boost in-store sales. Interested customers view CompUSA ads and click on the ad to open coupons for a $20 discount on purchases. To receive the discount, customers must bring their handheld device into the store for a salesperson to verify the coupon. The next phase of this solution may be a "click-to-buy" model, where a single click completes the transaction and has the product shipped home.

Mobile coupons target women shoppers, who historically have used coupons the most. The technology gives department stores the ability to target customers while making shopping more convenient. Instead of hoping a female shopper reads the section of the newspaper containing the coupon, takes the time to cut it out, and then remembers to bring it with her, stores can electronically send digital coupons to preferred customers to alert them about special sales. Customers will have the discount code on their cell phones. It is too early to tell what the digital coupon response rates (the ratio of the number of customers to whom the coupons are pitched to the number who actually make a purchase) are likely to be. Newspaper coupons typically generate a response rate of about 3 to 4 percent. Direct-mail ads and consumer catalogs generate response rates of 1 to 2 percent and 4 to 5 percent, respectively.[2] If the digital coupon approach succeeds, it will force businesses to enhance their inventory control and promotional processes in order to support the new customer behavior.

Customers and Feedback

Businesses seeking to upgrade their service quality continuously gather improvement feedback from three primary sources: customers, mystery shoppers, and focus groups. Of the three, the fastest-growing feedback method is mystery shopping, where "Jane Doe" customers are hired to rate a company's service.

The primary assumption behind the mystery shopping approach is that experiencing a company's service firsthand leads to more realistic data than does delayed feedback. Mystery shopping feedback is also less biased and more objective than the delayed feedback provided by either focus groups or customer complaints. The traditional paper-based complaint model is both slow and error prone. In addition, mystery shoppers are less expensive than conducting focus group sessions.

Service companies rely on feedback processes to ensure the correction of service issues as they arise. For example, a restaurant chain hires a group of mystery shoppers to monitor the performance of its individual restaurants. The shopper visits the restaurant and looks and acts just like a regular customer, ordering a meal and paying at the end. However, the shopper is secretly making mental notes on every aspect of the dining experience in order to fill out a detailed evaluation. The evaluation covers topics such as speed of service, facilities, greeting, accuracy with regard to how an order is filled, and food quality.

For example, Taco Bell, the fourth-largest quick-service restaurant chain in the world, used mystery shoppers who completed paper evaluation forms and mailed them to a data-collection agency overnight. The agency scanned the information from the forms, analyzed it, and compiled the results of their analysis into an online report. The report was then uploaded by the agency into a database at Taco Bell's corporate offices. From that database, corporate managers generated their own reports, which they forwarded to the restaurant managers.

Under this paper-based evaluation system, it could take as long as four days to provide a restaurant manager with service feedback. Furthermore, paper-based evaluation feedback is not always specific enough, given the limitations of the forms, to be helpful or actionable. It is also difficult to customize the forms with questions targeting different regions of the country or other demographic or assessment criteria. Because mystery shopper feedback is so intricately linked with the company's quality assurance and reward programs, its accuracy is critical—as is the timeliness with which the corporation can obtain the information.

To speed up the evaluation process, Taco Bell implemented a mobile solution. The company selected Thinque Systems, producers of the Windows CE-based application Merchandising Sales Portfolio. Thinque developed an application to present the questions and record the observations of a mystery shopper. The application also provided the underlying communications infrastructure for transmitting the collected data to a computer server from which it could be moved directly into Taco Bell's corporate databases.[3]

Mobile devices are also beginning to replace the traditional customer comment card. For example, airline companies looking to improve service quality distribute "electronic comment cards" to people in their frequent-flyer lounges to gather their input quickly. The same technology can be used with frequent shoppers. By having customers fill out an electronic comment card on a handheld computer while they wait for their credit card to be processed, managers can gather valuable information about service quality.[4]

Channel Extension

Corporate channel extension strategies give customers the ability to conduct mobile transactions in addition to retrieving online information. As a result, many large firms view the mobile channel as a natural channel extension of their existing self-service, convenience, and value-added strategies. However, the technology required to enable mobile transaction processing is far more complex to both develop and deploy than is the technology behind simple information retrieval.

Channel extension models leverage a company's existing back-end systems rather than building new systems from scratch. For example, many brokerage companies are moving quickly to provide their customers access to real-time trading. Both E-Trade and Schwab have selected Aether Systems, a mobile application service provider, to distribute real-time price quotes and news to customers using the RIM BlackBerry wireless product. Users are able to trade stocks, check on stock quotes, and obtain news.

Channel extension strategies are a natural first step for many companies as they gradually venture into the mobile world. Time-consuming and repetitive processes such as order tracking, ticketing, and replenishment are ideal candidates for channel extension strategies.

Order Status and Tracking Is a Killer APP

Nothing frustrates customers more than not knowing where their order is or its status. This is especially true with just-in-time inventory orders, where time-critical shipment information is so important. To address the order status and tracking problem, companies such as Sun Microsystems, ADC Telecommunications, and United Parcel Service (UPS) are offering customers self-service order-management capabilities on mobile devices.

At UPS, the world's largest express carrier and package delivery company, the personalized order information accompanying each package has become as important as the package itself. Managing and communicating this order information has been a key element of the company's value proposition since 1993.

In February 1993, UPS rolled out a nationwide cellular-based wireless data service in response to a similar initiative by FedEx, which had developed a wireless network application to keep track of document and parcel shipments. The cellular network provides the connection between UPS vehicles and UPSnet, the UPS private telecommunications network. With its delivery information acquisition device (or DIAD, a custom-built data collector), Motorola-supplied cellular telephone modems, and the cellular network, both delivery information and customers' signatures are transmitted from the company's 50,000 vehicles to the UPS mainframe in Mahwah, New Jersey, enabling UPS to provide same-day package-tracking information for all air and ground packages. Previously, this information was not available until the day after delivery.

Since then, UPS has shifted its focus from field data collection to enabling customers access to the information that is located in its mainframe. To complement its successful Web site and increase customer self-service, UPS looked at ways to address the needs of the mobile customer. Customers told UPS that they wanted to be able to access shipment information while traveling, as conveniently as they can from their office desktops, without having to telephone the call center or find a place to plug in a laptop to look at the Web site. With the majority of mobile customers having access to handheld devices, UPS felt that the best way to meet their needs would be through a wireless solution.[5]

UPS designed its wireless solution with the help of Air2Web, a mobile solutions provider. It gives UPS's customers the ability to (1) track a package; (2) find out how much it would cost to ship a package using either next-day, 2-day, or 3-day air or ground service; (3) know the exact in-transit time; (4) find the nearest drop-off box; and (5) know when an urgent shipment has arrived or been received through the automatic notification service.

UPS's solution has been extremely successful since its launch. Thousands of the company's customers actively use it. The more customers who use UPS's wireless service, the more traffic is diverted away from the company's call-center channel—and the greater the savings to the company. In addition, customers' satisfaction increases since they have more knowledge at their fingertips.

M-Tickets

It's 6:00 P.M. A young urban commuter is sitting in traffic on her way home from work. The traffic is at a standstill, so she pulls out her pocket PC. She goes online and buys tickets to the Elton John concert she remembered she wanted to attend the following weekend. She enters the number of tickets she wants to purchase, selects the location where the tickets can be either picked up or delivered, and pays for them. The transaction confirmation code is sent to her e-mail address.

Customer-facing firms are eliminating paper tickets and implementing m-ticketing strategies. The benefits of m-ticketing are not readily apparent. But if you have ever arrived at the ballpark and realized that your tickets are still sitting on the kitchen counter, its benefits are probably obvious. With m-ticketing, event tickets can be delivered electronically to a PDA or cell phone.

M-ticketing applications can increase "impulse sales," create new sales channels, and streamline current ticketing workflows. Customers will be able to place their orders using a telephone, the Internet, or a wireless device. But instead of opting for conventional delivery through the mail or will-call pickup, they can specify electronic delivery to their wireless device. When they arrive at the event, they use their mobile device to send an infrared signal with the ticket information to the vendor's receiver, where the ticket information is verified. The transaction remains electronic from beginning to end.

Security and validation are two major concerns involved with developing electronic transaction and delivery applications. Firms such as Mtickets are working to ensure the security of the electronic storage vaults that house purchase information. Printing bar codes is an alternate delivery option, providing additional security for customers who are not comfortable sending order information using an infrared signal. The customer prints out a Web page containing a bar code and takes this bar code to the event, where it is scanned by the ticket taker.

Mobile Replenishment

Mobile shopping, particularly for frequently purchased items, has significant market appeal for obvious reasons. Replenishment oriented processes, such as weekly shopping lists, do not require an in-store shopping experience. Frequently purchased items can be placed on a customized shopping list and reordered by customers on a regular basis. Replenishment e-tailers—drugstores, office supply, pizza delivery, and supermarkets—are giving serious consideration to implementing mobile replenishment strategies, especially since the delivery delays associated with receiving online orders is being steadily reduced as e-tailers increasingly take ownership of inventory management and distribution.

Successful mobile reordering and replenishment strategies use a "single-action" feature. For example, Amazon.com developed the "one-click" method to streamline the online purchase process and address customer frustrations with what is known in e-commerce as the "shopping cart model" of purchasing. A purchaser selects an item from an electronic catalog, typically by clicking on an "Add to Shopping Cart" icon, and thereby places the item in a "virtual" shopping cart. Other catalog items are added to the cart in the same manner. After selecting the items to buy, the purchaser proceeds to "checkout." On the checkout page, they enter order-related information such as the purchaser's identity, billing and shipping addresses and payment method. Finally, the purchaser "clicks" on a button displayed on the screen to execute the completed order. The shopping cart model of online purchasing thus requires the customer to take multiple steps before an order is complete.[6]

With "one-click" reordering, the number of steps required to place an order is reduced to one or two. However, "one-click" ordering is available only to purchasers who have previously visited the seller's Web site and entered all of the billing and shipping information needed to effect a sales transaction. Thereafter, when the purchaser visits the seller's Web site and wishes to purchase a product from that site, only a single action is necessary to place the order for the item. Once the item is selected, the purchaser simply presses the "one-click" button and the order is complete.

Single-click instant buying is a powerful customer-loyalty enhancer, because it drastically reduces transaction time. It is perfectly suited for use in a mobile replenishment environment.

M-Commerce Channel Design

Consumers gravitate toward shopping experiences that offer quality service, provide fast delivery, and are easily engaged. For example, the Sears, Roebuck catalog radically changed the shopping experience. The catalog traces its history to 1886, when Richard Sears, then a twenty-two-year-old agent working at a train station, got stuck with a load of watches that a local merchant had refused. Sears sent letters to other agents along the line, selling the watches and turning a nice profit. Sears then quit the railroad and began selling watches full-time. Alvah Roebuck, a watch repairman, soon joined the firm to run the service department.[7]

The R.W. Sears Watch Co. published its first catalog in 1888. By 1897, the Sears catalog was 500 pages long and was distributed to 300,000 homes. The cover of the 1894 edition proclaimed Sears "the cheapest supply house on earth." It offered America's rural customers a variety of products at attractive prices that small-town merchants were hard-pressed to match. The company used its catalog to sell a vast assortment of goods, from groceries to kits for full-size houses. Customers experienced the different products through the medium of a catalog and made their purchases without actually seeing or touching the product. Sears built company credibility by instructing customers not to pay in advance but to wait until they had received and inspected their order.

Sears pioneered a new business channel. Today, many companies are seeking to do the same by providing distinctive, interactive mobile experiences to their customers. For example, customers can walk up to an airport kiosk and download digital books to read or games to play on their handheld PC, videos to watch on their laptops, or digital music to listen to during a cross-country flight. These products target consumers who want something to do during the flight. Airline companies have long known that consumers are more tolerant of long waits, flight delays, or sitting on the tarmac if they have something that diverts their attention. Airport television monitors and magazine stands help flyers kill time. Virgin Airlines took this strategy further. The airline redesigned its Upper Class lounge to include entertainment options such as Sony PlayStations, model railways, and free massages.[8] Instead of providing time-killers, Virgin introduced the notion of "time-fillers," an ostensibly more productive use of time. It is a powerful concept in any environment where the customer must wait. Time-filler products, such as digital music and games, are the perfect complement to mobile devices.

By definition, the new mobile channels craft new customer experiences based on an assessment of unmet customer needs. The objective is to provide a compelling, personalized experience for each and every customer in the hope they'll return for more. Not only can the new channel be used to introduce new mobile products and services through its direct connection to customers, it can also serve as a platform offering applications that entertain and educate the customer. Perhaps the greatest benefit is that it provides a way to distribute new combinations of digital information and creates new transaction models without incurring the overhead costs that exist in the physical world.

M-channel innovations, which simplify the purchasing process while providing distinctive customer experiences, will put pressure on a company's competitors to implement a similar initiative or risk losing their customer base. Take, for instance, Amazon.com. Amazon's goal was to create an outside-in e-commerce business model unlike the inside-out channel extension models of Barnes & Noble, which extended the firm's assets outward. Success depended on innovation and creating unique customer experiences. For example, Amazon.com's "one-click" feature reduced the complexity that had characterized online shopping until that point. In so many ways, Amazon.com set the standard for e-commerce. Irrespective of the economics of the company's business model, it is hard not to applaud Amazon.com for its success at creating truly novel customer experiences.

Digital Products Retailing: The Case of Bertelsmann AG

From the consumer's perspective, shopping experiences for digital products—digital music, books, content—are brand new. Several companies are engaged in a variety of mobile experiments, from pilot projects to full-blown Internet ventures, to refine their buying-selling-delivering-paying-storing approaches to digital products. A leader in these efforts is Bertelsmann, a German media conglomerate.

Bertelsmann ventures span the entire spectrum of communications media. They own book publishers, music companies, book and music clubs, newspaper and magazine publishers, television and radio stations, TV production companies, print and media service companies, and multimedia and professional information companies. Its best-known companies and brands include Random House (books), BMG (music), Arvato (media services), Gruner+Jahr (magazines and newspapers), RTL Group (TV and radio), and BertelsmannSpringer (professional information).

For much of its 165-year history, Bertelsmann was known for publishing prayer books. Today it occupies a leading position in the global media and entertainment industry. It is the world's largest general-interest publisher, and the largest publisher in the English-speaking world. Bertelsmann's book and music clubs are both positioned at the top of the industry in Europe and internationally. Through its RTL Group and Gruner+Jahr, the company is the market leader in the European broadcasting and magazine sector. Lastly, its Arvato AG is one of the largest media services companies.

Bertelsmann is also a leading Internet company. With Bertelsmann Online in Europe and Asia and barnesandnoble.com in the United States, the company is number two in the world in media e-commerce. Much of Bertelsmann's e-commerce success is due to intelligent investing. In 1995, Bertelsmann bought 5 percent of outstanding AOL shares for $50 million and in subsequent years netted more than $1.5 billion from periodic stock sales.[9]

Digital Strategy: Paving the Way for M-Commerce

Two of the fastest-growing industries in the world—entertainment and mobile communications—are converging as lifestyles change, with people experiencing more rapid bursts of free time. Bertelsmann, anticipating the convergence, has realigned its media empire into three strategic business units: Content (books, music, magazines, newspapers, TV, radio, and professional information), Media Services, and Direct-to-Customer Businesses.

Bertelsmann's holdings provide it with an incomparable combination of media content and distribution assets. As part of its realignment, the company made a strategic decision to focus on creative content development as its key competitive factor in the media business. In Bertelmann's vision, distribution channels and media carriers may change, but content will remain king since it is the identity-providing commodity in free TV, in best-selling novels, in musical hits, and in magazines. When companies compete for consumer mindshare and budgets, content is the deciding factor.

Bertelsmann offers its content wherever consumers wish to use it. The firm is actively creating scenarios in which some countries bypass PC adoption and move directly to mobile devices. For example, there will be more handheld devices in China and India within seven years than there will be in all of Europe. This is one socioeconomic event for which all m-commerce companies must plan and adjust their business models and infrastructure technologies accordingly.

Bertelsmann's strategic goal is to provide consumers with entertainment content through as many channels as possible. In the area of music, Bertelsmann is actively formulating a digital strategy through its involvement in the Internet music exchanges CDNow, Napster, and consortium MusicNet. Bertelsmann owns CDNow and is one of the major investors in Napster. Napster, a person-to-person file-sharing community, provides music enthusiasts with a platform for discovering new music and communicating their interests with one another.

Bertelsmann and Napster are collaborating to create a "pay-to-play" business model for the 60 million registered members of the Napster community, while at the same time providing payments to copyright owners such as artists, songwriters, record labels, and music publishers. Another alternative music channel is MusicNet. It is a collaboration of three of the Big Five record labels: AOL Time Warner, Bertelsmann, and EMI Group. MusicNet, powered by Real-Networks, promises a cafeteria-style way of purchasing songs.

The Future Outlook

Fast and easy access to entertainment is always appealing to customers. But the new twist is the emphasis on a future in which consumers use mobile devices—phones, handheld computers, and a new generation of hybrids—to gain easy access to entertainment content. As the mobile Internet begins to offer more sophisticated services, the race is on to see who can become the leading mobile entertainment company in the world.

Bertelsmann, AOL Time Warner, and Vivendi are all jockeying to play a key role in digital services that are user-friendly, convenient, fast, and mobile. These companies understand the dynamics of the digital markets and are building barriers to entry for competition. For example, for an m-commerce company to enter the European market successfully, they must have a local presence and be multi-cultural. They must not only offer the European market quality technology but exhibit the ability to function across borders, in multi-lingual environments, and with an understanding of both foreign currencies and diverse payment customs.

As the network bandwidth improves to support fast downloads, Bertelsmann is poised with the necessary content to service customers. The early adopters are expected to be techno-savvy and entertainment hungry teenagers and young adults. The most probable first offering to this target group will be digital music, followed by digital books. Random House is working to digitize its entire backlist of books. Bertelsmann has a ready-made audience: their book clubs, with 25 million subscribers throughout the world. The clubs are already fully Internet-operational, giving Bertelsmann an instant subscriber base.

However, a barrier to mass-market adoption of mobile entertainment is the pricing model. The mobile Internet has ushered in a good deal of confusion around the revenue models for the new data services. Mobile entertainment services are particularly vulnerable to this confusion. There is an expectation among end users that entertainment should be free and bundled in with the service provider fees. To get around this problem, companies like Bertelsmann are experimenting with tiered models where certain basic services may be free but premium services are not. Expect to see a lot of turmoil in m-commerce revenue models as different options are experimented with and discarded. But whatever happens in the next five years, we expect Bertelsmann to come out ahead.

Multi-Channel, Multi-Technology Synchronization

Customers prefer a choice in the channels through which they do business. No matter how much a company tries to get customers to use specific channels, the customers ultimately use the one they want. They will read pages of mail-order catalogs, wander the shopping malls, call an 800 number, and surf the Web.

Instead of attempting to limit the number of channels available to their customers, both storefront and online retailers are recognizing the customer need for choice. They are seeking to enhance the quality of service and customer experiences with new multi-channel models. Customers can "click or brick," shop with a salesperson or not, and receive service through the wired or wireless Internet as well as the call center. Every channel is integrated to anticipate what the customers need at any point in their shopping or request for service.

Multi-channel, multi-technology strategies represent the next frontier. The concept of integrated channels is altering the way industry leaders conceptualize their channel strategy. For example, Home Depot's strategy is to differentiate itself in the do-it-yourself, home-improvement industry by ensuring a consistent customer experience regardless of the channel chosen. Companies, such as Home Depot, that adopt this strategy believe in a fixed/mobile convergent world. Even if a customer transaction is initiated in the mobile environment first, these companies want to make other channels available to customers in a seamless way to provide a richer experience. The primary objective is to avoid disorienting the customer with conflicting messages from the different channels.

To create a blended-channel experience, retailers are experimenting with the different ways m-commerce can positively impact the blend. For example, a number of retailers are experimenting with customers entering or scanning a UPC or bar code using a mobile device. This allows the customer access to relevant product, price comparison, and store information, from any location, at any time.

While the multi-channel vision of the 5R's—the right content to the right person at the right time at the right place on the right device—has been around for a while, its technical execution has proven to be difficult. The banking industry provides an excellent example of the challenges the 5R's present.

Banking: Building Relationships Across Channels

The financial services industry—brokerage, banking, and insurance—is leading the way into the m-commerce arena. The industry's goal is simple: achieve first-mover advantage or risk being left behind. Brokerage customers of firms as diverse as Schwab (United States), Fraser Securities (Singapore), and Fimatex (France) can now trade stocks using a mobile phone or personal digital assistant (PDA). Banks ranging from Royal Bank of Canada, HSBC (Hong Kong), and Barclays Bank (United Kingdom) are deploying mobile applications that let customers check bank balances and pay bills on the go.

The target market for these types of services are ultrabusy individuals who want the flexibility to bank anytime they want. The value proposition: remote access to account balances and transfers, cleared transactions, notifications, and credit-card statements, and the ability to pay bills without having to log on to the Web. For banks, the result is a closer relationship with customers through the mobile touchpoints.

The ultrabusy customer is looking for convenience. However, convenience means different things to different people. Is it time-related, is it dependability, or is it the ease of use? Socioeconomic factors such as lifestyle, household incomes, household composition, and even education can change a person's perspective on convenience. So, before building a solution, banks need to identify what the word *convenience* means to their customers.

The first-generation mobile banking services are extremely basic. They offer account balance and stock quotes and permit customers to transfer money between accounts. Since banks' basic service offerings are currently undifferentiated, any competitive advantage is likely to be temporary. Competition will increase, however, as more complex transactional services become available and as banks gain experience with the mobile channel, technology, and customer behavior.

Complex Transactional Services

Every customer contact creates a moment of mediocrity, a moment of despair, or a moment of satisfaction. In a competitive market, banks and other financial institutions are constantly looking for new, groundbreaking delivery channels for their financial services—innovative channels designed to help retain existing customers, attract new ones, generate revenue, and differentiate their services. A number of banks are aggressively pursuing a variety of m-commerce initiatives:

- **Providing the payments infrastructure for mobile commerce services.** Banks control the existing payments infrastructure and understand the security issues. They can also easily play a key role in m-commerce services such as ticketing, auctions, and providing value-added information. However, the banking industry's record in providing e-commerce payments infrastructure has been rather spotty, and it has found that changing people's payment behavior is a costly and slow battle.
- **Launching mobile portals for customers.** Most banks have millions of customers who are looking for a trusted brand rather than new brands after the "boom-bust" cycle of e-commerce. So creating cobranded portals—Web sites that aggregate information—is a strategy being pursued by some banks.
- **Launching private banking portals for high-net-worth customers.** Account aggregation for affluent clients is a growth business. Creating private wealth management portals that provide clients with a consolidated view of their net worth through mobile channels is a natural step for banks.

- **Launching private portals for small business customers.** Most large banks have huge numbers of small business customers who are juggling many things as they run their businesses. This both increases transactional efficiency and creates added value for customers.

Banks have two primary advantages in the m-commerce environment: (1) access to a ready-made customer base, and (2) a trusted brand with a reputation for protecting clients' assets. However, financial institutions most likely don't have the skills needed to successfully create different channel options that target niche mobile segments such as individual investors, traveling executives, or owners of small businesses. However, they can assemble the right set of partnerships—for example, a mobile-network operator, a specialist portal provider, and a handset manufacturer.

Most banks need to make sure that their internal processes have been optimized before undertaking a mobile channel initiative. Also, they have to make sure that the various applications can talk to each other. To accomplish this, they are investing in middleware that will help link mobile devices to proprietary back-end systems. A typical bank's back-office infrastructure is based on highly reliable mainframe applications that run every facet of its banking and trading operations. These legacy systems were not designed to connect with the Internet or even to be accessed by anyone but trained personnel. More importantly, systems-enabling products such as account management, trading, mortgages, and bill payment applications are often stand-alone tools and cannot be easily integrated.

Revenue Models

Currently, the financial services industry is focusing on building a few powerful applications to develop a user base. The thought process is as follows: Once the user base is established, service can be expanded and charged for. But determining the appropriate revenue model is a major issue. It requires determining how large the potential mobile market is, how to generate revenue from it, and the cost of doing so. The industry has much work left to do developing its mobile business model.

Creating revenue models is made more difficult by the fact that most market research shows that customers are unwilling to pay for mobile services, such as account balances, that they already receive free through another channel. So it is important to isolate what services customers are willing to pay for and which ones they are not. Some services customers appear willing to pay for are mobile transaction services, such as stock trading and other time-sensitive content, that they couldn't receive any other way. Even if customers are willing to pay, how much banks can charge customers for mobile services will vary by market.

What about costs? In some ways, mobile should be a cost-effective channel, since the customer will bear most of the expense of accessing the services. But this doesn't mean that banks see reduced costs once the channel is established. Many bankers are haunted by their experience with e-banking and telebanking. Both promised to be low-cost channels, and banks invested billions in them. But while unit costs per transaction plummeted, the volume of transactions rose because customers found these channels so convenient. The infrastructure and support costs per customer escalated.

It is far too soon to know the true economics of creating next-generation multi-channel products. In the near term, the majority of the value created by mobile banking is likely to go to other participants in the value chain—most probably consumers and network operators. However, banks will not be able to let the mobile revolution pass them by, and they must discover ways to create sustainable value from the mobile channel if they are to realize any return on their mobile investment.

Linking Mobile CRM to E-Business

Over the next three years, many companies across multiple industries will adopt a mobile CRM strategy that will increase the number of channels through which they can communicate with customers. As part of this effort, companies will require a systematic way to leverage and integrate with their e-business investments. Figure 7.2 shows the various applications through which the mobile framework will be linked to e-business applications.

However, bridging the mobile, Web, and traditional channels will entail some careful planning. It will require defining the customer experience, business processes, content, application infrastructure, and governance models. This overall architecture forms the basis for launching mobile CRM initiatives. Not doing the necessary planning will result in a disjointed approach.

Slowly but surely, click-and-brick CRM strategies are going to evolve into mobile, Web, and brick. This is not going to be easy. Moving from brick to click is a journey that many companies are still in the middle of. For them to adjust and extend their Web strategies to mobile will require a significant retooling. However, before they undertake any application and process modifications, companies are asking to be shown the return on investment (ROI) from a mobile scenario. The ROI can come from any of the following processes:

- **Experience differentiation:** offering personalized or customized service.
- **Profitable customer acquisition:** reducing the cost of acquiring new customers.
- **Self-service solutions:** more efficiently delivering what the customer wants, how they want it, and when they want it to maximize profits and revenue.
- **Customer retention:** building and sustaining customer loyalty. Also, increasing the "share of customer" through greater cross-selling of products and services.

Breaking these abstract process improvement benefits into quantifiable ROI measures is quite tricky. Estimating ROI is not an exact science. It depends on many assumptions about market conditions, customer adoption, and even competitor reaction. But it is something skeptical companies are looking for as they try to justify new technology investments given what has taken place in the topsy-turvy e-commerce wave.

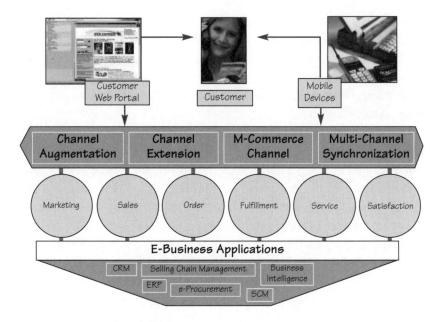

Figure 7.2: Customer Framework

A Final Thought

A cookie store is a bad idea. Besides, the market research reports say America likes crispy cookies, not soft and chewy cookies like you make.
　　—response to Debbi Fields's idea of starting Mrs. Fields' Cookies

A sound mobile customer applications strategy begins by articulating what is possible. It is amusing to read articles and listen to discussions about 3G infrastructure. Few seem to be grasping the fundamental problem: If there are no customer applications that are interesting or useful, all the billions being invested in mobile infrastructure is going to be wasted. Therefore, craft your business's strategy based on the value it provides your customer. Doing so requires a total commitment to understanding customers, to meeting their needs, and to helping them solve everyday problems.

　　Customers will pay for applications meeting these criteria. Up to this point, companies have tried to sell consumers on the notion that m-commerce means using your cell phone to buy a can of Pepsi from a vending machine, using Web-enabled phones to buy gas, or inputting real-time stock orders into a Palm. The hype has led to disappointments for consumers, many of whom have been turned off by cumbersome four-line, black-and-white displays that require extraordinary patience to use.[10]

As the mobile possibilities begin to augment traditional customer interaction models, companies are beginning to experiment with a wide array of channel alternatives. However, for managers in established businesses, mobility will be challenging for two reasons: One, it is easy to establish a mobile channel presence, but it is quite difficult to create a profitable business model servicing the customer. Two, determining exactly what mobile services the mainstream market is willing to pay for is often not easy. Most of the current mobile users are the tech-savvy early adopters and represent an extremely small percentage of the population. They aren't and never have been a very good indicator of what the majority will do or want.

One thing is certain: The changes made possible by the mobile economy are strategic and fundamental. However these changes play out in individual industries, in the foreseeable future they will unquestionably affect every company's value propositions and its relationship with its customers.

Supply Chain Focus

Compared to consumer applications, the breadth of mobile applications in the business-to-business (B_2B) market is far more breathtaking. To really understand what mobility can do to improve the efficiency of supply chains and B_2B commerce, it is important to look at the transformations taking place in the management of supply chains.

The modern supply chain is built on the concepts developed by Henry Ford. In 1913, the demand for Model T cars was so great that Ford developed new mass-production methods and introduced the world's first moving assembly line for cars. He also developed the concept of vertical integration—full ownership and management of the entire value-creation process to reduce waste and increase efficiency. Every step in the production and distribution of goods and services, from raw-material extraction and processing to the marketing of finished products, would be under the control of a single company.

As a result, the Ford Motor Company implemented an integrated supply chain strategy. The company owned rubber plantations, ships, foundries, and manufacturing plants capable of converting raw iron ore into a finished car in seven days. However, such vertical integration required tremendous capital investment and an incredibly complex organizational structure if it was to succeed.

Since Ford's time, the vertical integration model has undergone significant changes. Today's businesses are typical collaborative multi-enterprise supply chains consisting of several specialists. Figure 8.1 illustrates the five basic roles within the typical supply chain: suppliers who produce raw materials or components; manufacturers who assemble these components into finished products; distributors (or wholesalers) who deliver the finished goods; retailers (or e-tailers) who sell the products; and consumers who purchase them. Under the collaborative multi-enterprise model, the goal is to bring together the production, delivery, and service capabilities of multiple partners and to have them operate as though they were one seamless organization.

Making this vision a reality requires a highly coordinated sequence of transfers—materials, information, and funds—from the raw material supplier to the ultimate consumer. The focus of coordination varies by industry. For example, electronics supply chains are focused on shorter product life cycles, whereas retail supply chains are more focused on collaborative forecasting and demand fulfillment areas.

However, the objective of supply chain coordination remains the same: enhance end-customer value. Orchestrating this can be quite challenging. The difficulty lies in integrating the processes of the various companies who contribute to a finished product. Coordination challenges also occur in the downstream supply chain, where manufacturers, distributors, and retailers have to collaborate closely to deliver products.

As the end-to-end supply chain gets compressed, coordination up and down the supply chain becomes more intricate. Imagine the complexity when a large company uses multiple global supply chains for their different product lines and all these supply chains are sharing data with each other. In the real world, supply chains are highly interdependent. However, much of the literature on supply chain management assumes a single supply chain for a company with a linear flow. The reality is far from that. Supply chains are nonlinear, messy, error-laden, and full of complexity.

As a result, supply chain change initiatives have proven to be difficult to manage, as the case of Nike illustrates. The company decided to automate its entire supply chain so that when retailers ordered

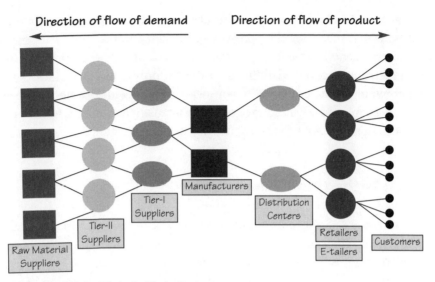

Figure 8.1: Typical Supply Chain Structure

shoes, they could then manufacture them at their partner facilities. The project's objective was to implement a supply chain system to process orders, collect payments, notify the shoe manufacturers, and manage the shoes' delivery. Instead, Nike wound up with excess inventory in some shoe models and not enough in other models that were in demand. Nike chairman Phil Knight commented: "This is what we get for our $400 million [investment]?"[1]

Even the most finely tuned supply chains are vulnerable to inaccurate information. For example, Cisco was considered by many business analysts to have one of the best build-to-order supply chains. The company grew at a phenomenal rate until the 2001 economic downturn. As a result of the slowdown, the company had to take a surplus inventory markdown of $2.25 billion. Cisco's poor performance was due in large part to the inaccuracy of the data its systems were using. Prior to the downturn, Cisco customers had hedged their bets on product lead times by placing orders with Cisco resellers as well as with the manufacturer itself. Consequently, components were procured by fixed contracts rather than short lead-time ordering. Cisco was simultaneously processing the same orders from two different sources: its customers and resellers. When the duplicate orders were withdrawn, Cisco was left with warehouses full of excess parts.[2]

Large-scale global supply chains are made up of numerous components, which increases the complexity of their interactions. In today's competitive environment, even large and medium size enterprises must gain better control and visibility over their supply chain processes. Supply chain management is no longer just a good idea. It is a necessity, as market share and revenue growth are increasingly dependent on getting the right product to the right place at the right time.

What Is the Business Problem?

Uneven demand, more frequent and shorter order-to-shipment times, and stricter customer compliance requirements are the key parameters shaping twenty-first-century business practices. As a result, companies are reexamining their business processes from a business-to-business (B$_2$B) commerce perspective in an effort to be more effective and efficient. Such an evaluation has the potential to transform a company's supply chain practices from a group of ad hoc and fragmented processes into a cohesive system capable of delivering value to the customer.

Traditionally, supply chains created value through efficiency and low price. Today, however, supply chains have to create value through their flexibility. Their design must accommodate a customer changing his mind after the order is placed so the company retains control of the manufacturing and fulfillment processes.

The advent of more sophisticated information and demand flows has led to the creation of a variety of new supply designs, such as build-to-order, configure-to-order, and fulfill-to-order. However, the reality and vision are often in conflict. The reason is that fragmented supply chain processes are characterized by many unnecessary handoffs or additional process steps, resulting in inefficiency and increased cost. In essence, the problem is not a technology issue as much as an inter-enterprise process issue. Solving this process problem has been the theme of many B$_2$B solutions.

However, the core focus of B$_2$B commerce remains the same: Compressing the end-to-end supply chain increases efficiency and savings by reducing the number of handoffs and inventory stops.

As a result, a megatrend has been the use of Internet and enterprise technology to increase supply chain velocity—the fast and accurate collection and manipulation of information—while maximizing service levels. Supply chain basics such as purchase orders, invoices, advanced ship notices (ASNs), and bills of material are still the same; they are just being handled more quickly, more cheaply, and more accurately through the Internet.

Another business trend that is impacting supply chains is the replacement of inventory with information. In such a scenario, companies can track inventory flow better than ever before. The real-time transfer of inventory information helps companies create a more realistic demand picture. Under today's current practices, order information is sent to warehouses, distribution centers, and retail stores in batches by telephone, fax, e-mail, or EDI. Since the order information isn't matched with demand in real time, manufacturers often get caught in the "bullwhip effect," making too little product, and then too much, in an attempt to keep up with the fluctuating market.

The need for faster and more accurate fulfillment is also transforming supply chain coordination. Faster end-to-end order processing is dramatically affecting product handling and logistics. For example, consider JCPenney. Traditionally, manufacturers shipped full truckloads and full pallets of product to the JCPenney central warehouse. As e-commerce became popular, JCPenney wanted to minimize shipping time, so they asked manufacturers to ship direct to the customer. As a result, the manufacturer's logistics function might be shipping to several thousand customer locations instead of a few warehouses. Also, this meant that the manufacturer was looking at item picks, small package shipments, and priority handling—all new processes they did not have to deal with before.

To improve supply chain coordination, new tools are required. Mobile applications are beginning to play a central role in enabling real-time supply chains. Most traditional supply chain applications have been hindered by the inability to get real-time data—things like accurate customer demand and the ability to track assets in transit. With the advances in technology, some amazing things are taking place that promise to take supply chains to a new frontier.

Mobile Solutions in the Supply Chain

The time it takes to procure, make, and deliver a finished product to a customer is often longer than the customer is prepared to wait. This is a basic problem companies have always faced. Several market trends are driving mobile supply chain investments in projects to shorten lead time.

- **Streamlining the order-to-cash process.** Customer orders drive supply chains. However, the complexity of the ordering process and the need for order information upstream to support supply chain planning has resulted in unusual pressure to streamline the entire order-to-cash process. The recent emergence of private exchanges, consortiums, and public exchanges will alter the order-to-cash process dynamic.
- **Accuracy in coordinating the order fulfillment process.** Once an order is placed, effective, timely order fulfillment requires a significant coordination effort. Customer demand for faster and more customized delivery has disrupted traditional inventory management policies and transportation models. Successful order fulfillment requires local, regional, national, and global coordination. This requires sophisticated synchronization of multiple distribution channels.
- **Better asset tracking and utilization.** Customers want real-time order status information. Customers are demanding greater visibility into the supply chain execution processes. As a result, companies are investing more in real-time asset tracking. These investments help companies achieve inventory reductions, eliminate sources of order fulfillment variance, reduce leakage, and cause fewer returns.
- **More responsive service management.** Companies have to accept lower profit margins in order to maintain and increase market share. In response to lower margins, many companies are redesigning their postsale service and support functions to eliminate unnecessary tasks and process complexity. The benefits include reducing delays, errors, and cost. For example, reverse logistics is an area of increasing focus. Reverse logistics implies that due to customer dissatisfaction, items must be shipped,

accounted for, and returned to the manufacturer or disposed of in a secondary "gray" market. Reverse supply chains in outsourced contexts are causing a whole new set of challenges for companies.

Figure 8.2 captures the four major segments in which mobile solutions will have significant impact on supply chains.

E-Procurement Applications

Corporate procurement functions are undergoing significant changes with the advent of new requisition applications, private portals, private exchanges, auction markets, and public exchanges. Traditionally, companies conducted business using paper- and fax-based processes. While well-suited to past business conditions, such order-processing practices have gradually become inadequate in the fast-paced supply chain environment.

Retail order processing provides a good example. Under the paper-based regime, it was difficult to obtain an accurate idea of what was

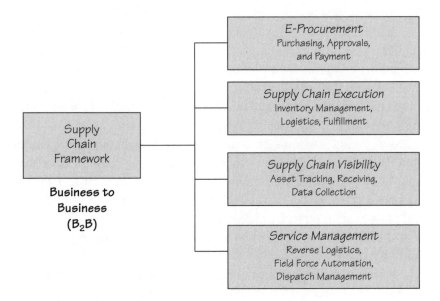

Figure 8.2: Supply Chain Framework

on the store shelves. Paper-based data took days or even weeks to make its way back to the manufacturers. This made it difficult to match production schedule to actual demand.

Orders represent the tip of the supply chain iceberg. The true end-to-end supply chain is represented by a concept called the order-to-cash cycle. This cycle begins when a customer places an order, which triggers the sourcing and procurement of materials. The items on the order are then manufactured and/or assembled and distributed. The cycle concludes with the receipt of payment from the customer. Three types of mobile applications support the order-to-cash cycle: order and transaction enablers, approval workflow enablers, and receiving and payment enablers.

Order and Transaction Enablers

Supply chains are increasingly market driven. In other words, they are capable of reading and responding to real customer demand. In support of this trend, new mobile applications are changing the face of order taking, especially in the B_2B context. For example, a corporate buyer in a high-tech industry is in charge of ordering parts for a printed circuit board production line. Since it is a 24/7 line, it is important that the parts be procured immediately in the event of an exception. As a result, the buyer's handheld device is configured with the item list. The user simply enters the order quantity for the selected item into the handheld and hits the order button to reorder the needed supplies. Once entered, the order is transmitted automatically over the network using a background process. The order is sent to the private exchange and is then routed into the order-approval process.

Order taking technology is undergoing significant change. For example, Kroger, the largest grocery chain in the United States, has recently entered into an arrangement with PocketScript. Through this partnership, Kroger expects to become the first food and drug retailer to use an electronic-prescription interchange. Physicians, using a handheld device, will be able to send e-prescriptions directly to any Kroger-owned pharmacy. Doctors traditionally rely on phone calls or handwritten prescriptions to communicate medication orders to retail pharmacies. Handwritten prescriptions can be illegible to pharmacy personnel, who must then make a follow-up call to physicians to verify the prescriptions' contents. E-prescriptions are expected to reduce the number of illegible handwritten prescriptions and decrease time spent making callbacks to physicians.[3]

Approval Workflow Enablers

Workflow applications such as document approval, expense reporting, payment, and purchase orders are another area to which mobile innovations are bringing considerable benefit. The concept of workflow management for procurement and related approval processes has been around as long as accountants and auditors. Procurement in ancient Rome and Egypt probably involved a papyrus purchase order requiring the signature of a bureaucrat.

Mobile applications hold promise for improving order-approval workflows, where purchase orders are approved by the appropriate authority in order to track and control spending. Traditional approval workflows are paper-based. The recent advent of e-procurement applications has meant purchase-order approvals can now be automated. Expense tracking and control is critical in current fully automated procurement environments. Not paying attention to expenses at various levels can get companies into trouble in the form of high overhead.

So keeping track of orders being placed is a priority at many companies. However, e-procurement applications still require the approvers to be at the office and by their desktops. They assume a tethered workplace.

Mobile applications relax the tethered constraint and allow the approving manager to authorize a requisition from anywhere, at any time. This means critical purchase orders, such as those impacting important customers or projects, must no longer wait in a queue until the manager returns or be expedited as an exception because the approval process is slow. Exception purchases often mean companies must pay more for products and services than necessary simply because the purchase is rushed and a lower price or more favorable shipping terms can't be negotiated with the supplier.

Mobile applications can play an important role in streamlining and monitoring approval workflows. Managers can receive alerts on a mobile device that orders await their approval. More advanced order-approval applications allow mobile managers to review an order and either approve it, deny it, or submit questions to the requisitioner about the order. They can also append comments about why certain purchase requisitions were denied or ask for clarification.

Receiving and Payment Workflow Enablers

While the product supply chain is being actively reengineered, the payment supply chain lags far behind, with most companies still working under 60- to 120-day payment cycles. Many companies are focusing their efforts on implementing mobile solutions to improve their order workflow while ignoring the need to bring the same types of solutions to two processes: receiving and accounts payable.

Receiving and payment processing are long-neglected business areas where only minimal technological and business process innovation has occurred. Managers at many firms don't even know where the company's receiving dock is or how the accounts payable process functions. It is important to remember that errors made during the receipt of products dissipate the efficiency gains that result from improvements to the front end of the procurement process. With the compression of the supply chain, receiving and inventory putaway processes are being carefully reexamined. Optimization of these processes should allow companies to save time, cut costs, reduce inventory, and speed up service to their customers.

The workflow associated with receiving is full of inefficiency.

In large companies, central receiving is responsible for the receipt, general inspection, and identification of all incoming product shipments. Receiving is responsible for promptly notifying all interested parties of the receipt and condition of incoming shipments. They must also deliver the merchandise to the requesting party and provide them with a receiving report verifying delivery. The receipt of partial shipments and shipments containing damaged goods are far more involved tasks. Lastly, upon receipt of a shipment, the quantity received is noted and forwarded to accounts payable for invoice processing.

To improve efficiency, mobile scanners are being used by corporate receiving departments. Over the past twenty years, handheld technology has advanced well beyond simple scanning. For example, today's handhelds can download the original PO at the time the shipment is received, allowing the checker to display each item and confirm its receipt. Verifying the receipt of all purchase-order items initiates the accounts payable process. As with all reengineering efforts, reducing the number of steps and paper-based transactions involved in the receiving process through automation can bring substantial benefits.

Supply Chain Execution

Keeping customers satisfied means companies must fulfill customer orders correctly and within the time frame promised. Supply chain execution—the process of fulfilling customer-specific needs for goods and value-added services in a timely, efficient, and cost-effective manner—is a key differentiator in competitive markets.

Take, for instance, the trillion-dollar grocery industry. Behind the products at any local supermarket is a massive industry that is undergoing structural changes. With global consolidation reshaping the retail grocery industry, producers, suppliers, and distributors are seeking new ways to inject efficiency into a business that is hampered by outmoded processes—from fax and phone orders to paper-based forms sent in triplicate via mail. Also, consolidation implies that few major players control the supply chains, and in turn they are forcing their suppliers to be more efficient. As a result, supply chain execution is gaining in strategic importance.

Current trends show that companies need more and more detailed information to better coordinate, optimize, and execute the supply chain. The market for supply chain execution apps is growing due to two major factors:

- **Lack of visibility increases risk, cost, and time.** During the past decade, many businesses reengineered their internal processes to increase efficiency and improve the quality of the goods and services they provide. Their current focus is on achieving the same operational improvements by enabling better visibility in their relationships with their supply chain partners.
- **Ability to manage bottlenecks.** As part of their new external focus, company executives have discovered how supply chain

planning applications often produce unrealistic and idealized plans. For these applications to work, they must be updated constantly with real-time data to adjust the plan's projections to real demand.

Traditionally, mobile applications were used extensively in managing warehouse and transportation operations. But now the focus is shifting to integrating these operations with planning systems and other enterprise software. The results of this trend are new applications of mobility in three key business functions: warehousing and inventory management, inbound logistics and transportation, and outbound finished-products distribution.

Mobility in Warehousing and Inventory Management

Warehousing and inventory-management strategies seek to minimize inventory risk and out-of-stock situations, and to maximize inventory turns. These strategies track and manage the movement of product from the supplier to the customer. They focus on providing exceptional customer service and faster, more accurate order delivery. Today's mobile solutions support warehousing improvement efforts by offering a wide range of wireless handhelds and truck-mounted readers that are being deployed to increase the efficiency of the warehouse operations.

A typical warehouse deals with a large array of items. Bar code scanners are used to track pallets of inventory that are shipped and received. The scanners update the master inventory records for the item received or shipped, providing an accurate, real-time count of on-hand amounts. For example, when a product comes into the receiving bay at the warehouse, the bar code tag is scanned. The code contains the product description, quantity, lot number, and pallet number. The item information is then instantly transmitted to an access point, which in turn is linked to a warehouse PC and corporate server. The warehouse PC processes the product data and generates a putaway list, indicating the warehouse storage location. This putaway task is automatically downloaded to the appropriate forklift operator, who retrieves the pallet of product and places it in the required location. Technological advances such as these are responsible for significant increases in warehousing efficiency.

Inventory management is also performed at the store level. Most retailers count every item on the shelf twice a year. The cost of this process for an average grocery store is estimated to be around $20,000 to $30,000. Now imagine the cost if you are a grocery retailer like Kroger, with more than 1,500 stores. To speed up the process and also make it more accurate, many store workers conduct in-store inventory using industrial handheld computers (HHC) with laser scanners. The simple process is similar to the warehouse process discussed above. Scan an item, verify its information, and log it to the inventory master file on the company's corporate server. In both scenarios, important information is collected instantaneously—and manual rekeying and volumes of paperwork are eliminated.

Mobility in Transportation and Logistics

Transportation and logistics are integral to every supply chain. Today's logistics and transportation industries are characterized by widely dispersed assets, tight delivery schedules, and minimal room for process error. Transportation management is required at key points throughout the entire shipment's life cycle, from acquiring the raw materials or components to making the product, sending it to the distributor, and delivering it to the customer. Transportation management applications provide customers with the ability to track their shipments across a network of multi-modal transportation.

The U.S. Postal Service provides an excellent example of where improvements can be made to the logistics and transportation functions within the supply chain.

The Postal Service moves millions of parcels across international borders. Unlike UPS or FedEx, each of which has its own fleet of jets, the U.S. Postal Service relies on a variety of third-party transportation resources to move mail. Each handoff increases the chances that a shipment will be mishandled. When mail arrives at its intended destination, ramp clerks go from plane to plane and manually complete a series of paper forms to document and track "mail-handling irregularities." These include anything from weather damage to mechanical problems that may have been responsible for the flight and the mail being delayed. The completed forms are later given to other employees for processing. Often, the information is incomplete or improperly recorded, or the handwriting is illegible.

As a result of these problems, the U.S. Postal Service initiated a program to improve the mail delivery process. Their goal was to implement an automated data-collection system to monitor process performance. With the aid of systems integrator Ciber and Aether Systems, the Postal Service developed a performance tracking system to monitor the airline carrier and shipment delivery performance. Using handheld scanners, ramp clerks enter data for each mail container and synchronize it, via an Ethernet connection, with the U.S. Postal Service's corporate databases, eliminating manual data entry and the need to interpret handwriting.

The system works as follows: International letters and parcels are placed into large containers before they are loaded onto an aircraft. Each container is bar-coded with the flight number, mail container number, and its final destination. Ramp clerks scan each container's bar code and send this information to the corporate database, where it is instantly available to the entire network. The system enables the tracking of any mail-handling irregularity, such as an airline's failure to load a bag of mail onto a plane.

It is expected that the system will greatly improve the flow of mail and reduce mishandling fines for airline carriers. Data collected by the system will be used to improve existing process performance, identify routings that need to be changed, allow trend analysis on types of incidents, and enable the Postal Service to work with its vendors to improve their performance.

Mobility in Distribution "Last Mile"

Distribution management encompasses the entire process of transporting goods from manufacturers to distribution centers consumers. Mobile applications give distributors faster access to shipping, tracking, and delivery data. For example, Kraft Foods uses handheld computers to capture delivery quantities for the products it distributes. The company includes the world's largest cheese brand (Kraft) and the world's number-one cookie and cracker maker (Nabisco). Other well-known Kraft brands are Oscar Mayer meats, Post cereals, and

Maxwell House coffee. The firm distributes products directly to local supermarkets with a company-owned truck fleet.

Handhelds are a key component of Kraft's service delivery process. Kraft's first-generation mobile system is based on handheld computers with six-line screens, a built-in keyboard, and a DOS operating system. When delivering an order to the back-door receiving area of a local supermarket, a truck driver unloads the shipment and then records any changes to the order in the handheld. In cases where the supermarket chain supports Electronic Data Interchange (EDI), the driver connects the handheld computer directly to the supermarket's computer system and transfers the delivery data. When the driver later returns to the distribution center, the daily transaction data is uploaded from the handheld into the company's back-end systems and any updated delivery information for the next day's route is downloaded.

Many mobile systems experience a key design problem. Information from the handheld device is often sent to multiple back-end systems through a number of transfer points. Just as having too many handoffs in a manual work process increases the risk of errors, too many transfer points increases the risk of system failure. If the mobile platform is not carefully chosen and the architecture is not properly designed, there will be daily problems resulting in extremely high cost of ownership. Kraft is deploying a new-generation handheld system to address the transfer point problem. Using a Windows CE–powered pocket PC as the solution's platform, the company upgraded handheld capabilities with enhanced communications and development tools to provide improved back-end system integration.

The use of mobile applications in the delivery chain is commonplace for trucking companies and delivery services. A pioneer in this area was Frito-Lay. In the early 1980s, the company developed handheld applications that helped delivery drivers keep track of products they delivered and also to count the amount of product on the shelf. More recent distribution management applications have been designed to integrate with transportation planning and scheduling.

Within the next decade, global positioning satellites (GPS) and automatic vehicle location (AVL) are expected to be widely used in the delivery industry. Firms will deploy these state-of-the-art communications tools in order to have continuous contact with their drivers and to map delivery routes. For example, Roadnet and Descartes routing systems use a satellite geocode to plot customers on a longitude and latitude grid and calculate the most logical delivery route. This tool also enables truck dispatchers to know where drivers are at all times.

Supply Chain Visibility

Customers increasingly expect to be able to find out the location and status of their orders whenever, and from wherever, they want. To better monitor and optimize asset utilization, they need visibility into inventory in motion (incoming raw materials and outbound finished goods), inventory at rest (inside a factory or distribution center), and a real-time view of their assets. Customers also want immediate notification if supply chain performance fails to meet the standards outlined in the company's delivery terms and service agreements.

Supply chain visibility requires the technological ability to match a unique customer transaction with that customer's products as they flow through the supply chain. This matching process is often done manually or through visual inspection and increases the potential for error. Today's companies are seeking technologies that, using either a customer serial number or pallet ID, enable the tracking of products from the original product components to the product's receipt by the customer.

Many manufacturers, suppliers, and retailers are banking on real-time supply chain visibility to make them more competitive. The U.S. Postal Service and Kraft Foods examples illustrate the importance of bar coding as a way to identify product shipments and to gain greater visibility into a product's physical location and status as it moves through the chain. The bar code is an excellent historical example of the power a single technological innovation can have in changing core business process functions.

Bar Code: Changing Supply Chains Forever

On June 26, 1974, a pack of Wrigley's spearmint gum was passed across a newly installed NCR scanner at Marsh's Supermarket in

Troy, Ohio, earning its fifteen minutes of fame as the first consumer item bearing a Uniform Product Code (UPC) code ever to be scanned. From that point on, retail supply chains were never the same.

The UPC system, which assigns each type of food or grocery product a unique code, was created when the Ad Hoc Grocery Committee, a group of supermarket executives and food manufacturers, jointly agreed to establish a standard product identifier for all packaged foodstuffs, regardless of where the products were manufactured or sold. The committee also agreed to develop automated checkout stands containing technology capable of processing the code. The new code would be a universal identifier represented by a small rectangle of black and white bars.

The need to improve supermarket efficiency was the primary driver behind the bar code's creation. Supermarket net margins had dropped to less than one percent by 1970. The industry had limited control over rising shipping, commercial space, air-conditioning, and other service costs. However, one large expense was controllable: They could improve their margins by reducing personnel. Costs for checkout clerks and baggers were a significant part of a supermarket's costs. With an automated checkout line, clerks could use the time saved to bag the groceries themselves, thus eliminating the bagger's position. If manually labeling each product with a price could be eliminated, staff size could be reduced even further, resulting in more payroll reductions. Automating the checkout line would also reduce human error at the register.

Alan Haberman, governor-at-large of the Uniform Code Council, provides another key reason for the bar code's creation: "As an industry, we were so damned conscious of the fact that the checkout experience was the least pleasant experience in a store. It was the thing that people hated! They hated having to wait in line! They hated having to watch the checker's action. It was an unhappy place."[4] By focusing on improving the quality of the customer's checkout line experience, the industry pioneered a symbol and systems that have transformed supply chains worldwide.

During the twenty-five years since its adoption, the bar code has enabled the creation of important new applications ranging from tracking customer buying habits to managing inventory. For example, bar code technology was key to breakthroughs such as Efficient Consumer Response (ECR) and Quick Response (QR). Both of these technologies capture on-demand data using point-of-sale or point-of-use devices. ECR and QR transformed the retailer's ability to hear the voice of the market and to respond directly to it. Bar codes are a case in which technology sought markets, markets found unappreciated properties, and retailers exerted themselves to translate properties into supply chain capabilities that resulted in tremendous value.

RFID Tags and Auto-ID

In recent years, new applications have been developed that complement bar-code functionality. These applications permit the tagging and tracking of physical goods. For example, Radio Frequency ID (RFID) tags are tiny computer chips and miniature antennas that are often packaged together and are smaller and lighter than a postage stamp. The tag's readers, known as "interrogators," allow companies to track products and materials. RFID systems use low-power wireless signals to read and update information on a "tagged" item or component. They provide the same levels of supply chain visibility, from manufacturing through postsale asset tracking, as do bar codes. However, unlike bar codes, the signals don't require line of sight or manual scanning.

One of the big benefits of RFID technology is that it streamlines the movement of goods through a supply chain. As a result, RFID systems are being used in airport baggage handling systems. For instance, at the San Francisco International Airport, RFID tags are affixed to passenger bags. The tags are then used to move the bags through a labyrinth of conveyor belts and security checkpoints. Another application of RFID tags can be seen in libraries, where the tags are affixed to books. Patrons insert their library cards into a self-checkout kiosk and then scan the books, which updates the library inventory and deactivates the RFID tag.

Auto-ID technology is a recent extension of the RFID method. MIT's Auto-ID Center has developed a numbering scheme—the "Electronic Product Code"—that is embedded in a microchip with wireless antennas. The microchip transmits a unique item-level product code signal when exposed to energy from a reader. This code identifies products individually, not just by product type, as today's

UPC codes do. When the Auto-ID readers in warehouse or retail stores intercept a tag's radio signal, which contains the product code, they use the code to identify the product and track it as it flows through the supply chain. The microchips used in Auto-ID technology are currently too expensive to place in individual products and instead are being used on pallets, totes, and containers. In the near future, as the price drops, individual item tracking within the supply chain will become a reality.[5]

The bar code, RFID, and Auto-ID technology extend visibility more deeply into supply chain performance. However, despite today's sophisticated technology, successfully managing supply chain visibility and performance hinges on the accuracy of transaction data captured at the item level.[6]

Visibility in Health Care: The Case of Clinical Trials

Process visibility is important not just to well-functioning product supply chains but to complex information chains as well. Clinical trials in the pharmaceutical industry are one example. Clinical trials are undertaken to determine the effectiveness and side effects of a drug and to compile data used in the making of new products. Many of these studies are performed using patients in remote locations and require them to record data in a diary on a daily basis.

However, manual data collection in a clinical trial setting is error prone. Patients participating in the trial make data entry errors and are not always reliable when recording the information the drug companies need. For example, some patients dislike completing lengthy data-collection forms because of the effort it takes. Other patients procrastinate and may update their patient diary at the last minute, perhaps attempting to re-create several weeks' worth of experiences while sitting in their doctor's waiting room. In spite of the pharmaceutical companies' monitoring of diary data, the companies cannot be certain of the data's validity and consistency.

Phase Forward is one firm whose offerings address this data-collection problem. The company provides software to the pharmaceutical industry for research and development, sales and marketing, and clinical trial management. It has designed an electronic patient diary, the "NetTrial CE-Diary," to solve many of the logistical challenges posed by large-scale clinical data management and paper-based data collection.

Patients use the handheld device to record their status from home. The NetTrial CE-Diary application gathers the patient data using online forms. The electronic diary supports self-administered clinical trial questions. In addition to capturing a patient's medical condition, the application time-stamps every entry session, which lets the physicians and the drug company better understand the side effects of dosage and other harmful interactions by tracking what the patient is eating and other drugs the patient is taking. The application also has an alarm that notifies patients when it is time to enter data. During the course of the trial, a patient visits the physician's office to submit the data. The doctor transfers the information from the NetTrial CE-Dairy to Phase Forward, where it is collated and forwarded to the drug company for analysis.[7]

The CE-Diary increases the speed and accuracy with which drug companies, such as SmithKline Beecham, can obtain clinical trial data. Using electronic data collection, the drug companies can review data far more quickly than they could if they had to wait until the study ended. Such quick access to information gives drug companies the option of contacting a study site or patient to ask questions or following up with physicians. The application also allows the drug company and physicians to manage patients more carefully. The use of mobile devices in speeding up clinical trials will be a huge advantage for forward-looking pharmaceutical companies.

Six Sigma and Supply Chain Visibility

Asset utilization and quality improvements are the focus of many supply chain efforts to achieve sustainable growth. The Six Sigma methodology applied to supply chains is the cornerstone of these initiatives. Simply stated, Six Sigma is a method that concentrates on eliminating defects from work processes. A defect can be anything that results in customer dissatisfaction, and as defects go down, so do costs and cycle time, while customer satisfaction goes up. Six Sigma literally means 3.4 defects per every million occurrences.

Traditionally, Six Sigma has been applied to processes within the company. More recently, there has been a growing tendency within companies like GE and Dupont to apply Six Sigma techniques to improve quality in supply chains. To reduce supply chain defects, companies are increasingly focusing on tools that enable better visibility through more real-time data collection.

One company that is doing innovative work in supply chain visibility is Savi Technology. Their product, Smart Chain, enables every supply chain event across land, sea, and air to be tracked and monitored in real time. The objective is to enable immediate responses to unexpected events, preventing time-critical, expensive catastrophes from occurring. Real-time visibility provides insight as to what product is flowing through and where it is at all times. The data collection is done by leveraging existing EDI data and legacy interfaces, or tracking in real time via RFID. The Smart Chain platform collects data and translates it into meaningful supply chain information about assets, inventory, shipments, and orders.

One interesting example of supply chain visibility comes from the defense arena. In 1990, the U.S. Department of Defense was preparing for war. The Army shipped 40,000 containers to the Persian Gulf for Operation Desert Shield (later called Desert Storm), then had to open up 25,000 of them to see what was inside. The Army estimated that if an effective RFID way of tracking the location and content of the cargo containers had existed at the time, the DoD would have saved roughly $2 billion.[8]

The problem that the Army faced is not unique. It is something every large enterprise is wrestling with as supply chains get more compressed and pieces of it get outsourced. Watch this convergence of Six Sigma and supply chain visibility for some significant innovations.

Mobile Service Management

Service delivery is the final task in a finished-goods supply chain. A variety of new mobile applications are currently being deployed to increase asset utilization and speed of service delivery functions.

Sears, Roebuck, for example, wanted to maximize the time employees spent with the customer. Currently, employees have to leave the customer to go to the stockroom, where the company's point-of-sale and inventory workstations are located. In what may be the largest deployment of handheld computers, Sears is giving its stockroom staff and salesclerks handhelds to use for inventory tracking, shipping, receiving, and price checks. Sears sees the handhelds as a means of increasing customer face time because they help to reduce the number of trips to the stockroom for inventory checks.[9] Also, the handhelds' simple interface helps compress new-hire training time, which is important because workforce turnover in the retail industry is high, with some employees staying only a few months.[10]

Service companies are positioning themselves to help meet customers' demand levels of product quality and service performance by offering solutions in three primary service areas: reverse logistics, field force management, and mobile dispatch.

Reverse Logistics

Generous product warranties have resulted in a growing trend of customers returning products. The returns process at many companies is the least customer service oriented. Indeed, it often seems that a company will go out of their way to create a negative returns experience, in some cases even antagonizing or humiliating their customers. On the other hand, some firms, such as Nordstrom and Wal-Mart, deliver an exceptional returns experience. It is no coincidence that both of these companies enjoy high levels of customer loyalty and satisfaction.

Reverse logistics manages the movement of goods back through the supply chain from the customer to their point of origin in the most efficient and cost-effective way possible. However, supply chains are designed for products and services to flow in one direction only—downstream to the customer. As a result, product returns, whether due to a product defect, spoilage, or customers changing their minds, present significant challenges for a business process optimized to move products forward. In addition to the strain they place on the supply chain, returns also impact company financials since they must be reconciled with the company books as the purchase transaction is rolled back.

Mobile technology is especially useful in returns processing. For example, Webvan, the now-defunct home delivery service, delivered a high-quality customer experience by using handhelds to track deliveries, client accounts, and other information. When couriers went into the distribution center to pick up their deliveries for the day, all the information they needed was downloaded into a mobile handheld. When the delivery person arrived at the customer's home with the order, the mobile handheld displayed the customer's name, address, phone number, and the items included in the order. During the dropoff, if the customer wished to return certain products, the delivery person entered the information into the device and generated an instant credit that was applied against the new bill. The driver also had a small printer, which printed out an updated customer receipt.[11] The entire returns process was easy and convenient.

Most companies neglect reverse logistics because of preexisting inadequate systems, inefficiency in personnel distribution, and/or cost implications. As a result, companies are wasting billions of dollars in returned goods. This is bad for profit margins. We expect reverse logistics to be an active area for mobile applications.

Field Service Management

AAA is one of the largest providers of roadside assistance, with a membership of more than 45 million people. Not surprisingly, the volume of service calls the company receives is astounding. In 2000 alone, AAA answered more than 30 million calls for roadside help to fix flat tires, fill empty gas tanks, boost car batteries, tow vehicles, and open locked cars.

In the past, AAA used a two-way radio system to dispatch its field units. However, only limited amounts of information could be transmitted to the company's fleet vehicles and field contractors with this system. Using two-way radios also resulted in miscommunications between dispatchers and drivers, which ultimately increased waiting times for customers.

To address these problems, AAA initiated a mobile strategy whose primary goal was to reduce customer wait time. The project's secondary objective was to make roadside service information gathered by AAA's drivers available to the company's other software systems. For example, the firm's billing process would be streamlined by having drivers enter service information and billing details directly into the records management system using their mobile data terminals.

Under the new mobile system, customer assistance calls are wirelessly routed over the Cingular Network to the nearest call center. The call center verifies the caller's membership and obtains other incident information. Incident details are then forwarded to the RIM 950 Wireless Handheld of the closest available driver. An estimated 2,100 AAA fleet vehicles are equipped with the service. AAA's mobile strategy achieved the company's primary goal, reducing customer wait time by up to fifteen minutes per call in some regions.[12]

Field service companies, from small repair businesses to large corporations, are seeking to automate the costly, unproductive and paper-intensive processes associated with performing field service. The improvement efforts focus on every major field service process, including communicating with company headquarters, receiving work assignments, completing work orders, submitting billing information to accounting, and ordering parts. The primary goal of these efforts is to increase field technician productivity by removing mundane and time-consuming data-entry tasks.

In the typical mobile field service scenario, the customer contacts the call center. A call center representative enters a work order. Once the work order is processed, the job notes, billing, and parts information from the order are automatically updated in the system's dispatch and accounting applications. This information is then sent to the relevant field technician's handheld PC, and the technician performs the work. In case of a problem, the technician can use the handheld device to communicate with the dispatch center directly. The dispatchers thus have real-time, accurate status information about any technician or work order. Once the order is completed, the billing information, including time and materials, is sent by the technician to the accounting system. Such immediate invoice updates greatly improve cash flow and enable billing to be accomplished in hours or days rather than weeks. Billing clerks no longer waste time entering job information. This reduces data-entry errors, further speeding up the billing process.

Field service processes can also be improved through the deployment of telemetry applications. These applications use wireless modems installed in equipment assets from computers to elevators at the customer's location to replace expensive dial-up lines or private data networks. Many organizations can use telemetry to monitor remote equipment such as vending machines, security systems, and meter readers. Telemetry applications proactively monitor the status of equipment assets by sending an alarm when certain threshold conditions are reached. The result is automatic dispatching, reduced field service management costs, and faster service.

Emergency and Non-Emergency Vehicle Dispatch Solutions

Vehicle dispatch and identification applications complement field service solutions. There are two types of vehicle dispatch and identification applications:

- Civilian emergency—police, fire, and ambulance
- Non-emergency—taxi, shuttle, private fleets, and couriers

For obvious reasons, emergency and public safety technology has historically been an area of steady innovation. Today, police vehicles have applications that allow officers to obtain real-time information from local, state, and national databases. These onboard devices give law-enforcement officers remote access to filed incident reports and other paperwork. Ambulances are also enabled with applications used to transmit patient data before the vehicle arrives at the hospital, which reduces time and thus saves lives.

Mobile solutions for commercial vehicle and private fleet management are also an active area of innovation. For example, Boston-Coach began operations in 1985 with three cars and has now grown into a service providing 935,000 rides a year in 450 cities. The business quickly set the standard for high-quality luxury vehicle service. The service is entirely reservation-based—no payment is accepted or tipping allowed in a BostonCoach vehicle. The company uses the same computerized reservation systems that travel agents use and also takes reservations via its Web site. BostonCoach passengers—typically corporate employees with a travel account—simply sign a voucher at the end of their ride.

In its early years, BostonCoach used traditional methods—voice radio—for linking drivers and dispatchers. But by 1993, there were simply too many drivers vying for the limited radio bandwidth. Drivers trying to get an open channel to call dispatchers often experienced delays, and deciphering directions garbled by static radio transmissions was frustrating. The problem became a major concern for the company's management, which had prided itself on the company's reputation for reliable, high-quality service.

To solve the problem, BostonCoach upgraded its communications technology by installing mobile data terminals (MDTs) in each vehicle. The MDTs allowed drivers to communicate directly with a host computer system, freeing dispatchers to devote more time to ensuring efficient use of the fleet. Drivers received text instructions and directions on their MDT displays. Most driver-to-dispatcher communications were accomplished with a simple press of a button. The use of MDTs led to a doubling of daily ride volumes, with only minimal additions to back office staff.

Initially, the MDT systems greatly enhanced dispatch operations. However, they also had their limitations. The systems were expensive, limited in functionality, and used proprietary operating systems and hardware. The bulky terminals were not portable, which was a major disadvantage at locations, particularly airports, where meet-and-greet drivers needed to leave their cars.

To support the company's growth and improve efficiency, Boston-Coach developed a new system using handhelds running Windows CE.[13] There were three primary system requirements:

- It had to be small, mobile, and easily removed and operated. This would allow drivers to carry the unit with them when they were out of the vehicle greeting customers.
- It needed to function on a ubiquitous wireless network. This would ensure that the system solution was not constrained by one wireless provider or mobile service with limited service coverage.
- It had to work on an operating system that could enable easy integration with the company's back office systems.

At the end of each ride, the trip's data is sent via a wireless modem to the dispatch office over the wireless network. It takes only a few seconds from the time the driver presses the "Send" button until the system acknowledges receipt of the data. Ride billing data is transferred directly from the driver's data terminal into the back office systems, which ensures that customer billing is done quickly and accurately.

Linking Mobile Supply Chain Scenarios to E-Business

Everything a business does is under the umbrella of either a supply or service process—from developing and selling products to supporting customers and ordering materials from suppliers. It should be obvious by now that these processes have gone through unprecedented change in just a few years. Processes have changed, relationships have changed—and technology has changed everything. Once you get beyond all the glitter and hype, the fact remains that the Web and mobile technology are fundamentally changing the way supply chains operate.

Faced with change of such incredible magnitude, it's critical for companies to avoid major missteps as they reconfigure and speed up their supply chains to meet new threats and opportunities. There's simply no rational way for a traditional business to evolve into a mobile business while tenaciously holding on to the supply chain architecture of the past; the demands of speed, complexity, and internal conflict will inevitably transform the existing processes.

Incorporating mobility into the existing supply chain framework is a process, not a one-time event. As Figure 8.3 illustrates, the linkage between the mobile framework and the e-business application framework is a complex one. Depending on the size, complexity, history, politics, and leadership style of the particular organization, there are any number of different choices and trade-offs that have to be made in aligning the mobile scenarios with the e-supply chain initiatives.

As the relentless drive toward supply chain efficiency and velocity builds during the next few years, deciding how to respond using mobile tools and new processes will only become more important. However, it is important to remember that mobile applications are the means and not the ends. Companies must question whether the promised benefits are real, whether they should participate in mobile activity now or wait, and which supply chain scenario is right for them.

This means that companies will need to understand clearly the broader impact that mobile solutions will have on their business. In particular, managers have to link mobile scenarios directly with the ongoing developmental and decision-making processes within the supply chain. From return-on-investment standpoint, the new mobile applications must serve to improve the efficiency of the supply chain

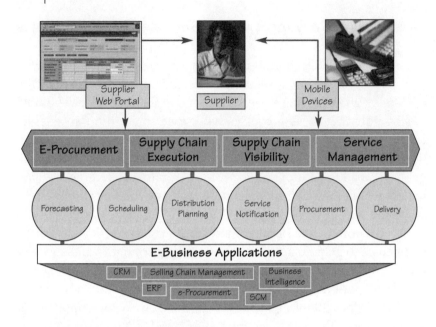

Figure 8.3: Mobile Supplier Framework

or effectiveness of the service chain. If it does not meet this simple test, then it is time to go back to the drawing board and ask: Why are we doing this again?

A Final Thought

The greatest challenge in working with suppliers is getting them in sync with the fast pace we have to maintain. The key to making it work is information.

—Michael Dell

According to Peter Drucker, continuity is a prerequisite for prediction. Prediction fails when it encounters a discontinuity, which Drucker defines as an event or social structure beyond which a prognosticator cannot see. An example is the transition from an economy dominated by tethered models to one dominated by mobile models.[14]

Mobility represents a discontinuity with tremendous implications for real-time supply chains. Already, supply chain management is changing radically with the advent of mobile and embedded devices. Many businesses are currently in the early stages of a multi-year supply chain infrastructure build-out. Automating customer and supplier relationships means upgrading existing systems architecture, infrastructure, and applications from their current PC-centric orientation to one that supports multi-device mobility.

To be competitive, companies in many industries must evolve their supply chain strategies to accommodate increasingly complex issues, including guaranteed delivery of products on a daily basis, the challenge of globalization, and the ability to respond quickly to changes in market demand and competition. It seems intuitively obvious that increasing the quality and speed of information along the supply chain is a strategy that most companies will adopt.

Executives in all firms should think about the implications of mobility on their supply chains. What adjustments need to be made to the infrastructure to support the next generation of real-time supply chains? Starting from a clear understanding of opportunities along the chain will make it easy to build solutions. Unfortunately, it is very hard for managers who are charging ahead to stop and say, "I now want to think deeply about the future."

Well, that is exactly what they will have to do.

Operational Focus: The Next Generation of Business-to-Employee Applications

A growing number of companies are using technology to personalize service for each individual customer. However, few companies have figured out unique ways to address the needs of white-collar knowledge workers and blue-collar manual workers. Increasing employee productivity by reducing "information access blackouts" is a nonstop challenge for companies. Leading firms are addressing this challenge by extending their enterprise applications beyond the four walls of the enterprise to a workforce on the move.

Knowledge is information in motion. Over the past decade, the trend has been toward more effective and easy use of knowledge tools. The purpose of these tools is to increase productivity through the efficient dissemination of managerial, administrative, or customer support information. As a result, companies are deploying more knowledge applications on handheld devices, often distributing a palmtop as employees' primary mode of accessing and inputting data. For example, Weyerhaeuser, a Canadian logging company, sends inspectors out with handheld devices to gather forestry data. The inspectors must be able to work in tight spaces such as helicopters and small planes, so a notebook PC is too large.

Mobile access to critical information is occurring in a number of industries. For example, in the military, the long-term goal is to increase a soldier's efficiency through real-time targeted information. An example is Motorola's Combat Identification System (CIS).[1] Combat identification is the difficulty of distinguishing between friendly and unfriendly forces in the midst of battle, an issue that has plagued battlefield commanders for centuries. The issue is made even more problematic by the increased accuracy, range, and lethalness of modern weapons. Innovations in weaponry have outpaced the current technological capability to accurately identify potential targets.

As a result, individual soldiers need better situational awareness tools than those currently available for determining that an object or person they are targeting is the enemy.

To address the combat identification problem, the military is using mobile technology to deliver a need-to-know view of customized battlefield information for each soldier. CIS is an active interrogation system used by a soldier to quickly determine the status of an unknown target. Its deployment aims to improve situational awareness and reduce the incidence of "friendly fire."

Civilian companies fight process improvement battles daily. Companies worldwide are driven by the fierce competitive environment of restructuring operations to slim down the company, get the lines of communication more open, and reduce layers of management so that they can be more nimble. They are looking at mobile employee applications to deliver improvements by focusing on specific business opportunities.

For example, at a Big 5 consulting firm, managing partners are constantly on the move. Consequently, decision making is slow and simple issues take months to resolve. To solve this problem, the firm is developing an "information at your fingertips" engine to deliver a complete desktop-on-the-road to its traveling managers. The application provides access to e-mail, calendars, and pertinent applications such as profitability analysis, time tracking, and customer data. More-sophisticated features—real-time conferencing and project management—are planned for the second phase of the project.

More and more companies are examining mobile employee applications for three primary reasons:

1. **Business.** Companies realize that employee time is both a limited and costly resource. As a result, they have to fulfill each employee's information needs while keeping costs as low as possible.
2. **Technology.** Always-on mobile networks with continuous data connections are becoming more reliable. Mobile devices are also becoming less expensive and richer in functionality, and more employees are becoming comfortable using them.
3. **Financial.** The payback for a company's investment is quantifiable in the form of cost reduction, quality, and speed.

New Tools for New Times

Mobile relationships are the centerpiece of a new employee customization trend. Employee customization means responding to employee needs efficiently and specifically. Employee focused solutions, such as corporate portals, have widely been acknowledged as being vital to business success. However, the application of information technology to improve the productivity of white-collar, so-called knowledge work has been disappointing over the past two decades.

Peter Drucker has described the failure of technology to improve knowledge worker productivity: "The first thing we have learned—and it came as a rude shock—is about what does not work [in knowledge work]. Capital cannot be substituted for labor. Nor will new technology by itself generate higher productivity."[2]

So, it is unrealistic to believe mobile technology will succeed where other "silver bullet" technologies have failed. Mobility alone will not magically increase productivity. However, it can serve to enhance existing investments in ERP, CRM, and other system frameworks. A mobile infrastructure complements these solutions but is not a substitute for them.

Clearly, corporations must learn to use mobile technology in conjunction with existing technology investments to address three key knowledge management problems:

- The usability of enterprise applications
- Fast, accurate, and streamlined decision support
- Information and data visibility

Current enterprise applications are quite sophisticated at capturing and managing transaction data. However, given their heritage, they tend to suffer from a serious lack of usability. Although functionally rich, their standardized design ignores the specific needs of business users in unique work roles. For instance, if I am a manager in manufacturing, do I really care about marketing information? Give employees information relevant to their job.

Over the years, enterprise applications have been overengineered to the point of being almost unusable. Call it the "all the features that you may ever want but will probably never use" syndrome. As a result, companies are left with oceans of inaccessible repositories with no effective tools for their employees to quickly manipulate or retrieve information. Mobility's value in this context is to solve two problems: provide the information I need in a simple form and do so when and where I need it.

Companies operate based on decisions. Thousands of corporate decisions are made daily, from the office of the chairman to the shop floor. To enable superior decision support, every company wants to enable worker empowerment. The first step is to create a data-access infrastructure to support decision quality and responsiveness. Yet few companies currently have such an infrastructure to support this vision. While the vision is all about empowerment, the reality is pretty far removed. Despite spending millions of dollars, most companies have been unable to create an application foundation to support the movement of information across various departmental and intracompany boundaries. The idea itself goes against every principle of modern organizational theory. To realize its full potential, mobile technology must integrate with large-scale process changes to break down the barriers to information access and to help, rather than hinder, information visibility.

Therein lies the paradox. To be useful, real-time process and transaction data must be both accurate and visible. Quick decisions based on inaccurate or incomplete data cause more problems than they solve. Information visibility is a major problem for many firms. Much of a company's most useful information remains unconscious. This is largely due to "information silos" built over the years, which often characterize large enterprises. These silos typically result from political and turf conflicts where knowledge and information often equal power, status, and job security whether for senior management or line staff. These information barriers fragment corporationwide processes. The problem is magnified when two large companies with completely different cultures and application frameworks merge. Typically, the balance sheets get integrated but the firm's business processes and knowledge bases don't. So enterprise data capture and integration is the pivotal first step of mobile enablement.

Information visibility and process integration issues are even worse in an outsourcing business model. Companies worldwide have forged alliances, decentralized, and downsized based on an outsourcing strategy. Those who argue for outsourcing do so in the name of flexibility and the increased freedom to focus on the firm's core competencies. Outsourcing is a common practice, but the resulting intricate information flows are not well understood.

Companies are looking for new ways to solve existing problems. It is no secret that most enterprises are facing relentless pressure to do three things: reduce the cost structure, improve quality, and increase the speed of processes. Imagine trying to provide mobile access in a typical Fortune 500 company that operates on four continents with as many as 100,000 employees, 200 applications, and 5,000 servers. A nightmarish scenario! Clearly, the challenge is not simply creating new solutions but solutions that can scale effectively. One thing is clear: Implementing mobile technology in many companies is going to take some unnatural acts of process integration. Companies will be forced to deal with deep-rooted integration problems.

Mobile Employee Applications Framework

The objective of business-to-employee applications is to provide employees with control over the various forms of communications they deal with every day. This means having access to the corporate data needed to do their jobs effectively and efficiently, regardless of the employees' location or type of device they are using. To meet this need, companies must deploy a variety of applications to facilitate mobile transactions. A review of different business-to-employee applications can illuminate how mobility can improve employee efficiency. The following scenarios illustrate the different nuances of mobile access in a corporation:

- Company A has more than 1,000 sales representatives who work in groups to sell complex solutions. These representatives need to monitor sales leads, update schedules, access contact information, and coordinate customer responses.
- Global company B has 500 factories worldwide, with divisional managers who constantly travel. To optimize production line scheduling, these managers need to monitor inventory data, production bottlenecks, and incoming customer "expedite" requests.
- Company C has 100,000 employees worldwide who need access to internal applications for expense tracking and time accounting applications. These on-the-go professionals want to use mobile devices to support job-specific tasks and manage workflows in the context of projects.
- Company D is an airline with more than a million customers who interact with it at various touchpoints. To provide outstanding service, the field employees need access to legacy applications that can quickly enable them to help irate customers.

The applications required to address each of these scenarios might, on the surface, appear similar. However, the first requires a mobile office solution, whereas the second requires access to an enterprise application such as a CRM solution. The third context requires a mobile information portal, and the fourth access to specialized or legacy applications. Figure 9.1 shows these four types of mobile employee applications: mobile office applications—messaging and personal information management (PIM), enterprise applications, corporate portals, and specialized solutions.

Mobile Office and Messaging Applications

Handheld devices change the way employees organize their work, manage their tasks, and communicate with coworkers, suppliers, and customers. As enterprise users discover and leverage the benefits of personal information management (PIM) applications—such as contact, address, and schedule management—they quickly come to expect even more PIM functionality and applications. Manufacturers such as Palm and Microsoft realized the need to extend their platform functionality to include:

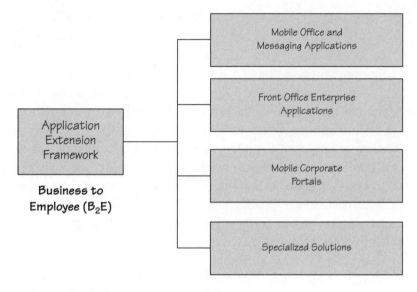

Figure 9.1: AOL Mobile Capability Framework

- Access to corporate e-mail communications such as Microsoft Exchange and Lotus Notes
- Instant peer-to-peer messaging
- Unified or mixed-mode messaging

In the near term, e-mail access and use will drive mobile adoption more quickly than any other feature. Microsoft estimates that there are more than 70 million users of Microsoft Outlook and more than 90 million users of Hotmail. Employees need to access e-mail at work, at home, while out of the office, and while on vacation. Mobile e-mail applications are not only driving the purchase of handheld devices; they are laying the technological foundation for an expanded set of enterprise handheld applications.

Unified and Mixed-Mode Messaging

Today's employees are mixing the modes or channels of modern telecommunications. The following example illustrates how mixed-mode communication works. Tom types a meeting request on his handheld computer and sends it to Jane, Jack, and Bill. Jane is able to retrieve the message on her cell phone, Jack views the request on his pager, and Bill views it on his screen phone. As the number and type of communication devices grows and collaboration between the different channels increases, employees will expect consistency in quality and content between the service and experience on all mobile devices—cell phone, pager, and handhelds.

Mixed-mode messaging is a unique form of collaboration, as the following example illustrates: Barb has dropped off her son, Joey, at soccer practice. Practice ends early, so Joey takes out his cell phone and calls his mom. "Mom," he says, "my practice is over. Please come and get me." However, Barb, a senior VP at a Fortune 50 firm, is sitting in a meeting with her notebook PC opened in front of her. It's wirelessly enabled, and her cell phone is on meeting mode. Barb wants messages received during meetings to be handled in a unified-messaging "store and forward" fashion. Using a speech-to-text translation feature, she gets an instant message from Joey on her laptop. She looks at it and says, "I can't deal with this right now." She forwards it to her husband and writes, "Jim, I can't get Joey for another two hours. Can you please pick him up?" Jim is driving home from work in a car equipped with telematics capability. He gets the message from Barb on the dashboard with an attachment (message from Joey) and the soccer practice location. Jim clicks on the location link and gets the navigational information he needs to go and pick up his son.

A variety of complex technologies support the above scenario, including unified messaging, wireless instant messaging, text-to-speech, speech-to-text, and location-based services. However, the most critical component of each of these scenarios is the context. It is the context that tailors all communication to the needs of a specific individual, device, location, and situation. Context requires the technology to know who a person is, what role they are in, how many mobile devices they carry, which devices are on, and how and from whom they prefer to receive their communications. To meet these contextual requirements, a highly sophisticated infrastructure must be in place.

While mixed-mode messaging may sound futuristic, several solutions that represent the convergence of channels are already widely used. One such application is created by Research in Motion (RIM), which has nearly achieved cult status by offering very usable integrated e-mail solutions.

Research in Motion (RIM)

Research in Motion, headquartered in Waterloo, Canada, was founded in 1984. The company designs, manufactures, and markets innovative wireless solutions for the mobile market. RIM provides "always-on, always-connected" solutions for seamless access to time-sensitive corporate information, including e-mail, messaging, and intranet-based applications, through the development and integration of its hardware, software, and services.

In the beginning, RIM designed and manufactured radio modems for embedded wireless applications, primarily targeting vertical markets. For example, RIM's modems are used in stand-alone automated teller machines, for wireless dispatching in the trucking industry, and in vending machines. These wireless modems are also used in notebook PCs and handheld devices.

RIM's growth is a direct result of the emergence of the two-way pager network. Ericsson's two-way cellular network, Mobitex which is now under Cingular Wireless; and Motorola and IBM's comparable network called Ardis, which is now called DataTAC under the Motient Corporation, created the perfect environment in which RIM could succeed. The company exploited the introduction of these networks by adding a keyboard and monitor together with software to turn their paging product into a user-friendly e-mail device.

RIM's key breakthrough was its ability to address three main barriers to on-the-road usage: the inconvenience of managing multiple e-mail accounts, instant synchronization with the desktop, and corporate security issues. Every CIO was aware of these issues, and RIM was the only solution that addressed them.

Products

At the core of RIM's products is leading-edge radio technology. This technology has been incorporated into RIM's product portfolio, which includes the RIM Handhelds product line, the BlackBerry e-mail solution, embedded radio-modems, and software development tools.

RIM Wireless Handhelds—RIM Handhelds allow users to send and receive wireless e-mail from a device no larger than the palm of their hands. These devices (think of them as pagers on steroids) include pager-size handhelds—the RIM 850 and 950—and palm-sized handhelds—the RIM 857 and 957. Each features a wireless modem, an Intel processor, 4 MB of memory, and integrated e-mail/organizer software. All of RIM's handhelds feature powerful transmitters, sensitive receivers, and long-lasting batteries. Even though the products are "always on," they run on two AA batteries for up to 500 hours.

BlackBerry—BlackBerry is a fully integrated package that includes software, nationwide airtime, and a choice of RIM Handhelds. Black-Berry allows users to send and receive e-mail and integrates with the user's own e-mail mailboxes and addresses. It is also a full-featured connected organizer, with PC synchronization and a wireless handheld with an Intel processor, embedded wireless modem, QWERTY keyboard, and a backlit screen. Recognizing the wide range of e-mail platforms currently in use, RIM customized BlackBerry offerings for different e-mail systems and thus comes in a number of editions—the Exchange, the Notes, and the Internet editions.

Embedded Radio Modems—Computer and radio technology are converging to create a complex technological environment. RIM's radio-modems are high-performance transceivers designed for enterprise applications. The modems are embedded in a broad range of products such as handhelds, laptops, point-of-sale terminals, bank machines, billboards, metering equipment, vending machines, GPS systems, and automobiles.

RIM Wireless PC Card—The RIM Wireless PC Card provides wireless connectivity to laptops, palmtops, and PDAs. The product is compatible with the BellSouth Intelligent Wireless Network and other Mobitex networks worldwide.

Revenue Model

RIM has three sources of revenue: (1) BlackBerry subscriber and service fees; (2) sales of RIM wireless handhelds through channels like AOL, Aether, BellSouth Wireless Data, Motient Corporation (formerly American Mobile Satellite Corporation); and (3) sales of OEM radio-modems.

The company's revenue model may soon be affected by RIM's ability to enforce a key patent. On May 17, 2001, RIM received a patent protecting its method for routing e-mails to wireless devices. The BlackBerry Single Mailbox Integration patent is on both the system and the method used to redirect information between a host computer system (such as an office PC or server) and a mobile communications device (such as a wireless handheld). This is done while maintaining a common electronic address between the host system and mobile device. Using this patented technology, BlackBerry integrates seamlessly with a user's existing e-mail account to provide a wireless extension of the user's regular e-mail mailbox. Users can read, compose, forward, or reply to messages from their mobile devices while maintaining their single, existing e-mail address and mailbox. While other two-way pagers can forward e-mail, their capabilities are limited. For example, if users edit a pager message, the changes won't appear on the desktop version. This patent potentially means that RIM can force a diverse set of wireless-device makers to pay royalties to the company. The long-term value of RIM's patent and its eventual impact on license fees is unclear.

Competition and Corporate Messaging Market

BlackBerry's value proposition is ease of use. More and more corporate subscribers want the ability to send and reply to e-mail in real time using a wireless device, without having to dial in or initiate connections. As a result, RIM's BlackBerry has established itself as a strong presence in the corporate market.

Users of BlackBerry devices are easy to recognize. They enter e-mail messages by typing on PDA-size devices with their thumbs—in the airport, in conferences, at restaurants, or anywhere the network is available. RIM wireless devices are as easy to use as a remote control and allow users to accomplish tasks simply and elegantly. RIM has attained a significant lead over its competition, but it is too early to tell if the company can sustain its current competitive advantage.

Its main competitive concern for the future will be the introduction of Microsoft's Mobile Information Server.

RIM's current competitive advantage stems from technical superiority, lengthy battery life, efficient transfer of data, and simple user interface. There is also considerable technological sophistication behind RIM's wireless "push" solution. One key advantage the company has is its ability to facilitate the transmission and receipt of e-mail in the corporate environment without compromising the corporate firewall. Other wireless e-mail solutions using a common e-mail address, such as Motorola Timeport, have appeared on the market. However, to achieve the common mailbox objective, RIM's competitors' solutions require a company to allow access through the corporate firewall so the vendor's server can synchronize with the company's mail server via remote access. Most security-conscious companies will be highly reluctant to implement any solution with such a requirement.

RIM's competitive advantage also comes from its strong distribution relationships. RIM has partnerships with some of the largest messaging service providers in the world, including BellSouth, AT&T, PageNet, and Skytel. Furthermore, the company has entered into distribution agreements with AOL Time Warner, Dell Computer, and EarthLink to resell the firm's BlackBerry Solution.

RIM currently dominates the e-mail market that is based on infrastructure deployed in the 1980s. A major strategic challenge for RIM will be the coming 2.5G network upgrade, which will accelerate the entry of many new competitors, threatening RIM's near-monopolistic control of the corporate e-mail market. To compete, it is likely that RIM will acquire the firms it needs to fill out the gaps in its product lines. While other wireless companies falter, RIM's balance sheet is strong. As it appears now, RIM is well positioned to evolve from a wireless e-mail provider to a more broad-based mobile platform company.

Front-Office Enterprise Applications

Employees want and expect almost instant access to information. Mobile front office enterprise applications streamline and speed up the flow of information and data to and from mobile workers in the field and the corporate office.

As a result, there are a variety of mobile enterprise applications currently on the market. In the preceding chapter, we reviewed several service management scenarios where mobile solutions "extend the boundaries of the enterprise" by enabling field employees to work while away from the office and still remain fully connected to their organizations. In this section, we will review several sales and merchandizing scenarios that will soon become commonplace.

Many companies are seeking to leverage their existing information technology investments and extend them to the firm's mobile employee. Over the past two decades, most major corporations have spent considerable time, effort, and resources to both automate and reengineer their sales, finance, manufacturing, distribution, human resources, and general office operations. Today's employees are demanding secure, real-time mobile access to their enterprise applications and corporate databases.

ERP applications providers, such as SAP, Siebel, and J. D. Edwards, are enhancing their products to work seamlessly with emerging mobile technologies. This will lead to a wide range of mobile functions in the near future—mobile order entry, inventory management, direct procurement, materials management, and customer management information—increasing an enterprise's operational efficiency beyond that achieved from its ERP system alone.

Enabling Mobile Sales

Selling is a complex and information-intensive business activity, particularly for high-end goods and services. It requires a tremendous amount of preparation—in fact, preparation distinguishes high-performing sales executives from those who are merely average. The latter typically call their office and ask for the customer's account information just before they meet with the customer. This call can be time consuming and unproductive for the office staff, since they are taken off other tasks in order to respond.

The business problem is how to provide the sales force with real-time, immediate access to leads, contact, contract, and current purchase information to support their visits to existing customers and prospects. Some innovative companies are experimenting with mobile solutions to provide their field representatives with accurate information at the point of customer contact. Sales forces everywhere want to bypass the complicated customer relationship management (CRM) applications and instead use lightweight mobile applications to make selling easier.

Consider the following example: A major pharmaceutical company sought to increase the efficiency and productivity of its field sales operations.

In the competitive pharmaceutical marketplace, physician adoption is critical. From the salesperson's perspective, convincing a physician to adopt and use a drug in his or her medical practice requires a considerable amount of face time. Often the sales meeting is conducted over a meal, away from the distractions of the physician's office. Whipping out a laptop in a crowded restaurant to check a price is unwieldy and professionally awkward at best. Also, pricing and configuring orders on a laptop can be time-consuming and cumbersome. As a result, the standard response was "I will get back to you with that information tomorrow."

Mobile information access during a meeting between a sales representative and a prospective customer can reduce the back-and-forth communication that is so time-consuming for both parties.

The pharmaceutical firm adopted a mobile desktop strategy where the salesperson can access needed information from a remote setting, such as a restaurant. The strategy's goal was to create a pocket PC mobile desktop that integrates with the company's SAP R/3 ERP system, is easy to implement, and is continuously upgradable.

The solution the drug company developed was a personalized entry point through which users access mySAP.com MiniApps. The application provides salespeople with product and pricing data, a cost calculator, and inventory and distribution information as well. Salespeople can thus quote prices and delivery information remotely and accurately. They can also check on open issues related to the status of prior orders. Above all, customer satisfaction is greatly enhanced, because questions about products are being answered quickly and correctly.

The next phase in the pharmaceutical company's mobile deployment is to use the application to improve competitive intelligence, identify new selling opportunities, improve the sales closing rates, and increase revenue per customer. For example, the sales force can now use their handheld devices to record which competitors' products are being used by prospective and existing customers. As a result, management has better quality and more accurate data—data that was difficult to obtain in the past—to support decision-making. In addition, as the company's database of detailed information grows, the marketing group anticipates numerous benefits from leveraging this extensive customer knowledge base. Using this data, specific marketing feedback can be generated to identify which campaigns are working and which are not.

Kodak: Enabling Field Merchandizing

Stock market analysts are demanding better visibility into a company's sales pipeline. A major management concern for many firms, particularly global ones, is the ability to gather field data quickly in a usable form. For example, Eastman Kodak, a market leader in traditional, digital, and online photography, with sales of $14 billion, was having considerable difficulty obtaining accurate merchandising data from its field operations. It needed this data to better understand the needs of its customer segments.

Kodak is truly a global company. Its products are manufactured in a number of countries in North and South America, Europe, Australia, and Asia and are marketed and sold through thousands of retailers worldwide. As customer demand patterns became increasingly unpredictable in several of its customer segments, the accuracy of sales merchandizing data from the field declined, seriously impacting the company's decision-making process.

A significant part of Kodak's sales come through its field-merchandizing representatives who work with the retailers. These representatives spend most of their time selling and then reporting to corporate about their sales calls. Under Kodak's old system, the sales representatives submitted their reports verbally using a cumbersome interactive voice response (IVR) system with the ubiquitous "dial 1 for this and dial 2 for that." Typically, the salesperson wrote down information about the sales call after their meeting with the retailer and then made their reports by telephone each evening. Each phone call took five to ten minutes per sales call; with six to eight site visits each day, this resulted in a significant amount of nonproductive time. It took approximately thirty days for the field representative's information to make its way to Kodak's sales account managers and other company decision makers.[3]

Not only did the IVR system make data entry awkward, it was not flexible. Updating information about out-of-stock questions or display compliance rates would take account and field managers a long time. To streamline its data-collection processes and improve information flow, Kodak chose to implement the Field Performance Group's FieldWeb, a handheld sales merchandizing application. The application adds value by increasing the consistency and efficiency with which the field reps capture data. The reps enter sales call information while still on the customer's premises. They can also summarize the results of a sales call, record details about a customer's preferences, and add a new contact's information into the company's account files. At the same time, sales managers get same-day sales call results and more accurate reporting of out-of-stock situations.

The greatest benefit was the resulting real-time data flow directly from the sales force's mobile applications in the field to the firm's financial system. The financial system can use the data to gain better earnings visibility and satisfy stock analyst needs. While the technology itself may seem simple, its successful implementation in a global corporation was a major accomplishment.

Mobile Corporate Portals

Mobile technology is tailor-made to support on-call software applications. In today's 24/7 real-time economy, it is not an exaggeration to say "Isn't everyone on call?" The following scenario illustrates what being on call means today compared to only a few years ago. A physician is on call and gets paged by an application built into his pocket PC. The physician opens her handheld, clicks on the patient identifier, and pulls up all the pertinent patient information by accessing the health maintenance organization's (HMO) secure portal. The portal, accessible to authorized users only, consolidates information from a variety of sources, including patient information files, correspondence, schedules, and clinical information.

Time-sensitive real-time transactions are becoming commonplace. In recent years, enterprise information portals, or corporate portals, have played a major role in making such transactions a fact of daily life. Corporate portals evolved from the concept of the intranet. A lengthening list of vendors, such as SAP, SAS, PeopleSoft, Plumtree, Oracle, J. D. Edwards, and Sybase, have portal products. Corporate portals pull together disparate types of information, including business transactions, customer leads, and inventory information. For example, from a personalized portal, sales representatives can access and manage customer information, view product catalogs, check inventory availability, place orders, and communicate with coworkers, partners, or customers.

Simply put, the business rationale behind the corporate portal marketplace is to provide personalized destination sites containing a variety of useful applications. These applications aim at making it easier for employees to locate the specific information they need in what is often a highly fragmented information environment. Faster access to quality information enhances and speeds decision making. For example, a portal application is linked to an ERP system. The link allows managers to view receipts, invoices, and payment data. Corporate portals seek to provide a single point of access to structured and unstructured information by mimicking the approach pioneered by consumer portal sites such as Yahoo!.

As competition for customers increases, and the speed of response to customer requests becomes more critical, sorting through file cabinets or performing tedious database queries is an unacceptably slow means for acquiring the information a company needs. Consequently, major companies are investing billions in developing corporate portals. The challenge these firms face is how to extend corporate portal functionality to a mobile device. The issue is not whether such extension is technically feasible; it is understanding the business scenarios in which it makes sense to do so. Let's look at three potential scenarios: business intelligence applications, financial portals, and human resource portals.

Business Intelligence Applications

Executive management must determine their strategy for providing their decision-makers with real-time business intelligence applications. The information and knowledge base resulting from the use of such applications will be critical to successful business performance. For example, Sears Home Services implemented a mobile business intelligence application developed by the software company River Run. The application provides 12,500 mobile technicians with wireless dispatch, parts queries, and invoicing capabilities. The goal of the application is to enable Sears to deliver superior customer service, reduce costs, and increase its business volume. The application also allows the mobile technicians' managers to monitor the technician's work activities by tracking key performance metrics such as the time it takes to close a ticket, the number of stops per day, the dollar amount per visit, and the cross-sell ratio.

Mobile performance monitoring and measurement applications provide managers with important process information as to how well the business's operations are functioning. Performance monitoring measurement is not only critical to increasing quality and service; it is the bridge between a firm's operations and its strategy. By using key performance indicators linked to a scorecard, companies can continuously monitor actual performance against the strategic targets. For example, a key trend in manufacturing, especially in Six Sigma organizations, is to increase real-time performance monitoring in order to correct problems in real time.

Companies will be under increasing pressure to develop effective business intelligence strategies as customer demands and expectations increase and the pace of business accelerates. Today's managers are expected to do more in a shorter period of time with fewer resources. Gone are the days when large teams of analysts supported major business units within an organization. Today, rather than a business specialty, analysis has become every manager's responsibility and may soon be the responsibility of everyone in the firm. In such a tense, fast-paced environment, managers need consistent access to relevant business process information and analytic tools tailored to their specific needs. In short, business intelligence solutions must enable decision makers to:

- Minimize the time required to collect all relevant business information
- Automate the assimilation of the information into personalized intelligence
- Provide analysis tools for making comparisons and intelligent decisions

With accurate, real-time data a manager can identify and correct potential problems before they escalate. Accurate real-time information is also vital for companies who wish to capitalize on new business opportunities quickly or adapt when the customer response to a promotion exceeds expectations.

Financial Portals

In the early 1990s, GE and Motorola pioneered delivering consolidated year-end data to their top executives in a matter of days. Since then, the fast financial close has attracted considerable attention from finance departments worldwide. Today, the fast close is becoming even faster and virtual. Cisco's financial systems can close the company's books within a few hours' notice.

Financial portals enable the continuous monitoring of sales amounts, cash flow, product margins, and returns. Efficient management of a company's financials is critical to the firm's successful operation. For example, the hotel operator Carlson, whose chains include Radisson and Country Inns & Suites, requires its managers to oversee financial performance of the regions for which they are responsible. The managers must constantly monitor key financial and guest satisfaction metrics. As a result, Carlson is deploying Compaq's iPaq pocket PCs to its regional managers, each of whom oversees between twenty and eighty hotels. Carlson's solution, Mobile Access to Carlson Hospitality (MACH), began as a way to force managers out of their offices and into the field to monitor hotel financial operations.[4]

The managers configure their mobile units to "subscribe" to different applications. These applications then alert the manager with a tone when important events occur. For example, the device can be programmed to monitor occupancy rates at various hotels. The managers can also monitor a specific hotel's average daily rates to see if excessive discounting has occurred. Monitoring for fraud in high-employee-turnover industries, such as hospitality, is an internal auditing best practice.

Human Resource Portals

HR portals are employee self-service sites and can result in significant cost savings for many companies. Major applications in this category include travel and expense management. Their self-service functionality reduces administrative costs. They are also ideal for reducing the time employees spend making travel arrangements, since they can be customized to comply with a company's travel policy.

For consulting companies with thousands of employees onsite at client locations, HR portals are excellent tools for collecting time and materials accounting data. These portals eliminate the problems associated with paper-based time-sheet systems by allowing team members to record the time they spend on specific projects and submit time sheets in compliance with the company's reporting processes. Providing mobile access to the consulting firm's project management system could save considerable amounts of time. For example, work could be rescheduled due to a delay and those affected would be notified. The link could be used to locate a replacement for a worker when a consultant is unexpectedly unavailable. Each of these examples illustrates how mobile solutions complement Web portal applications.

Mobile portal solutions have to be carefully designed and tailored to meet a company's specific needs. Text entry on current mobile devices is inefficient and unwieldy since there is no mouse or keyboard. Personalizing applications to fit an end user's unique needs can help minimize the amount of data entry and navigation the application requires. Personalization "presets" can be enabled from the PC to reduce the number of steps the user must take. Examples include frequently used parameters such as login/passwords, and start/home pages and menus that automatically load. Minimum data entry with maximum information value is the key to quality mobile device design.

Specialized Solutions

Mobile solutions can also address specialized needs beyond the common requirements of most businesses. For example, in the event of a natural disaster, such as a tornado, mobile applications could prove to be an invaluable aid. For example, a claims adjuster steps through the remains of a house. His company has prided itself on responding more quickly than any of its competitors in helping customers put their lives back together. The adjuster's mobile device works with a digital camera. He completes the claims forms online and attaches the supporting photographs. No time is wasted reentering critical claim information or filing documents back at the office, so claim processing can start without delay. The check to the customer is issued within twenty-four hours.

This scenario illustrates how a basic mobile application, working together with specialized insurance software, can deliver tremendous value. Over the next decade, the mobile enablement of legacy systems will be a major growth business. Most large companies have hundreds of legacy systems that have been built up over the years. In recent years, two major organizations, the New York Stock Exchange (NYSE) trading floor and Hertz, have extended their existing legacy systems into the mobile environment to meet each organization's unique needs.

New York Stock Exchange (NYSE): Trading-Floor Applications

The New York Stock Exchange began with the signing of the Buttonwood Agreement by twenty-four New York City stockbrokers and merchants in 1792. The NYSE is an agency auction market. Trading at the exchange takes place through open bids and offers by exchange members acting as agents for institutions or individual investors. Buy and sell orders meet directly on the trading floor and prices are determined by the interplay of supply and demand.

The Anatomy of a Trade

The dynamics of the trading process are reflected in how investors place their orders. For example, an investor places an order to buy or sell shares in IBM, a NYSE listed company, with a NYSE Member Brokerage Firm such as Fidelity Investments. The broker checks the customer's account, provides the customer with bid-ask pricing information, and enters order details into an order match system. The order is then transmitted to the NYSE trading floor. The order is stored and then, based on the order details and programmed parameters, is routed to a broker's booth or directly to the trading post specialist for the stock.

At the NYSE, each listed stock is assigned to a single post where a specialist manages the auction process. The stock exchange has seventeen post locations. NYSE members bring all orders for NYSE listed stocks to the exchange floor either electronically or by a floor broker. At the trading post, the order appears on the specialist's display screen. The specialist displays the order in the agency auction market and makes the trade, seeking price improvement for the customer whenever possible. As a result, the flow of buy and sell orders for each stock is funneled to a single location. This heavy stream of orders is one of the great strengths of the exchange. It provides liquidity—the ease with which securities can be bought and sold without wide price fluctuations.

At one of the 1,500 broker booths lining the periphery of the trading floor, Fidelity's clerk receives the order on a display screen or by telephone and then enters it into the system. The clerk contacts the firm's floor broker by pager or telephone to alert him that a new order has arrived. The order may be wired, phoned, or physically picked up. The floor broker takes the order to the trading post, where the stock is traded.

Speeding Up the Process

As trading volume increased dramatically in the 1990s, the paging system described above was found to be inadequate. The buy message delivery speed took between thirty and forty seconds. In the real-time business of stock trading, problems with delivering critical messages could have monumental financial repercussions. The New York Stock Exchange needed a fast and reliable system to facilitate communications among associates, brokers, and specialists executing the huge volume of trading that occurred on the floor. In

1997, the NYSE implemented a new paging system developed by JP Mobile and Motorola to reduce the time it took orders to reach brokers on the exchange's floor.

Today, the NYSE operates on a wireless data system (WDS). Its individual traders now use handheld computers. The WDS moves information to and from the point of use with great speed and accuracy. Brokers use their handhelds to both receive orders and to disseminate reports from anywhere on the trading floor with great efficiency. The results are impressive: The wireless messaging system successfully delivers each message in less than four seconds.

Hertz: Laying Out the Gold Carpet

In 1918, Walter L. Jacobs began the automobile rental industry in Chicago. His first fleet was twelve Model T Fords, and within five years his company's revenues had reached $1 million annually. Jacobs then sold his firm to John Hertz, president of the Yellow Truck Company. General Motors acquired the Hertz Drive-Ur-Self System from Hertz in 1926. Today, Hertz is the world's leading car rental organization, with 6,500 locations in 140 countries. They operate a fleet of 525,000 vehicles. In 1994, Hertz became an independent, wholly owned subsidiary of the Ford Motor Company, and in 1997 became a publicly traded company listed on the New York Stock Exchange.[5]

Hertz as a Pioneer

For eighty years, Hertz has been providing its customers with quality service that exemplifies a company's commitment to continuous service improvement. They were the first to offer a "fly-drive" car rental program, which combined the use of a rented car with a plane trip. In 1984, Hertz introduced computerized driving directions, making it easier for customers to find their destinations. The driving directions system allows customers to use touchscreen terminals at airport counters to select a specific hotel, restaurant, or other destination and print out the detailed driving directions.

Another first was the Hertz Instant Return, introduced in 1987, which further streamlined the return side of the car rental transaction. At the car-return lot, a Hertz agent meets the returning customer with an Instant Return handheld computer. Even before the customer gets out of the car, the Hertz agent has begun the return transaction. The agent processes the return on the spot and issues the customer a receipt from a portable printer—usually in less time than it takes to remove the luggage from the trunk.

In 1995, Hertz introduced its NeverLost onboard navigation system. The NeverLost global positioning system (GPS) provides route guidance in the form of turn-by-turn driving directions to virtually any destination within a specified geographic area. The information is displayed on a four-inch video screen, with computer-generated voice prompts, mounted between the driver and passenger seats. In 1998, Hertz released an upgraded NeverLost system through an exclusive joint venture with Magellan Corporation. Navigation Technologies produces the mapping software used to interface with the Magellan-manufactured GPS system. Hertz's customer focus continues to make the company easy to do business with and is a major key to its continued success.

Hertz Continues to Innovate

Hertz's Worldwide Reservations System handles over 40 million phone calls and processes approximately 30 million reservations annually. Ensuring the happiness and satisfaction of all these customers is a top priority. Hertz never stops seeking ways to improve its customer service. For example, the company recently undertook a project to reduce the amount of time customers spend waiting in line. For most business customers, time is money. The typical business traveler is often hurriedly en route to a meeting or to catch a flight. Hertz realized that too much time spent waiting in line might send its customers to competitors.

Since 1989, Hertz has deployed a number of systems designed to streamline the rental process. What began as a voice radio network has evolved into a wireless data network. The Gold Electronic Manifest (GEM) system allows curbside attendants to use small handheld devices to wirelessly transmit the names of arriving customers to the Gold booth. At the Gold booth, Hertz representatives make sure that the customer's car is ready to go and that the customer's name and stall number are displayed on the digital sign. Customers get off the courtesy bus, look for their name, go directly to their cars, where the rental paperwork and map are ready to go, and drive away.

While the current GEM system offers powerful results, it is dependent on an array of complicated technologies. The DOS-based GEM handheld devices communicate via internal or external wireless modems. These modems connect to multiple public wireless networks through specialized middleware residing on both the device and the host server. The host servers are integrated not only with the wireless networks but also to Hertz's legacy Unix-based point-of-sale system.

Hertz's existing system did well at streamlining customer service.[6] But the company is always seeking new ways to improve their customer care strategies. As a result, Hertz redesigned the original GEM system to include centralized processing and use of "open" components to improve supportability. Their new system design also replaces the current local wireless networks with national wireless networks. The goal of these system enhancements is to provide a more positive rental experience for the customer.

The Future of Hertz

The competitive landscape of the automobile rental industry changes daily. It is a fiercely competitive environment where low price alone is not a significant enough differentiator to ensure success. To maintain its strong position in the industry, Hertz differentiates itself not through price, as many of its competitors do, but through its customer-centric service strategy. As part of this strategy, they are now seeking to provide personalized customer service through multiple channels.

For example, Hertz.com Web site visitors are able to download city guides to their handheld computers and PDAs for use when traveling. The Hertz version of the Port@ble Guide, a mobile application from Portable Internet, includes information such as a Hertz location finder, telephone numbers, and operating hours for each branch. The Port@ble Guide also includes interactive maps, local business listings, reviews of local restaurants and hotels, and full address search and driving directions to selected points of interest.

To remain competitive, Hertz must also lower its insurance and liability costs. In the near future, Hertz could conceivably track their cars' locations and build a detailed database on which to base their rental rates and new rate offerings for specific destinations. Furthermore, such location-specific data could reveal usage patterns leading to more favorable insurance rates.

Hertz has been a profitable firm since 1918, with a current #1 Club Gold membership of more than 2 million customers. The company continually seeks new and innovative ways to offer the best and most efficient service to its customers. This customer-centric strategy has served the company well in the past and will continue to do so well into the future.

Linking Mobile Workforce Scenarios to E-Business

Helping employees do their jobs better is a key business driver that necessitates integration with existing e-business applications. Mobile employee needs usually take two forms: the need to know about and respond to unusual events, and the need to monitor ongoing activity. To address these needs, mobile employee solutions must give users personalized access to content and services from inside other enterprise applications and from other sources, such as databases and external content sources.

Mobile employee portals basically present a relevant snapshot of activity within e-business applications. Figure 9.2 illustrates the integration between the mobile employee scenarios and the behind-the-scenes e-business applications through several mini-apps that act as filters or access points. Because not all information is equal in importance, the filters need to be able to define which information is accessible to the users based on their user privileges.

Users can avail themselves of these filters to personalize their own view so they see only the information they need, which makes their interactions much more efficient. This way, users can be instantly notified about events that require their immediate attention. They also can manage the distribution of alerts so they aren't notified about events that don't require immediate action.

How do you initiate the integration effort? As you think about the mobile employee interaction problem, consider where you could produce better experiences for your employees. Don't worry yet about the technology; focus on the business results you want to achieve. The following questions may help identify leverage points in the various processes to improve business results:

- How are your employees' needs and expectations changing?
- What are the missed productivity enhancement opportunities?
- What new capabilities do your employees crave?
- What opportunities to expand employee effectiveness would you most like to enable? What process changes would be required?

Your answers will suggest areas where you should investigate integration with e-business applications. Next, evaluate and prioritize opportunities. Opportunities should be evaluated based on their level of business impact, their market urgency, their technical achievability, and their cost. Managers should look for simple, high-impact appli-

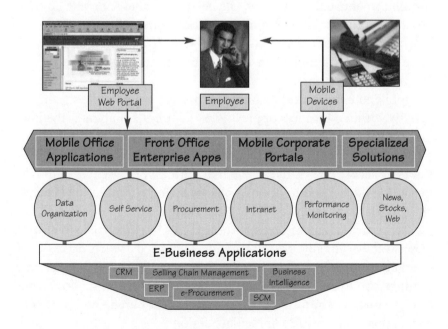

Figure 9.2: Mobile Employee Framework

cations that can deliver short-term return on investment. Quick wins can often justify the cost of establishing a mobile platform on which future applications can be built.

A Final Thought

Airplanes are interesting toys but of no military value.
—Marechal Ferdinand Foch, Professor of Strategy,
Ecole Superieure de Guerre (1911)

"Tools or toys" is the debate raging in companies over employee-facing mobile applications. In a 24/7 environment, companies want their employees to be always available—with access to all the tools and knowledge they need, when and where they need them. Equipping mobile workers with not only e-mail access but with critical corporate intranet information and transaction capabilities is now possible with new application extension technologies. Application extension means expanding the Internet desktop functionality to the mobile device.

The trend toward enterprise application extension is in its earliest stages. As the business velocity increases, companies will have no choice but to implement new employee-facing solutions to improve their competitiveness and service. Managing and streamlining employee-centric information flows will be key to any firm's ability to compete in the marketplace. By thinking broadly about the work challenges employees face, rather than narrowly about job tasks, companies can almost always find ways to not only improve the work process but make it easier for the employee.

Of all the areas of mobility, we expect business-to-employee applications will have the fastest adoption. However, the extension of desktop functionality to mobile devices will most likely take a decade to occur. During this time, companies will experience serious change-management issues. Emerging mobile applications will change the nature of "white-collar" work itself. Mobile technologies not only affect tasks, activities, and processes, they also transcend the boundary between work and private life. They blur the limits between our personal time and space and that which we commit to our employers.

The ability to empower employees with information 24/7 is both liberating and intrusive. Clearly, the challenges mobility presents aren't just technological. They are social and ethical. Unless these challenges receive as much attention and discussion as has the technology, the mobile economy's tremendous potential will be only minimally realized.

The Art of Mobile Strategy

In the 1980s, a Motorola-led consortium envisioned establishing a dominant platform for mobile telephony. The pursuit of this vision led to the founding of Iridium LLC and inspired the development of a system of sixty-six small satellites deployed in low-Earth orbit, enabling communications over virtually the entire surface of the Earth. Operational in 1998, Iridium linked existing terrestrial communications systems, including faxes, pagers, computers, and telephones.

Iridium was designed to address two broad trends in the communications market: (1) the worldwide growth in the demand for uninterrupted portable wireless communication; and (2) the growing demand for communications services to and from areas where landline or terrestrial wireless service was not available or accessible, such as oil rigs in the Gulf of Mexico and towns in remote regions.

The Iridium satellite network was a technological marvel but a business disaster. Iridium embraced a new and unproven technology too quickly, overlooking many of the marketing and sales "red flags." For example, the special brick-size satellite phone was heavy, it needed a host of attachments, and it couldn't be used in a car or building—exactly where users needed it most. Its prospective customers saw no compelling reason to purchase a $3,000 satellite phone when a $200 cell phone would suffice.

In the end the "If you build it they will come" mantra did not work. Iridium declared bankruptcy. It was on the verge of destroying $5 billion worth of satellites by doing a controlled burn in the atmosphere before it was bought for $25 million. Iridium learned the hard way about market timing. The Iridium story illustrates the risks associated with being a first mover in a new and untested market. Even the most highly respected firms can produce spectacular technological failures if customers don't adopt the proposed solution. Any company can put a new platform on the market before it's ready or at the wrong price.

The Iridium case also illustrates the pitfalls of relying on market forecasts. Most market forecasts tend to present a rosy and optimistic outlook that takes much longer than initially thought. In retrospect, Iridium completely misjudged the customer price-versus-value trade-off and underestimated the impact of digital technologies in the mid-'90s . Both of these factors conspired to make its solution either customer unfriendly or obsolete. The vendors who are pushing 3G platform innovation should pause and see if they are not repeating Iridium's mistakes.

The Art of Mobile Strategy: Innovation Versus Renovation

Creating a radical strategy that deals with new opportunities is more art than science. The probability of getting it right is extremely low. It is often easier to focus on an improvement strategy that is less risky and simply extends current markets or processes.

The innovation-versus-renovation dilemma captures the essential difference between evolutionary and revolutionary change. Evolutionary change can be seen in the catalog business. Shortly after the Internet arrived in the 1990s, many pundits began predicting that the Web would kill the printed catalog. It was not unlike predictions that television would be the death knell for printed magazines. Of course, not only did magazines survive, but within a relatively short period the magazine with the largest circulation was *TV Guide*. Most technology predictions almost always hype revolutionary changes, scenarios that seldom come to pass. The lesson: Most change is gradual and incremental; seldom does it take the form of revolutions.

While we are not against revolutions and wholeheartedly believe in the need for innovation, it would be disingenuous to write about yet another "six principles" or "ten laws" of creating innovative strategy. Our experience has been that there is no such thing. Can you learn to paint like Picasso or acquire the sheer inventiveness of Edison by reading a manual? Innovation is discovery. It is hard work and takes both patience and luck. Also, it is one thing to study innovation in the abstract, but entirely another thing to put theory into practice under different circumstances, against different kinds of competition, and on different customer segments. As the Prussian general Carl von Clausewitz wrote, "In war everything is simple, but even the simplest thing is difficult."

On the other hand, the practice of renovation is more fully understood. Renovation is where the dynamic of value creation is examined, taken apart, analyzed, and assembled back into new business models that allow companies to move forward. There are some established guidelines that can help in creating incremental improvement or renovation strategies. Enterprise renovation requires a well-articulated plan, carried out in a coordinated manner by a diverse, multi-functional team that is equipped with different tools. And one thing is certain: Most companies practice renovation rather than innovation. This will also be true in the case of most m-business efforts.

M-Business as a Renovation Strategy

M-business holds tremendous potential for renovating a company's products and services and streamlining its processes. However, as is always the case with corporate change initiatives, successfully moving from a vision of technology's possibilities into a concrete strategy for how to realistically achieve them requires considerable analysis, planning, and discipline. As a result, we anticipate that creating an m-business strategy will be a common concern of both established and entrepreneurial firms in coming years.

Developing an m-business renovation strategy is a lengthy, detailed, and difficult process. Formulating the strategy involves assessing customer and employee needs, developing an m-blueprint based on these needs, and using the blueprint to prepare a comprehensive business case/plan for gathering the resources—capital, labor, and talent—required to make the strategy a reality.

Envisioning how a mobile strategy can improve company performance is far easier than executing the strategy in a way that ensures profit. What makes execution difficult is often the behavioral change needed among the users—customers or employees. Mobility isn't just a product or technology. It can't be purchased and installed. Mobility is a fundamental structural change in business. Before any of mobility's benefits can be realized, it must become integrated with the user's way of doing things. Indeed, mobility's potential contribution can't even be envisioned until the solution has been fully adopted and used by a company's employees and customers.

Remember, first-generation e-commerce conceived of a Web site as an "Internet strategy." First-generation mobility does not need to repeat this mistake. Underestimating the effort required to deploy a mobile strategy wastes time and resources over the long term.

Making M-Business Real

Making m-business a corporate reality involves four key elements: the solution strategy, capability evaluation, the blueprint formulation, and tactical execution (see Figure 10.1).

M-business will work only if it provides a complete solution to a problem. All too often, mobile is simply novel technology in search of a business problem. The first step of any solution strategy is to find and structure a business problem. Simply paving the cow path is not enough. You need to find something that couldn't be done the old way. In established companies, this is most often done by studying the customers in their natural environment to determine gaps between existing solutions and customer needs. For instance, mobile sales force solutions solve the problem of providing remote users almost instant information, a capability unavailable through any other means.

Based on a solid needs assessment, the first step of a solution strategy is to formulate a customized approach for meeting the market's needs and structuring the mobile value proposition. The solution strategy states why the company is pursuing a mobile strategy and what value it will provide its customers.

Once a problem has been articulated and structured, the next step is to figure out what capabilities are needed and what capabilities are at hand to solve the problem. The capability analysis feeds into a high-level blueprint. The blueprint is a statement of the strategic, operational, and technical issues the company must address before its mobile strategy can succeed. Why is a blueprint necessary? No sane person would think of building a house without an architectural plan. Yet many corporations attempt to build large complex applications without a blueprint. The high-level blueprint lays out how the solution strategy is to be implemented and when the firm's customers can expect to experience its benefits.

Lastly, tactical execution is in the frontlines, where strategy is converted into action. Here, usability experts create the user experience, whereas programmers create the applications and integrate the front-end user interface with the company's back-end infrastructure. This phase also focuses on how the mobile applications and devices will work with a firm's existing systems.

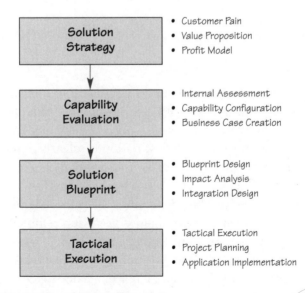

Figure 10.1: Typical Supply Chain Structure

Phase 1: M-Business Solution Strategy

Formulating a strategy requires taking the general concept of mobility and turning it into a viable business concept. Its outcome should be a concise statement of what the company's mobile capability will look like, including the products and services to be developed, a description of the customer, the sales approach, and the revenue model. Ability to articulate the strategy crisply demonstrates that the business concept has been thought out with care and thoroughness.

Today, m-business is still in the realm of hype and potential. Few examples of "success stories" exist. Since no prior models of how it should be done exist, developing a mobile strategy takes considerable effort. The problem? The chicken-and-the-egg dilemma. It is very difficult to justify an m-business investment, since either the customers are not there, the return on investment (ROI) is not clear, or the risk is too great. As a result, companies developing these strategies must adopt an early-stage entrepreneurial mentality and focus on the destination before attempting to map the journey. The following questions help define this focus:

- After our firm implements its mobile solution, the customer is going to do _____.
- After our firm implements its mobile solution, the company is going to be _____.

A clear statement of the destination is critical to formulating a successful mobile strategy. As with any corporate initiative, a clearly defined goal minimizes the risk of a project deviating from its original strategy. Not only must the destination be clearly defined, it must also be measurable. In other words, the company and its customers must have a tangible, verifiable sense for knowing "we've arrived."

Specifying a quantifiable destination requires significant background work and analysis. Companies are often tempted to select a destination quickly, to pick one that has been widely written about or talked about in conferences. Such "momentum strategies" are similar to momentum investing in the stock market. They reflect a company's unwillingness to focus on its own internal issues, unique characteristics, and customer needs when shaping its mobile strategy. Formulating a strategy takes patience and focus—both rare commodities in the time-deprived world of instant everything.

The key to crafting a successful business strategy is well documented in business literature. However, it is seldom followed because it is difficult to do. The first step in developing any business strategy is determining the unmet needs of the customers and knowing what the customer seeks that is novel or unique. The second step is to honestly assess the company's capability for meeting these customer needs and preferences. A capability assessment identifies the skills and resources the firm currently has and identifies how to acquire the ones it doesn't have. Formulating any strategy requires a company to be conscious of its own abilities and limitations. M-business is no different.

M-business strategy formulation involves answering the questions in Table 10.1. It is important to follow the questions' sequence. The questions analyze the customer and business environment first, performing an "outside-in" rather than an "inside-out" analysis.[1] This approach forces managers to take a broader perspective by first focusing on how the customers are changing and then on how these changes will affect the firm.

Is There a Need or Preference?

Any serious attempt to map m-business strategy must start with the customer, his pain, his needs, his expectations, and his values. This is hardly a new insight. Every manager knows that companies should assess the current state of their customers before introducing something new and unproven. Most business processes have inefficiencies

Table 10.1: Questions to Ask When Implementing M-Business

Value Identification	• *Is there a need or preference?*
Value Validation	• *Is there a market?*
Value Creation	• *What is the focus of the value proposition?*
	• *What is the scope of the value chain?*
Value Capture	• *What are the economics of this market?*
	• *What is the profit model?*

that can best be identified by listening to customer dissatisfaction with a company's products or services. Removing the sources of customer dissatisfaction or offering customers a breakthrough on performance can result in major business opportunities.

But awareness of customer service and business process gaps is not enough. You must also understand how to address them. Take, for instance, eBay, which was formed on the very simple premise of facilitating consumer-to-consumer auctions. There was no inventory, no guarantee that merchandise was authentic, and no easy way to purchase or receive goods—it might take a customer a week to buy a $20 item, and another two to three weeks to receive it.

Pierre Omidyar, the founder of eBay, saw an unmet market need and used technology in a unique way to address the need. It is often said that the first prototype of the technology behind eBay took a few weeks to build. Now contrast eBay with Motorola, which has hundreds of employees and consultants conducting customer research. Motorola probably understands the wireless world and mobile customer behavior better than any other company. Yet it frequently falters when attempting to introduce the right product at the right time. The lesson: Opportunities often come from viewing the world differently and from simple insights.

For a new venture, failing to address customer needs can be disastrous. The following scenario illustrates this point: Sam started a B2B exchange linking buyers and sellers in the large but fragmented chemicals industry. He raised a lot of funding very quickly based on the strength of his vision. The new B2B exchange started to ramp up, with Sam purchasing expensive market-maker software from Ariba. He convinced customers to place a few sample orders. He hired a Madison Avenue PR agency to promote the company. After a year, the exchange had only minimal adoption. After spending $40 million, he finally had to declare Chapter 11 bankruptcy.

What went wrong? He never really understood what the customers' needs were in the complex chemical marketplace. Sam's business, like many other Internet ventures, started with a 100,000-foot perspective focused on the cool Web site, the company brand, and how much money the firm could raise. He and his staff seldom discussed in detail the reasons that customers would use their exchange. While they often discussed the potential billion-dollar market opportunity, they seldom discussed the specific customer need at the root of the opportunity.

Many dot.com failures have resulted from too much of a focus on identifying business inefficiencies and not enough focus on understanding the severity of the customer's problem (venture capitalists call this customer pain). Companies must ask if the value they are striving to create *exceeds the cost and effort required to switch or adopt on the customer's side.*

Figure out the customer pain and work to solve this pain. Customer pain can vary in degree. To use a medical analogy, it can be a body ache, migraine headache, or cancer. A body ache requires a nice-to-have solution, whereas cancer requires a need-to-have solution. A new venture must know the degree to which a customer needs its offering before it can have a realistic sense of the venture's potential for profitability and success.

Customers will pay to alleviate pain. The issue is how much they are willing to pay for a solution. Too high a cost for a body ache remedy may mean they forgo the purchase. This simple fact is a common denominator in most strategic failures. Business strategies that ignore this fact are built on a false premise of the degree of customer need. Far more people have body aches than cancer, but most strategies assume that just because everyone has this problem there is a huge market for it. Customers having needs often does not translate into their paying for costly solutions.

Finally, companies must clearly identify the real versus perceived value trade-off. Most strategies never really have a chance to succeed. From the very beginning, the strategy may be based on unrealistic expectations about the company's product and its target markets. Iridium is a prime example of this. The company presumed knowledge of why someone would buy its product without clearly demonstrating a real need for it. Validating the market before proceeding with a product or service offering helps avoid such risk. As we like to say: *Don't scale an imperfect model.*

Is There a Market?

The market-validation process asks the following questions: Who are the customers with this need? What is the size of the potential market?

When will the consumer demand actually materialize? Business executives often presume they know their customers because they've had a conversation with a few of them or have sold products or services to them. However, more often than not, what an executive thinks he or she knows about the customer is more likely to be wrong than right.

Understanding the specifics of customer needs and anticipating them requires in-depth customer knowledge. Such understanding and knowledge can result only from a continuous, ongoing inquiry into what the market needs and wants.

Market validation requires a company to test its product or service to enough customers and noncustomers to confirm the validity and soundness of the offering. Moreover, it provides confirmation of the customer's willingness to pay for the offering. Market validation also enables a company to uncover potential problem areas early on when they can be more easily corrected. For example, in early 2001, Amazon.com made a business decision to pull back on Amazon's Anywhere, their shop-by-phone-or-PDA effort. Although its wireless initiative was a high priority, it was scaled back because the company perceived insufficient demand. Also, the mobile initiative was not in line with Amazon top priority to "get profitable fast." However, this strategy changed by the summer of 2001 as AT&T Wireless launched their high-speed 2.5G network. Amazon Anywhere was relaunched with the same features that have made the retailer's online store so popular, such as one-click ordering, customer reviews, and recommendations.

One approach to market validation is building a prototype and experimenting with real users. This involves showing it to customers or prospects and asking: What will they pay for it? Vendors with whom a customer currently does business usually win a close decision based only on price. Are they willing to change their existing way of doing things? In addition to identifying the willingness to pay, the validation process should also present an argument for why a potential customer would choose the new product or service over the one they currently use. Are they really interested in the new features and functionality? Validation means ascertaining the new tie-breaking features and functions for each customer segment.

Another widely used approach for conducting market validation is to examine customer behavior in complementary markets. Customers who buy from one company also buy many other products and services. After extrapolating from their behavior in complementary markets, a company can apply this information to its own industry. The following questions help determine customer buying behavior in complementary markets: What new products or services in our industry have been popular in the last five years? What customer segments are buying these products or services? Why do these customer segments like these products or services? However, extrapolation techniques can often lead to false conclusions if they are used as a primary form of market validation.

Positioning: Focus the Value Proposition

Once a company has gone through the steps of understanding customers' needs and validating the market, it must further refine and focus its value proposition. Positioning is about addressing the following question: What aspect of your market is not being adequately served and what might you do about it? Very simply, the imperative here is differentiating your product or service. This means specifying exactly what customers will be buying from the firm. Customers buy value. Value includes selection, time savings, quality, lowest price, fashion, experience, brand assurance, or a unique niche solution.

In many markets, terms such as "we're high end" or "we're a discounter" point to how the firm and its product/service offerings are positioned in the marketplace, and how competitors differ on the dimensions of quality, service, and price. For example, compare the value propositions of Dell versus Apple. Dell Computer has a reputation for value and reliability but little creative flair. On the other hand, Apple Computer is all about innovation and style. Apple deliberately targets a customer base of people who enjoy having fun and being creative with their computers. Dell's target is the consumer using e-mail or games at home and businesspeople using the PC for e-mail or spreadsheets.[2]

Value is in the eye of the beholder. Many firms find that the best starting point for refining new solutions is to focus on improving those things customers care about the most, such as price, a fully integrated solution, or speed. Take, for instance, the well-known example of SouthWest Airlines, a no-frills airline. The no-frills aspect comes in the form of scaled-down services (no in-flight meals, no preassigned seating, no travel agents, no coast-to-coast nonstops). In contrast to SouthWest, when Virgin Atlantic, an all-frills airline began in the early 1990s, it had to offer a noticeably superior value proposition to get travelers to switch from British Airways (BA). It had to wrestle with the question: Why would business travelers who are accumulating frequent-flyer miles on BA want to try a unknown brand? To differentiate, Virgin introduced Upper Class service, which offered the larger seats and legroom of traditional first class at the price of business-class service. Virgin further enhanced its value proposition by offering to pick up and deliver Upper Class passengers from and to their destinations. Virgin is now a trend leader, having introduced value-added extras such as onboard masseuses. Many other airlines are now copying SouthWest and Virgin's service innovations.

It's important for companies to identify improvements and new offerings their customers request most often and take the time to document them. Collecting these ideas and focusing the company's efforts on them can reveal business opportunities.

Finally, differentiating the value proposition of a new product or service offering is central to connecting with customers. A common problem many companies have is that their concept of value is far too abstract. A typical example of a value statement is "to create a world-class company that serves its customers through multiple channels." This is a broad mission statement; it is not a value proposition. Value propositions should be measurable, tangible, and brandable.

What Does the Value Chain Look Like?

Creating a new mobile value chain requires an in-depth analysis of the following: What does the end-to-end value chain look like? How is information transformed as it moves along the value chain? What kind of skills are needed at various points in the chain? Who are the content providers, suppliers, resellers, or distributors that are likely to deliver value more effectively?

No matter the simplicity of the value proposition, it takes the well-coordinated effort of a number of companies to ensure its delivery to the customer.

Mapping the mobile value chain will clarify the scale and scope of effort required. It illustrates how information reaches the user and better defines who the customer is in the mobile value chain. In large-scale projects the value chain's complexity is increased, since it is actually composed of multiple chains that are often interdependent. As a result, focusing on a series of small-scale mobile projects has a much greater chance of success than a large-scale implementation.

A value chain perspective is useful in surfacing hidden assumptions about users. For instance, when determining the best approach to selling products and services, it is important to identify the customers at various points along the chain. For example, if a company believes its distributors are its customers, then it might tailor its solution to address distributor needs. The company would focus its solution on making sure the information they provide about products they distribute is accurate, relevant, and useful.

Lastly, it is important to understand how any future changes to the value chain might alter the dynamics of the company's existing relationships. Channel conflict issues must be addressed early on and are fairly common when implementing digital strategies. Existing channel participants naturally feel threatened by the new channels and react accordingly. For example, a traditional salesperson may perceive the mobile channel as a threat and discourage customers from using it. Channel conflicts are serious issues capable of derailing the most well-thought-out strategies.

Understand the Core Economics

Now the going gets tough. Understanding in detail the economics of the solution is what makes or breaks great ideas. Most strategies we have looked at failed because entrepreneurs and corporate intrapreneurs failed to develop a comprehensive and realistic understanding of the economics of their companies' target markets.

Too many executives in start-up firms and ventures talk about the mobile marketplace's potential value as hundreds of billions of dollars and growing. They use this to convince themselves, and possibly potential investors, that just capturing one percent of such a large market will ensure their venture's success. Surprisingly, even seasoned venture investors will suspend their own disbelief and proceed into large emerging markets such as wireless without thinking twice.

The suspended reality that surrounded the e-commerce models is being repeated all over again with many wireless ventures. Investment banking and research firms contribute to this investment frenzy by publishing their own speculations as to m-commerce's potential—sometimes calling it a multi-billion if not trillion-dollar market. As a result, there are already too many start-ups targeting the wireless market.

When analyzing the market, companies should assess exactly how value is distributed among the various players in the value chain. Separating the market into specific niches that will buy the product or service will render a more realistic picture. Such an effort takes careful modeling, and coming up with optimistic, realistic, and pessimistic estimations is essential. Finally, if you cannot model the market your value proposition is targeting, this is a warning sign of an immature strategy.

Profit Model: How Do You Make Money?

Any business idea must have an excellent chance for significant growth and return on investment before it is pursued. Otherwise the time, effort, and capital it requires will have been wasted. The path to profitability (P2P) should be detailed early on in the development of the mobile strategy plan.

Can you monetize enough value to be profitable? A company must know how to make money off the target customer. Entrepreneurs normally ignore profitability in an effort to gain initial market share. Market share without profits has been proven again and again to be an unsustainable strategy. As a result, many firms have spent millions of dollars before realizing how untenable their underlying assumptions were of how the business would generate a profit.

Without a clear profitability (or quantification of efficiency improvement) picture, companies should not proceed with large-scale mobile strategies. Experiment? Yes. Bet your company? No! Many experienced investors, like Warren Buffet of Berkshire Hathaway, say that they don't invest in the Internet because they don't understand how profits will be made. Addressing this concern is often the top priority of boards and top management. Management's performance is judged by its ability to produce returns from the investments it has made within the time frames it has agreed to.

Profitability analysis requires calculating the point at which a company breaks even on its investment. New solutions always seem to take more time and money than expected, and the project risks and uncertainties multiply over the course of the effort. Therefore, project budgets, work plans, and time frames should allow significant space for the unexpected. Implementation plans conform to the realities of the business environment and life; the opposite is seldom true. The expected profit margins and the dates when they will be achieved should be understood in as much detail as possible.

Phase 2: Capability Evaluation

Even the most well-intentioned business strategies are often visionary, abstract, and qualitative. They remain at the 20,000-foot level, never becoming pragmatic, concrete, or quantifiable. To take a vision out of the ethereal realm and ground it in solid everyday business reality, a business must analyze its objectives, organizational structure, channel conflicts, and current capabilities. In the belief that their own capabilities are well-known, most firms ignore this critical step when initiating a company project. The reality is that most large firms know very little about themselves in terms of concrete skills, abilities, and resources.

In our experience, we have found that far too often, corporate executives embrace a business vision but are incapable of focusing on the next step. For example, a Fortune 50 company wanted to develop a consistent customer experience regardless of the channel chosen. Everyone at the firm came to accept this vision during a two-day workshop. But their acceptance was only philosophical, and they left the workshop wondering what to do next. Luckily, this firm has a very strong leader who stepped in to show the way. Over the next quarter, a mobile task force was set up to drill into the specifics further. The task force spent time on understanding customers' needs and preferences, the mobile value proposition, and how to make the solution profitable.

Each of these tasks required an external focus—on customers, partners, and financial markets—before any thought could be given to what the company must do in response. A capability evaluation involves focusing on the company's internal operations and on how to extend them to implement the new mobile strategies. In this phase, the company is assessing whether or not it can achieve the mobile vision it has said it wants. It must take an honest look at its current organization, business processes, and people to support the new vision. It must determine what changes need to be made to ensure success. Lastly, a capability evaluation prioritizes each mobility project according to the firm's capabilities and the potential value the project brings.

The Socratic adage "Know thyself" is vitally important when planning any initiative. We have found that the simple questions listed in Table 10.2 are quite useful in helping a company center their vision of mobility on the firm's unique capabilities. It is important to note that capabilities of companies change frequently. Capabilities change because people leave, new products are created, new talent is hired, new companies are bought, and so on. So, don't underestimate the need for capability evaluation.

Capabilities Audit and Validation

Once the capabilities are evaluated and linked to the broad strategy, various strategic scenarios emerge. At this time, it is essential for companies to select a strategy scenario based on what they know is right for them. A capably executed strategy delivers better results than a seemingly more elegant one that does not reflect an organization's strengths. It makes sense to choose a sound strategy that meets financial goals and provides the best fit with the abilities of management.

When determining a company's "to-be" strategy, it is critical to assess the company's strengths and weaknesses. Such an assessment can challenge long-held beliefs, much to the firm's chagrin. However, strength and weakness are both relative concepts—relative to the competition and to customers' expectations. Yesterday's strengths may have become today's weaknesses without anyone in management noticing. A thorough corporate self-examination clarifies a company's readiness in the existing business environment, given the vulnerabilities and risks to which it is open.

It is also important to uncover and address any differences between the business philosophy of the various lines of businesses, the technology/infrastructure group, and that of the leadership.

Table 10.2: Questions to Ask When Implementing M-Business

Capability Audit and Validation	• *What capabilities do we have today?* • *What state are they in?*
Capability Assessment	• *What capabilities and resources do we need to create the proposed value proposition?* • *Do we build these capabilities in-house, do we outsource, or do we selectively partner?*
Capability Configuration	• *How do we structure this activity?* • *Where will the money come from?*

Often these differences are reflected in a business organized around application "stovepipes" resulting from political conflicts. Companies in which the application infrastructure isn't aligned with customer-facing or employee-facing business objectives must undergo housecleaning before they can embark on a mobile strategy. As a result, top management commitment will be crucial in going forward.

Capabilities Assessment: What New Capabilities Do We Need?

Once a strategic scenario is chosen, capability assessments identify what the company must acquire, improve, learn, or build in order to make its mobile strategy a reality. This requires having a fully developed statement of the effort's scope and focus. The key considerations outlined in Figure 10.2 can help structure a firm's capability assessment and ensure a clear alignment between a firm's vision and its capabilities. This leads to the creation of a business case.

The assessment will reveal gaps in the company's current capabilities. A strategy must then be developed for filling these gaps by either acquiring, hiring, contracting, or through strategic partnering. If these missing capabilities are ignored, the company risks "mobilizing" its existing inefficiencies. In other words, it automates a mess. Despite the investments in the project, the root causes of historical company problems remain, putting the project at risk.

A significant part of current capabilities assessment is the application and information infrastructure readiness. Infrastructure can either accelerate or impede an organization's ability to adapt to changing business conditions. The organization's underlying design must be flexible enough to integrate emerging technologies without compromising the existing enterprise architecture. The ability to fully meet new business requirements is revealed during the infrastructure assessment.

The capabilities assessment phase should also focus on the change management requirements. It must assess the cultural willingness to change and whether the initiative is something the employees approve of or is mandated by management. Never underestimate the changes required in culture, business practices, and operations when undertaking a company project.

The change plan should carefully phase in mobile initiatives with the company's overall strategy. A thorough change plan details how the current business operations will be performed while transitioning to the new way of doing business. The plan should provide a sense of stability and security as the firm moves from its current to its future state.

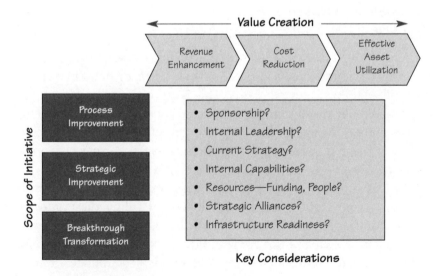

Figure 10.2: Capability Assessment

Capability Configuration: What Structure Is Right for Us?

Capability configuration links a company's m-business "to-be" strategy with its current "as-is" capabilities. It describes the unique combination of capabilities, processes, partnerships, and funding needed to support a strategy. It also describes the organizational structure of the new venture, whether it is a spin-off or an internal division, or is considered part of existing operations.

Determining the appropriate structure for a new initiative means addressing a variety of issues, including creating business and sales models for bridging the old and new, identifying potential margin pressure, creating a strategy to motivate and retain employees, and designing an incentive structure to overcome customer and employee inertia. Customer and employee inertia is a response to living and working in environments of constant change. It is essentially "innovation fatigue," and it creates a vicious spiral in which the pressure to perform leads to accelerated burnout. Employees become exhausted, with little energy for further innovation, and this stalls the change process. The result is greater disruption to the company's social structure.

This "law of diminishing innovation"—the more companies embark on frequent change, the less likely they are to change—must be dealt with by carefully examining the initiative and confirming that it is the right thing to do. Changing a project's goals in the midst of the effort can demoralize both the project team and the company's employees. It can seem as though the company is without clear leadership. Moving target management is a common and thorny problem in technology-enabled transformations.

When adopting any innovation, transitioning from the old to the new should be conducted in a way that minimizes disruption. Capability configuration helps define a high-level structure for making explicit exactly how the transition will take place and who will be responsible for making it happen. The structure and transition plan are documented in the business case.

The business case helps the executive team to fully understand the m-business efforts and objectives. It relates the project's objectives to each executive's functional area and informs executives of the project's impact. It defines the scope, specific milestones, deliverables, activities, and critical success factors for each function.

Phase 3: Solution Blueprint Formulation

A business case leads to a solution blueprint. The detailed solution blueprint explores different alternatives for executing the mobile strategy. The blueprint development process forces the company's management to consider all of the aspects involved in creating the mobile solution. A blueprint ties together all activities on a project. A strategy may be well conceived, the business case carefully drawn up, the project adequately financed, the technology very sophisticated, and consultants may be brilliant. But if the efforts of all the participants are not coordinated and skillfully managed, the project may fail to meet the schedule, overrun the budget, or fall short in expectations. The larger and more complex the project, the more critical is this overall solution blueprint function.

In preparing the blueprint, the firm must analyze all of the project's potential ramifications for existing technology, marketing, operations, and customer service strategies. The blueprint also outlines the human, physical, and financial resources the project requires. Further, the blueprint grounds the strategy in practical reality and saves time, energy, and resources that would have been consumed through trial and error. On a typical project, novel and puzzling problems have a way of cropping up constantly. And the ability to respond to these challenges and creatively resolve conflicts can spell the difference between success and failure.

In more mature organizations, solution blueprint planning links the strategy, applications, and infrastructure together in an iterative design. Figure 10.3 shows a three-tier model of the different elements of a solution blueprint. The challenge in solution blueprint planning is to try to preserve viable legacy assets, to replace outmoded assets, and to add new assets—all in the context of an infrastructure linking them coherently.[3]

When reviewing your blueprint priorities, be practical and balance expectations with reality. The mobile Internet is supposed to link applications and users effortlessly, ushering in an era of frictionless commerce. In this vision, the role of traditional infostructure elements—legacy systems, applications, databases, and networks—would be supplanted, enhanced, or bypassed with more efficient technology. Barriers to information would go down, even as the complexity increases.

We have seen these scenarios before. Instead of falling prey to disintermediation efforts, traditional infostructure elements have maintained their presence in the corporation. Most companies, from retailers to financial services, get 99 percent of their information from existing systems. Bypassing the existing systems is a fantasy for established companies. So spend time thinking through how to integrate and leverage existing infostructure. That is the hard part of solution blueprints.

In our experience, most "great strategies" have failed in linking the new with the old. Laying new mobile processes on top of the existing infrastructure often creates unforeseen problems. Today's typical corporate infrastructure is composed of a diverse mixture of application packages, legacy systems, and functional processes. Integrating them is often the most difficult part of any solution blueprint.

Similar to strategy formulation, the first step is to identify the services and features each target audience needs.

For example, the mobile consumers interact with the business

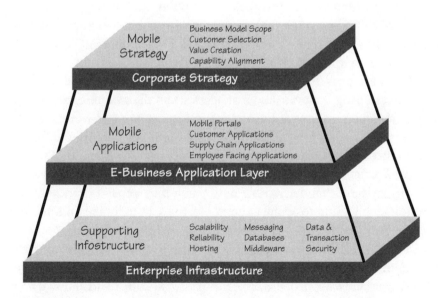

Figure 10.3: Elements of a Solution Blueprint

because they know what they want to purchase. The solution blueprint would contain a list of activities or transactions that meet this consumer profile. Once the profile is complete, the blueprint identifies the data sources to support these transactions, such as the corporate databases. With the transaction profile, a firm can determine which mobile devices are best suited for the user experience the company wishes to deliver and which features in the individual mobile platform best provide these services.

The solution blueprint evolves continuously. It requires considerable discipline to develop a blueprint that will evolve over the course of the next decade, as problems with device usability and slow Web access are overcome. A clearly thought out and adhered-to blueprint plan helps to ground a company's mobile strategy in the realities of a changing business environment. It is a living document able to adapt to business and technological innovations that will occur in the near future.

Phase 4: Tactical Execution

Given the relative novelty of m-business, we recommend that companies start with a pilot to test their assumptions and understand the terrain. It is to be noted that mobile business may require different approaches in design, development, and implementation of applications due to the inherent characteristics of wireless networks and mobile devices. Whenever a new period of innovation begins, software architects, programmers, and managers strain their intuition hoping to gain an understanding of the applications most likely to work.

It is likely that m-business implementations may be quite different from those of e-business. Corporations that want to gain a first-mover edge, whether by being the first into a market with new products or by launching new channels, know how much they depend on new application architecture to achieve their objectives. Usually, the architecture is a mix of costly and aging applications, hardware systems, and networks. Far from making it possible to achieve mobile application goals, it can make a mockery of them. So we often recommend that companies, especially large ones, not leap headfirst into the unknown, but rather prototype to understand the ROI, potential integration pitfalls, change management issues, and customer adoption patterns.

Only hard-won experience in the trenches will give us this knowledge. As Theodore Roosevelt once said: "It is not the critic that counts, not the man who points out how the strong man stumbled or whether the doer of deeds could have done them better. The credit belongs to the man who is actually in the arena, whose face is marred with dust and sweat and blood, who strives valiantly, who errs, and often comes up short again and again . . . if he fails, at least he fails while daring greatly so that his soul shall never be with those cold and timid ones who know neither victory or defeat."

A Final Thought

People who get on in this world are the people who get up and look for the circumstances they want, and, if they can't find them, make them.

—George Bernard Shaw

Whether you are an entrepreneur or a corporate intrapreneur, the answers to five questions—why, what, when, where, and who—form the foundation of business strategy. A constantly changing business environment makes strategy more, not less, important to business success. Yet we can safely predict that many organizations will fail to create effective m-business strategies. As a result, these firms risk investing valuable resources in poorly conceived initiatives that will at best return mediocre results.

Developers of mobile strategies must learn from the mistakes of the e-commerce era. The era's early exuberance quickly turned into a mood of gloom and doom. In optimistic times, numerous companies became convinced that the "new economy" would undermine their business models and their profitability. Many created "me-too" cookie-cutter plans and quickly jumped on the bandwagon, largely out of fear—not vision. However, e-commerce's "first wave" was only minimally adopted by customers, resulting in a number of bankruptcies. Highly speculative projections of online sales and growth potential led to unrealistic expectations that contributed to the boom-bust cycle.

However, e-commerce was only the beginning of an unstoppable technological trend that will continue to change companies and everyday lives for the foreseeable future. It is quite possible that a number of the companies that failed during the last business cycle will not participate in the next. For example, Silicon Graphics was a leader in the graphics workstation market and interactive TV world of the early 1990s. While the company's founder, Jim Clark, went on to form NetScape Communications, Silicon Graphics had no coherent strategy during the rise of the Internet. As a result, Sun Microsystems walked away with most of the Web business. By focusing too narrowly on its core, high-end graphics businesses, Silicon Graphics missed a number of extraordinary growth opportunities.

Established firms must decide for themselves whether or not to adopt a mobile strategy. If they decide to do so, the time has come for their management to understand the potential of new mobile applications and begin the necessary planning to integrate them into their business processes. If they choose not to pursue a mobile initiative, competition and new entrants most likely will.

Finally, in mobile strategy even more than elsewhere, a company must plan as though it is confronting a moving target. Hence, what matters is the ability to adapt the plan to the market and customer reactions rapidly and smoothly. Flexibility is thus a cardinal principle of mobile solutions. But flexibility will be of benefit only if it is bound by a rigid disciplinary framework. Moreover, flexibility and discipline are not easy to combine—in many cases, they can be achieved only at each other's expense. The next decade promises to be a very interesting one.

Epilogue: A Reality Check

It is a great nuisance that knowledge can only be acquired by hard work. It would be fine if we could swallow the powder of profitable information made palatable by the jam of fiction.

—W. Somerset Maugham

We are in the very early stages of a mobile innovation wave that will steadily transform the applications and infrastructure landscape. Like any innovation, there will be moments in time when irrational exuberance rules the day, as well as moments when extreme pessimism reigns. However, one thing is certain, the mobile revolution will create tremendous opportunities for some companies and be a terrible threat to those who insist on the status quo.

In many ways, the promise and perils of the mobile economy is similar to what is taking place in the biotechnology world. In June 2000, a scientific revolution was unleashed when two competing research groups—National Human Genome Research Institute and Celera Genomics—announced that they had completed the "first draft" of the entire blueprint of human life, described as the most important scientific effort humankind has ever mounted, eclipsing in importance even the splitting of the atom and putting a man on the moon.

Among their findings: People have about 30,000–60,000 genes, far fewer than was previously believed. What's more, the genetic difference between people and animals is relatively small. With this genetic map at hand, analysts predict a new world where drug treatments are customized to an individual's genetic makeup and gene-based therapy can root out cancer and other diseases before they take hold in the body.

This new science marks a milestone for biology, biochemistry, biotechnology, and the pharmaceutical sciences. It is expected to revolutionize the way medicine is delivered to individual patients. The potential influence on drug development is intriguing. A whole era of customized drugs ("designer drugs") is believed to be possible. Today's drugs can reach about 500 disease "targets" in the human body. With genomics, there are as many as 10,000 potential targets, creating hope for a host of drugs and therapies that can be tailored to individuals and result in far fewer side effects.

The point is that rhetoric about genomics and its potential is far removed from the reality of today. It will require significant investments in research, drug development process reengineering, and FDA regulatory changes to fill in all the gaps in our knowledge of how genes interact with proteins. Almost everything written about genomics is a potential scenario based on speculation rather than facts. Many things have to happen along the way for this immense genomics potential to come to Main Street and affect patient care.

M-business is following a trajectory very similar to that of biotechnology. Lots of opportunity—if you can survive the journey through the uncharted terrain. Like biotech, the mobile market is maturing rapidly, with new infrastructure, devices, and applications. However, for the next three to five years the reality of implementing m-business and extracting business value will be far removed from the marketing messages that are the focus of the media, Wall Street, and start-ups. In other words, it is going to take a lot of patience to develop innovative ways to apply mobile technology in solving Main Street business problems.

We see m-business as complementary to e-business. As e-business moves from the fringes into the core of the enterprise, it is no longer just an option; it is a matter of business survival. To extract value from e-business applications, new mobile applications are needed that enable unprecedented ease and speed of information access. Our goal in this book has been to give managers a compass to navigate the treacherous and disorienting waters of emerging technology. We tried hard to strike a balance between the possibilities and the reality of tying it back to e-business. As we describe in this book, the ultimate purpose of strategic management is to focus an organization's resources, capabilities, and energies in building a unique value proposition along one of the dimensions of our framework—new product or service innovation, new efficiencies in customer relationship management, supply chain efficiencies, or employee-facing productivity or operational improvements.

These dimensions represent distinct mobile scenarios or opportunities. The purpose of mobile scenario creation is not to predict the future but rather to understand how emerging technological forces can shape the business landscape in different ways. This exercise helps to identify strategic issues and challenges if and when they happen. The utility of scenario planning lies in its ability to anticipate the future and create what-if discussion around the question: What might our company do if these mobile scenarios were to unfold, and what might our value proposition become? When this question is answered, the ability to respond to future events is increased. It will take skill to get the right emphasis between anticipating the scenarios and using the scenarios for developing a new business strategy.

The macro- and micro-economic implications of m-business are quite exciting. Of these four potential marketspaces, the fastest adoption will be in the enterprise applications side, as companies will use the in-house technology to reduce operating costs. This will translate into more business-to-employee, business-to-business, and inter-enterprise applications, such as extended supply chains. We expect that the radical new business models being simultaneously developed and market-tested in consumer markets for mobile business are going to mature more slowly than expected. As a result, when the dust settles, expect to see a few firms win big on the consumer side and the rest struggle to survive.

So fasten your seat belts! The turbulence you've experienced in the last decade isn't over yet. In fact, it's probably going to get worse. Don't fight change—simply enjoy the ride!

A final thought. Throughout this book we attempted to create a roadmap through the chaos, provide insight into the mobile business opportunities, and identify some of the ultimate winners. We will continue to provide up-to-date content through a companion Web site: www.ebstrategy.com. We look forward to interacting with you through the Web site.

Notes

Chapter 1

1. "Nearly Half of U.K Kids Have Their Own Mobiles," NOP Research Group, http://itn.co.uk/news/20010129/business/07mobile.shtml.

2. Jim Suhr, "GM's OnStar Partners With Fidelity," APNewswire, Wednesday, February 14.

3. The term "Evernet" is used by venture capitalists John Doerr of Kliener Perkins and Roger McNamee of Integral Capital Partners. The term "Supranet" is used by the Gartner Group. The term "X Internet" is used by Forrester Research. The term "Hypernet" is used by Digital4Sight. While we are tempted to invent our own buzz-word, we refrain from it. Some of our final candidates were "OmniNet," "RealNet," and "EverySpace."

4. R. Milner, *Encyclopedia of Evolution* (1990), p. 169.

5. Jeremy Rifkin, *Algeny* (1983), p. 134.

6. John G. Spooner, "TI to Plunk Down $100 Million for Wireless Software," CNET News.com, February 22, 2001; http://yahoofin.cnet.com/news/.

7. E. M. Rogers, *Diffusion of Innovation,* 4th ed. (New York: Free Press, 1995). The concepts of this book were applied to high-tech marketing by Geoff Moore, *Crossing the Chasm.* For a more academic rendition, see V. Mahajan, E. Muller, and F. M. Bass, "New Product Diffusion Models in Marketing: A Review and Directions for Research," *Journal of Marketing* 54, 1 (January 1990), pp. 1–26.

Chapter 2

1. For a fascinating twenty-year retrospective on the personal computer, see the video *Triumph of the Nerds,* Robert X. Cringley. Also see Jim Carlton, "It Seems Like Yesterday," *Wall Street Journal,* November 16, 1998, for some insightful commentary on the PC industry.

2. Frances Cairncross, *The Death of Distance* (Boston: Harvard Business School Press, 1997), p. 18.

3. Deutsche Presse-Agentur, "Malaysia forbids Moslem men to divorce wives via SMS phone message," July 12, 2001, Thursday, International News, Kuala Lumpur.

4. Richard Hodgson, "It's Still the 'Catalog Age,'" *Catalog Age,* June 2001.

5. Jaye Scholl, "The Chips Are Down," *Barron's,* March 12, 2001.

6. For more detailed information on how Telematics really works, see www.telematics.motorola.com.

7. "Ten Trends for the Post-PC World," *Red Herring,* December 1, 1998.

8. For more technical information, see "Next-Generation Wireless: Far More Than Phones," Agilent Technologies, http://www.agilent.com/Feature/English/archive/E014.html.

9. "Bluetooth" is the name that was given to Harald Blatand, a tenth-century Danish Viking king who united and controlled Denmark and Norway. The name symbolizes the specification's ability to unify the telecommunications and computing industries using wireless technology.

Chapter 3

1. "Nokia's Poised for Its Toughest Challenge," *Computing,* March 1, 2001, p. 56.

2. Peggy Albright, "Is Intel 'Stalking' TI?" *Wireless Week,* September 25, 2000, p. 3.

3. Peter Benesh, "A Platform War Brews for Dominance of Wireless Web," *Investor's Business Daily,* February 15, 2001, p. 6. See also Lydia Lee, "Java Man's Second Coming," *The Industry Standard,* January 1, 2001.

4. Aisha Williams, "Doing Business Without Wires," *Informationweek,* pp. 22–24, January 15, 2001.

5. Ibid.

6. "JetBlue Adopts 'Roving,' Wireless Check-in System," *Business Wire,* May 14, 2001.

Chapter 4

1. For additional examples, see Michael A. Cusumano and Richard W. Selby, *Microsoft Secrets: How the World's Most Powerful Software Company Creates Technology, Shapes Markets, and Manages People* (New York: Free Press, 1995).

2. For additional examples, see Marc H. Meyer and A. P. Lehnerd, *The Power of Product Platforms* (New York: Free Press, 1997).

3. The MX1 processor will combine Motorola's MCore340 processor and a Star-Core 140 DSP, which the company jointly developed with Agere Systems, formerly Lucent Technologies Microelectronics Group. For more information, see Darrell Dunn , "TI Charts New Wireless Territory—Company Aims OMAP Platform At 3G Cellular Handsets," *Electronic Buyers' News,* February 19, 2001.

Chapter 5

1. Mbizcentral, "Analysis: Corporate Users Abandon WAP," May 29, 2001.

2. Interview with Larry Roshfeld, Senior Vice President Software Products, Aether Systems, June 14, 2001.

Chapter 6

1. "Boeing to Announce Airborne Internet Deals," Reuters News Service, June 12, 2001.

2. Bob Brewin, "Starbucks Takes Wireless Leap," *Computerworld,* January 8, 2001, p. 1

3. See www.nngroup.com/reports/wap for the complete report.

4. One of the most innovative location-based applications is NextBus.com, which is using wireless technology to help passengers and users of public transit track real-time transit arrival information. Currently available in six cities around the United States, NextBus.com allows commuters to determine what time their bus will actually arrive at the stop, recognizing that traffic variations, breakdowns, and day-to-day problems faced by any transit provider can interrupt or slow down service

5. Suzanne Baran, "Bloodhound Technology," *Internet World,* October 15, 2000.

Chapter 7

1. We strongly believe that universities should teach every student the fundamentals of solutions design and creating new customer experiences. In executive education, more corporations should focus on solutions thinking.

2. Pui-Wing Tam, "Show of Hands," Special Report on E-Commerce, *Wall Street Journal,* April 23, 2001.

3. See "Case Study: Taco Bell Corporation," www.thinque.com.

4. The Electronic Comment Card is an actual mobile touchscreen device manufactured by Boca Raton, Florida–based Jtech Communications, Inc.

5. Source: "UPS Case Study," Air2Web (http://www.air2Web.com/wireless_success.jsp).

6. Amazon.com has a business method patent on "one-click" reordering. This patent is being challenged in the courts by barnesandnoble.com. For more on this, see Amazon.com v. barnesandnoble.com (Fed. Cir. 2/14/01).

7. Mary Connors, "Closing the Big Book," *Women's Wear Daily,* January 26, 1993, vol. 165, no. 16, p. 27.

8. Holly Acland, "Slowing Down the Speeding Shopper," *Marketing March* 16, 2000, p. 25.

9. Bertelsmann AG—Questions and Answers on Corporate Strategy, http://www.bertelsmann.com/documents/en/FAQ_english_0401.doc

10. "Wireless at Work," *Business 2.0,* February 15, 2001.

Chapter 8

1. Tom Smith, "Call This Efficient," *InternetWeek,* March 12, 2001, p. 26.

2. Antony Adshead, "E-Supply Chain Savings Are More Than Just Dotcom Hype," *Computer Weekly,* May 3, 2001, p. 20.

3. "Kroger and PocketScript to Launch Electronic Prescription Interchange Service for In-Store Pharmacies," PR Newswire, January 12, 2001.

4. For a comprehensive history of bar codes, see Ed Leibowitz, "Bar Codes: Reading Between the Lines," *Smithsonian,* February 1999, vol. 29, p. 130. Also see

Stephen A. Brown, *Revolution at the Checkout Counter : The Explosion of the Bar Code* (Harvard University Press, 1997).

5. For more information on Auto-ID, see the Web site auto-id.mit.edu. For more on tagging technology, see the Web site www.aimglobal.org.

6. Antony Adshead, op. cit. p. 20.

7. See "Case Study: SmithKline Beecham," www.phaseforward.com.

8. Source: www.savi.com/index.html.

9. Mitch Wagner, "Handhelds Nudge PCs in the Enterprise," *InternetWeek,* Monday, May 14, 2001.

10. Ibid.

11. Anne Gonzales, "Electronics Keep Delivery Services on Right Track," *San Francisco Business Times,* March 23, 2001, vol. 15, no. 33, p. 29.

12.For more specific details on the implementation, see "Case Study: AAA" by Cingular Interactive Data Services (www.bellsouthwd.com).

13. For more technical information on the BostonCoach solution, see "Dynamic Mobile Data" (http://www.dmdsys.com/).

14. Peter Drucker, *The Age of Discontinuities.*

Chapter 9

1. Source: Motorola Warrior Focused Solutions. http://www.mot.com/GSS /SSTG/ISD/ws/index.html.

2. See Peter F. Drucker, "The New Productivity Challenge," *Harvard Business Review,* November–December 1991.

3. For details, see "Case Study; Eastman Kodak," www.pocketPC.com. Also for more information, see the January 2001 issue of *Field Force Automation* magazine, which features a case study titled "Picture Increased Sales" documenting Kodak's implementation of FieldWeb.

4. Mitch Wagner, "New Users, New Devices," *InternetWeek,* May 14, 2001, p. 1.

5. http://www.zambasolutions.com/learning/index.html?casestudies_hertz.html.

6. Source: Hertz Corporation, Hertz.com.

Chapter 10

1. Our approach is consistent with the strategy/innovation methodologies proposed by Adrian J. Slywotzky, David Morrison, and Bob Andelman, *The Profit Zone: How Strategic Business Design Will Lead You to Tomorrow's Profits* (Times Books, January 1998), and Gary Hamel, *Leading the Revolution* (Harvard Business School Press, June 2000).

2. Brent Schlender, "Steve Jobs: The Graying Prince of a Shrinking Kingdom," *Fortune,* May 14, 2001, p. 118.

3. For more details, see Ravi Kalakota, Marcia Robinson, *e-Business 2.0: Road Map for Success* (Addison-Wesley, 2001).

Index

Page numbers of illustrations appear in italics.

About the Authors

Ravi Kalakota is a noted pioneer and visionary in the area of e-business. He holds the distinction of having authored the first-ever book on e-commerce, *Frontiers of E-commerce* (1995), and continues to be at the forefront of "e" thought. His recent book, *e-Business: Roadmap for Success* (1999), was a national bestseller. Ravi is the CEO of e-Business Strategies, a worldwide research and consulting practice based in Atlanta. His current research focuses on multi-channel e-business, mobile business models, click and brick infrastructure models, and design of e-service platforms. Ravi has consulted extensively with Fortune 1000 companies. Before starting his consulting company, he served as the Georgia Research Alliance Chair Professor of Electronic Commerce and Director of the Center for Digital Commerce at Georgia State University in Atlanta. He also previously held the Xerox Chair in Information Systems at the Simon Graduate School of Business, University of Rochester, and has taught at the University of Texas at Austin. Ravi can be reached at *ravi@ebstrategy.com*.

Marcia Robinson is the President of e-Business Strategies, a research and innovation consulting practice designed to help companies create tomorrow's business models today. She co-authored *e-Business: Roadmap for Success* (1999), a national best-seller, which was the first book on e-business that looked at the organization and infrastructure changes necessary in order to compete in the digital economy. Her latest book, *e-Business 2.0: Roadmap for Success* (2001), further examines recent developments. Marcia has extensive experience in the service delivery and customer side of e-business. Her previous experience includes technical and managerial positions in a variety of industries including consulting (EDS), telecommunications (RochesterTel), and banking (SunTrust Bank). Marcia can be reached at *marcia@ebstrategy.com*.

For more information, please visit us at *www.ebstrategy.com*.